C O L L E C T O R ' S   L I B R A R Y

GOLF

♦ ♦ ♦

*Four decades of Sports Illustrated's finest
writing on the game of golf*

Manufactured in the United States of America
First Printing 1994

Published by arrangement with:
Oxmoor House, Inc.
Book Division of
Southern Progress Corporation
PO Box 2463
Birmingham, Alabama 35201

SPORTS ILLUSTRATED GOLF
was prepared by:
Bishop Books, Inc.
611 Broadway
New York, New York 10012

Cover photograph: Stephen Dunn/Allsport

The following stories are used by permission of
the authors acknowledged:
Golf's Greatest Putt by Grantland Rice;
'Man, I'm Dropping Your Bag Right Here'
by George Plimpton.

Contents

◆ ◆ ◆

Introduction

♦

Golf is a choke game. Nobody ever shanked a three-iron because his opponent threw him a curve or put too much topspin on the ball. When Scott Hoch missed a three-foot putt to blow the 1989 Masters, the ball was sitting perfectly still when he hit it and the crowd was perfectly silent. It was completely, entirely, totally him. That's why golf is also the cruelest game.

Golf writing is a choke game, too. It is sportswriting in the most pleasant surroundings under the easiest deadlines. Nobody ever shanked their story because the snow was blowing in the press box window or the winner was getting his femur set. Yet golf is a sport that writers often bogey, perhaps for the same reason that it is so hard to play.

When Jack Nicklaus won his improbable sixth Masters, in 1986, won it at the age of 46, won it when his eyes and his supporters and his swing were failing him, the press room at Augusta fairly groaned at the enormity of it. This story was too big, too delicious, too perfect to write. Grown men tugged at their collars. Longtime veterans sat bleary-eyed staring at unforgiving blank screens. One well-known American columnist finally led with, "My fingers will not work."

But through the years, the fingers of *Sports Illustrated*'s golf writers have managed to work quite nicely. Something about golf has been very lucky for us. Maybe it's because golf is so continually new—this hole is different from the last, this week's course is different from last week's, this tournament's hero is sometimes last week's goat.

Whatever the reason, we've had some of the finest names in golf writing working on our nickel—from the respected Herbert Warren Wind to the hilarious Dan Jenkins to the delightful Rick Reilly, the magazine has contributed richly to the literature of the sport.

Of course, this anthology isn't just a trophy case for deadline stuff. There's much more. Here is Frank Deford's unforgettable look back at perhaps the greatest tournament ever, Watson and Nicklaus's immortal battle at the 1977 British Open at Turnberry. Here is Grantland Rice on Bobby Jones, Sarah Ballard on Byron Nelson, Jenkins on Lee Trevino and Reilly on John Daly.

If you were to pick your favorite holes in golf, you would have to leave some great ones out. Same for us. We've included 25 great stories here and left a hundred good ones in the bag. To those writers we three-putted, we owe you a beer at the 18th hole.

Enjoy it. If this book can't help you keep your head down, you're hopeless.

MARK MULVOY
Managing Editor

MAJORS

•••

Golf's Greatest Putt

BY GRANTLAND RICE

JUST BEFORE HE DIED IN 1954, THE GREAT GRANTLAND RICE WROTE THIS ACCOUNT OF THE PUTT THAT BROUGHT BOBBY JONES BACK FROM THE MOUTH OF DISASTER TO WIN THE 1929 U.S. OPEN AT WINGED FOOT. IT WAS RICE'S FINAL STORY, AND IT APPEARED IN THE FIRST ISSUE OF SPORTS ILLUSTRATED.

On a late June afternoon in 1929, some 10,000 tense spectators crowded up to the 18th green at the Winged Foot Golf Course in Westchester County, New York. As they came running up to the green, crowding as close as they could get, you heard every type of sound from a whisper to a shriek blended into one vast babble of excited human voices. The startling news was passed from person to person—Bob Jones was on the verge of the worst catastrophe any U.S. Open had ever known.

As Jones broke through the crowd and came upon the green, the babble suddenly was stilled. This was the silence of suppressed nerves. Since the first Scottish herdsman addressed an early golf ball with a shepherd's crook, I doubt if any golfer had ever faced a moment so packed with tension.

It was one of the great moments I have ever known in

sports. The silence was complete. Only a few short minutes before, Jones had been six strokes up with only six holes to go. Now he had one putt left, for a tie. Bobby Jones had faced crucial putts before—more of them than any other golfer I have ever known—where important championships were at stake. But this putt meant more to Bob Jones than merely winning an Open. It meant the recapture of his golfing soul. It meant removing a dark stain from his pride, certain nation-wide ridicule that was to follow failure.

Let's go back a minute. The real drama of this, the 33rd Open, and of Bob Jones's career, started at the long 12th hole.

Here Al Espinosa, the only challenger, took a destructive 8. When Espinosa took this 8, he felt he had no chance. With the tension off, he finished with four 4's and two 3's for a 75 and a total of 294.

Even with this spurt on Espinosa's part, Jones could drop three strokes to par over the last six holes and still win. There never was a surer thing in golf.

Bob lost one stroke at the short 13, and then at the 15th he had a heartbreaking 7, three over par. Now he needed three pars to tie Espinosa. Here was undoubtedly the finest golfer in the world ... yet no duffer had ever blown so bad.

Jones got his pars on 16 and 17 and came to the final hole needing a par 4 to tie his Mexican-American rival. Bob's drive was good. His second shot hit the hard, keen green and ran down a grassy bank. He chipped from below, but the chip stopped 12 to 14 feet short. He stopped as he came up on the green and saw how far short he was—the putt he had to hole to even get a draw.

This wasn't the first 10- or 12-foot putt Bob had had to sink in his brilliant career ... I could name any number of 10-footers he had holed to keep from being beaten on some closing green. I might add here that over a long period of years I have seen five great putters— Walter Travis, Jerry Travers, Walter Hagen, Horton Smith and Bobby Jones. I believe Jones was the greatest for the simple reason that he saved himself more times by holing the important ones—the 8- and 10-footers against George Voigt, against Cyril Tolley, against Maurice McCarthy, to beat out Gene Sarazen and Hagen in so many championships here and abroad.

But this occasion at Winged Foot was different. Jones's competitive career, by his own choice, was nearing its end. He had been working seriously at the game since he was 7 years old. He was now 27. The 1929 title meant his third U.S. Open. He had finished 1-2 in this Open since 1922, eight years with only one exception—1927. Later O.B. Keeler, Jones's Boswell and the best golf writer this country ever produced, told me that if Bob had missed this putt he would never have gone abroad the next year to make his Grand Slam.

On the green, Bobby Jones crouched partly on one knee studying the slanting line of the treacherous putt. There was a dip or a break in the green of at least a foot-and-a-half that had to be judged. Bob was usually a fast putter. This time he took a few seconds longer than usual, for in addition to the speed of the fast green he had to decide how big the break was.

I was with Mike Brady, the club pro, when the putt was made. I was on the ground, peering between legs. Mike had a step ladder and was above the mob.

"He's short," Mike shouted. "He's missed it. He's short." I lost the ball en route. I picked it up again near the cup. Suddenly the ball hesitated, stopped—and then turned over once more and disappeared.

That's the way Bob always putted—to get the ball just up to the cup where it has 4½ inches to fall.

I have heard in my time a sudden roar—a great crash of noise, many, many times at many different games. I never heard before, or since, the vocal cataclysm that rocked the oaks of Westchester.

Jones beat Espinosa in the play-off by more than 20 strokes. The next year he won the Grand Slam. In the wake of that putt he went on his way to one record that may never be equaled. For, as George Trevor put it, "he stormed the impregnable quadrilateral of golf."

The Doc Shows The Masters How

BY HERBERT WARREN WIND

DR. CARY MIDDLECOFF, A "VOLUNTARILY UNEMPLOYED DEN-TIST" FROM MEMPHIS, WON THE 1955 MASTERS TOURNAMENT, THANKS IN PART TO AN 82-FOOT EAGLE PUTT HE SANK IN THE SECOND ROUND. HERBERT WARREN WIND, SPORTS ILLUSTRAT-ED'S FIRST REGULAR GOLF WRITER, GAVE THIS ACCOUNT.

The 13th hole of the Augusta National Golf Course, the scene of the annual Masters Golf Tournament, is a par five some 470 yards long which doglegs sharply to the left. Rae's Creek, which follows along the left side of the hole, cuts across the width of the fairway just before the green and then bends back to patrol the green tightly along the right. It is the strategic sinuosity of the creek, of course, that makes the hole one of the most demanding tests on America's outstand-ing inland course. The golfer who follows a fine drive with a daring second over the water and onto the green is in a posi-tion then to pick up a stroke on par, and sometimes two, and this can frequently turn a fair round into a good round and a good round into a great one. On the other hand, the golfer who follows a fine drive with a daring second that does not quite fill the bill generally receives a very stern comeuppance.

It is the rare Masters indeed when the 13th is not the stage for some dramatic turn of events, and the 19th Masters, which finished this week, was certainly no exception.

On the first day of the tournament, Sam Snead, the defending champion, came to the 13th two under par and playing just as precisely as those figures would indicate. He laced out a long drive and, with a little wind in his face, elected to play a spoon for his second. The shot cleared the creek with yards to spare, but Sam had pulled it a shade and the ball thudded into the wet sand on the far wall of a newly remodeled side-hill trap just off the edge of the green. After flicking away a little sand with his hand, Sam was able to identify the buried ball as the one he was playing, and then he got down to the bitter business of extricating it. Standing on the turf outside the trap, a foot or so above the ball, in his first attempt he succeeded only in driving it deeper into the sand. That was three. On his next attempt he hit the ball flush on the top with the blade of his wedge and moved it not at all. Four. Holding his poise, remembering that a ball lacerated such as his was now, legally can be deemed unplayable and a new ball substituted without loss of stroke, Sam, after checking with the officials, made just such a substitution. On his third attempt the ball trickled down the face and into the center of the trap. He was out in six, finally, and down in two putts for an eight. It was an utterly unfortunate, typically Snead, experience, and the wonder was that Sam could accept it with the stoicism he displayed and finish the round with four pars and a birdie. But Snead, who had come to the Masters exuding the sunniest disposition of his postwar career, was thereafter in a far less expansive and confident mood.

On the second day of the tournament, Dr. Emmett Cary Middlecoff, a "voluntarily unemployed dentist" as Bob Jones described him, and perhaps the most accomplished tall-man player the game has produced since "Long Jim" Barnes, came to the 13th five under par. Capable of very hot streaks, Cary was enjoying an extremely calorific day. He had opened with a birdie, followed it with four pars, and then had gone off on a terrific burst of four consecutive birdies. This had brought him to the turn in a record 31. Starting back, he had started to cool off, not much, mind you, but a few degrees nonetheless. He played three comfortable pars and this brought him to the 13th.

When a golfer is off on a hot round in a major tournament, the foreknowledge of the prodigies he may continue to perform and also of the sudden disaster than can overtake him heightens everything he does. Every little movement takes on a meaning of its own. This may explain, in a superficial way, why Middlecoff is one of the most exciting golfers to be with when he is off on one of his sub-par dashes, for few modern athletes can contrive to pack as many fidgety movements into an afternoon's work.

Middlecoff can rarely play a shot without working up to it with several tugs at the visor of his cap, a brief exploration of the territory stretching before him, a long gander at his target, a movement of repose as he hikes his trousers, a little unloosening of the neck muscles, a pause to dry his right hand on the seat of his trousers, another tug at the visor, another brief exploration, and so on—all this accompanied by a frown of furious concentration. Beneath the parade of gestures there is the complete absorption of a high-strung, intelligent, emotional individual playing an extremely nerve-racking game. And it is this abiding intensity, of course, that Middlecoff communicates to his galleries and which explains the charged atmosphere he creates when he is pouring it on. On the 13th he pushed his tee shot to the high or right side of the fairway. There was an absolute hush the length of the gallery—stretched out some 300 yards along the roped-off fairway—as Middlecoff went with his spoon on his second. He hit a fine, solid shot, and as the ball cleared the creek and landed on the green and rolled to the back edge, a series of shouts went up the length of the line of spectators. These salvos bounced off the pines on the ridge across the fairway and the area reverberated with a sound not unlike artillery fire on a distant battlefield.

Middlecoff strode to the green and inspected, sighted, scrutinized and deciphered the line of his long, long, putt. They change the location of the pins every day at the Masters, and on this, the second day, it was positioned at the front of the long, slippery green some 82 feet away. The precise distance is known, to be sure, only because Middlecoff sank that putt, and the curious thing was that everyone in the gallery felt he might very well do it. Middlecoff eventually tapped the putt, and no ball ever looked whiter than this one did as it ghosted its way just below the center folds of the shadow-strewn green and rolled and rolled and slowed down and then crept off a final slight break and fell into the hole. And then, those salvos again.

Cary Middlecoff's eagle, because of how and when it happened and the further fact that he went on to win this Masters Tournament, will undoubtedly be referred to time and time again as long as the game is played. Eight thousand persons may have been lucky enough to have witnessed it, but like the number of people who now claim to have seen Sarazen's double eagle and the small army that apparently came over on the *Mayflower*, the count will surely rise from year to year. Very possibly, it is the longest putt of any consequence holed in a major event since Bob Jones got one into the cup on the fifth green at St. Andrews from 120 feet away in the 1927 British Open.

After the 13th, Middlecoff came in in even par—a birdie on the 15th, a "bogey" on the 17th where he three-putted—for a 65, seven under par. Accordingly, he did not equal the course record of 64 set by Lloyd Mangrum back in 1940 when the Augusta National was younger and less difficult, but what he did do was to take charge there and then and he never did relinquish his grip until he finished his fourth round two evenings later with a margin of seven strokes over the runner-up, Ben Hogan. In this respect, the margin of victory, it was the most decisive triumph in the history of the Masters.

The only day of the tournament which Middlecoff did not dominate was the opening day. The Masters nearly always gets more than an even break from the weather and, sure enough, on Thursday morning, despite prediction of intermittent showers, the sun began to break through the overcast just as the first starters, Freddy McLeod, U.S. Open Champion in 1908, and Jock Hutchison, British Open Champion in 1921, drove off and ambled down the fairway accompanied by Johnny McDermott, the first American-born golfer ever to

win our Open. A short time later, Billy Joe Patton was called
to the first tee. Lurching into his drive with characteristic
abandon, he pushed into the small pines in the rough. When
he played a superb recovery 15 feet from the pin—why, it
seemed that last year's Masters was still going on. At the end
of Billy Joe's first nine, though, you knew it was another
year. He was out in 39 and he never really did get the bit in
his teeth from that point on. The old guard was up front, as
always in the Masters: Snead at 72 (despite his 8), Ben
Hogan at 73, Lloyd Mangrum at 74. The young guard had
fairly strong representation in Mike Souchak at 71, Bob Rosburg at 72. The in-between age group that, for lack of a better tag, must be called the middle guard was in good shape,
too: Middlecoff was 72, Julius Boros, 71 and Jack Burke out
in front of the pack by four strokes with a handsome 67.

If the scores ran somewhat higher than they generally do in
the Masters, the explanation was that the course was playing
considerably longer than in previous years. This was due to
the heavy, lush growth of the grass in the fairways which cut
down the roll on tee shots to a minimum. The course looked
different in one other respect. Two weeks before the tournament the southeast sector was hit by a severe "cold freeze,"
and among the many victims were the dogwood and the
other southern flora that line the fairways at the Augusta
National. They were missed, but the beauty of the setting is
founded on the greenness of the grass and the pines and the
golf values of the terrain, and the Augusta National looked
just about as lovely as ever. As one old Augusta hand put it,
"Son, let's face it. Here you have the Grace Kelly of golf
courses—beautiful from all angles and in all weather."

On Friday, the second day, until Middlecoff began to perco-
late, the key figure was the leader, Jack Burke. A member of
that talented coterie now being alluded to as the Claude Harmon Boys' Club—it is made up of the young men who have
served as Claude's assistants at Winged Foot and includes
such other top-notch young players as Mike Souchak, Al
Mengert, Dick Mayer, and Shelley Mayfield—a great deal has
been expected of Jack for quite some time, but he inveterately
has been unable to get through a big championship without

coming up with one poor round. Here, when it was important that he stick close to par, he had a 76. In some ways Jack played a sturdier round than his score would suggest. But he still misses his shots in just the wrong places. Middlecoff, on the other hand, played his poor shots when they hurt him least, and beyond this, throughout the tournament he putted far better than any man in the field, always holing the crucial ones. This was clearly evident on Saturday, the third day, when Middlecoff had taken over the leadership at the halfway mark with his total of 137, four shots ahead of Hogan, six ahead of Burke and Snead, seven over Rosburg, eight over Souchak and nine over Boros. It was patent that if any of these challengers was going to overhaul Middlecoff he had better get going, and quick. None of them could buy a putt. Hogan, emerging as the only serious challenger as the afternoon wore on, three-putted three of the four par 3s, and what could very easily have been a 69 became a 72. Middlecoff, on the other hand, confronted by a possible 74, got home in 72. On the 17th, with Hogan breathing down his neck, he holed a tough 10-footer after a very timid approach putt. And then on the 18th, lying two off the edge of the dipping green, he rapped in a curler some 25 feet long. They made quite a difference, those two clutch putts. Middlecoff entered the final round with his lead of four strokes over Hogan still intact, and you can use a lead of that size when Ben is stalking you.

On Sunday, the day of the final round, Middlecoff was not scheduled to tee off until 1:42, a half hour after Hogan's starting time. Waiting to get out is hard even on golfers of phlegmatic make-up. The five and a half hours from 8 o'clock, when he awoke, until 1:42 were murder for Middlecoff and by his own account the longest 20 hours he has ever spent. "I bought the Sunday papers on Saturday night," he recounted later, "but I purposely held off reading them till Sunday morning. Well, I read the funnies and drank some coffee, and it still wasn't 9 o'clock. Then I decided to play some records on the phonograph to kill some time, things like Glenn Miller. I thought I played those records for hours. I was ready to throw the machine out the window. I checked the time and it was still only 10 o'clock. Then I got out some magazines and read them for what seemed like hours. At 11 o'clock I bathed and shaved and ate a big breakfast here at the club and killed time in the locker room and hit a few shots down the practice fairway, and then it was nearly 1:42. I thought it would never come."

Playing about three holes in front of Middlecoff (who was partnered with Byron Nelson), Hogan (who was partnered with Boros) began his pursuit coolly and methodically. Ben's play during the tournament reflected to some degree that he hadn't had the time he would have liked to tune his game up. He had planned to give himself a two weeks' prep at Augusta but he had been called back to Fort Worth by a business problem. Nonetheless, he was hitting the ball well from tee to green, and had he been putting, on Sunday he might have been able to put Middlecoff under considerable pressure. He had an eight-footer for his birdie on the 2nd, a 12-footer for his birdie on the 3rd, and another 12-footer on the 4th. He missed them all. He three-putted the 5th from 35 feet. When he missed an eminently holeable birdie putt on the 6th from seven feet, his bid was over. The only man Middlecoff had to beat now was Middlecoff.

Cary was chattering nervously as he played, but he was hitting the ball hard, not taking too long over his shots, and all in all playing very efficiently until he came to the 5th, one under par. Then, on this rugged 450-yard par four, he tried to belt an extra-long one and duck-hooked his tee shot into a shallow trap. He hit a very wobbly recovery with his five-iron, catching the ball too high and rolling it only some 75 yards down the fairway. An unimpressive seven-iron shot put him on the lower deck of the two-level green. His approach putt from 30 feet below the cup slipped five feet past, but he holed the big one coming back and it did him a world of good. Nelson, who can bring in a horse like Eddie Arcaro, relaxed him further with a little chatter about nothing at all on the 6th tee, and Cary proceeded to pump a good iron toward the flag. It struck on the apron before the green and hopped up some 14 feet from the cup. He banged it in for his bird. Then he followed with a much more authoritative birdie on the 7th, holing for a birdie three after a crisp wedge approach to 10 feet.

He turned in 34, and thereafter he had only one other rough passage. He went two over par on the 10th with a six when he pushed his iron into a trap by the green and took two to get out. He was still shaky playing the 11th, and here he received an exceedingly good break on his approach to that dangerous green; he came up much too quickly on his two-iron and the shot never climbed more than three feet above the ground. It had the line, however, and kept bounding down the slope and over the mounds and finished well on the green. A weak approach putt again left him a five-footer and again, as on the 5th, he made it. His last attack of jitters was over. He played a fine birdie two on the 12th. "I don't see what can happen now, do you?" he asked Nelson as they walked to the 13th tee. "No," said Byron.

And nothing did happen. From that point on Middlecoff played wonderful golf shots and he played them with tactical intelligence. He played short of Rae's Creek with his second on the 13th and got his par, which is all he wanted. A very easy par on the 14th. A birdie on the 15th. Another easy par on the 16th. A harmless bogey on the 17th when he three-putted. Then the 18th, the last hole on the long journey home. A big drive. A six-iron—and Cary never did hit a more perfect shot. The ball spun around the rim of the cup and subsided three feet away. He holed that putt for a 70 on the round and a total of 279.

It was in all ways a magnificent victory for the 34-year-old son of a Memphis dentist who had trained for dentistry himself but gave up his practice in January, 1947 to try the much more precarious one of drilling irons for the pin. A year and a half later he won the National Open. "I was enough of a neophyte not to know what I was doing," Middlecoff remarked of that victory at the presentation ceremonies. "I found it was harder after that. I wondered if I was ever going to win another big tournament." Well, everything comes to him who waits and who outplays the opposition by seven solid strokes.

Eyes Right...but Wrong

BY DAN JENKINS

WHEN SCRAPPY LEE TREVINO WON THE 1968 U.S. OPEN, HE DID MUCH MORE THAN GIVE MEXICO A NATIONAL HERO. HE ALSO REJUVENATED THE GAME ITSELF, WHICH HADN'T SEEN SO APPEALING A PLAYER SINCE ARNOLD PALMER FIRST APPEARED IN THE '50S.

Super Mex is what he called himself. Super Mexkin. And there he was out there in the midst of all of that U.S. Open dignity with his spread-out caddie-hustler stance and his short, choppy public-course swing, a stumpy little guy, tan as the inside of a tamale, pretty lippy for a nobody, and, yeah, wearing those red socks. And here were all of these yells coming from the trees and the knolls of the Oak Hill Country Club in Rochester, coming from all of the other Lee Trevinos of the world. "Whip the gringo," hollered Lee's Fleas, a band of instant Mexicans enthusiastic enough to rival anybody's army, some of them $30-a-week guys like Trevino himself was just a little more than a year ago.

Lee Trevino whipped all of the gringos last week. He mainly whipped a gringo named Bert Yancey, the tournament leader for the first three days, in a head-to-head, you-and-me thing on the final day, the kind of match a hustler really likes; but in so doing, he knocked off everything else in Rochester, including a good golf course, a strong field, a couple of USGA records that looked untouchable, and a $30,000 check.

What Lee Trevino really did, when he won the Open championship last Sunday, however, was shoot more life into the game of golf than it has had since Arnold Palmer, whoever that is, came along. Trevino will not only go out and fight a course for you in the most colorful of ways, he'll say most anything to most anybody. He'll hot dog it. He'll tagline it. And he'll respond. In a gangsome of 30 or 40 visor-gripping Bert Yanceys, most of whom seem to have graduated from the yep-and-nope school of public relations, Lee Trevino had already made himself known to a degree. He had received more pretournament press than anyone simply because he talked a lot and said things like, "I used to be a Mexkin, but I'm makin' money now so I'm gonna be a Spaniard." Well, now, you take this kind of a fellow and give him a major championship and what you've got is instant celebrity.

It all happened in one day, actually, but that is all it ever takes. It happened on Sunday, the last day of the Open, when Trevino went out and did what no one thought he could do—turn Bert Yancey's game into a shambles, one on one, and totally ignore the near presence of Jack Nicklaus. Trevino did it although he had not won an event on the PGA tour, and, in fact, had only been on the tour for a short while—a couple of months last summer and all this season. Which is not so long, especially for a man who has not had a lifelong acquaintance with money. In winning, Trevino further had the audacity to tie Nicklaus' 72-hole 1967 Open record of 275 and set a record of his own by becoming the first player ever to shoot four straight rounds under par in an Open: 69, 68, 69 and 69.

The last round began with Yancey leading at 205, Trevino second, a stroke behind, and Nicklaus a distant third at 212. Yancey and Trevino started off as if they were playing for the Tenison Park municipal title in Dallas, which is a place where Lee used to hustle $5 Nassaus and where the U.S. Public Links tournament will be played in July. Yancey drove into the right rough, and Lee hit into the left trap, and they both made bogeys. Trevino steadied a trifle, but Yancey kept it up. He hit a big hook at the 3rd under a tree, chipped up nicely but missed the five-footer for his par. At the 5th he hit into a bunker, came out to within three feet but missed again. At this point he had lost the lead for the first time since Thursday afternoon. Trevino was one ahead, and Nicklaus, who had birdied the 3rd and 4th up ahead, was only three strokes away.

One more birdie right in there somewhere could have made a gigantic difference for Nicklaus, but he had already demonstrated in three previous rounds that he couldn't read consistently the subtleties of Oak Hill's greens. Hit the shots, sure. Nicklaus was hitting more greens in regulation than anyone; he was, in fact, playing superbly. But never did the putts fall, and they weren't to fall the rest of the day. Makable birdie after makable birdie slid past the holes, and a great amount of pressure was taken off Trevino.

On each hole Trevino could look ahead and see that Nicklaus wasn't catching fire, and on each hole he could look over in the woods or in the bunkers or around the cups where poor Bert Yancey's game had gone thataway. ("I guess I just must have choked," Yancey said later.) Bert was plodding dismally to the 76 that most people in the gallery would have bet their periscopes that Trevino would shoot.

If there was a big hole that wrapped it all up it was the 12th. They got there with Trevino having just birdied the 11th with his longest putt of the tournament, a 30-footer, and with the noise and joy of it still ringing in him. The crowd sensed he was the winner now. He had a three-shot lead, and he played this comparatively short par-4 nicely with a good drive and a pitch into the flag, only 18 feet away. He rammed this one down to go one under for the round—and four great big strokes ahead of Yancey and five in front of Nicklaus. It was, as a matter of fact, all over, even though Lee had to slash out of the rough on the last two holes to save a couple of pars and the record.

"I was tryin' to get so far ahead I could choke and still win," Trevino said afterward. And then he started firing all of those lines that made the press tent roll with laughter, and made him everybody's darling.

"I haven't got no shirts and shoes and cap contracts like the big-timers do," Lee Trevino said.

And: "Yeah, I been married before, but I get rid of 'em when they turn 21."

And: "When I first started winnin' those $3,000 and $4,000 checks last summer, I said, 'Say, how long's this been goin' on out here?'"

And: "Man, I like to go to the dog track over in Juarez. I been feedin' them dogs for years and they don't get no faster."

And: "Yeah, you got to speak Mexkin in El Paso. Man, you can't even buy gas if you can't speak Mexkin."

And, finally, after an overdue pause for breath: "No, I haven't called my wife, but if I don't have the $30,000 check there by Wednesday, she'll call me."

As Super Mex laid it out there for his new band of worshipers, over in the corner stood a hefty, medium-size fellow with short curly hair. Name of Bucky Woy. Bucky Woy is a manager like Mark McCormack is a manager, only it is Bucky Woy who is advising the Open champion, Lee Trevino, and the Masters champion, Bob Goalby, and it was Bucky Woy who was throwing a tequila party up at the Oak Hill club house after the Open Sunday night, where the new champion talked nonstop on such matters as hitting a wedge left-handed and the value of practicing on a pitch-and-putt course. Woy also invited everybody over to the Blue Sombrero for a Lee Trevino party. Tony Lema had champagne. Lee Trevino has margaritas. And golf has a brand-new guy.

There were really three unusual pairings for that last round, the best of which, of course, was Trevino-Yancey, who were playing their own tournament. But there was also one with Bob Goalby and Roberto De Vicenzo, which naturally led everyone into the same joke trap: Oak Hill will settle the Open *and* the Masters. Finally, there was another. Arnold Palmer, who had been posting all sorts of psychedelic scores, found himself in the very last insulting group with a couple of amateurs. One was Jack Lewis from Wake Forest, the other 18-year-old John Simons from the vicinity of Palmer's Latrobe. Palmer, it could thus be said, was only playing for two things: the Wake Forest Alumni Championship and the West Penn Open. He won the latter and lost the former, finishing with twin double bogeys to let Jack Lewis beat him 74 to 75.

Palmer, who still drew the big crowds, finished his catastrophic

Open at 301 in 59th place. Except for Nicklaus' last round of 67, which lugged Jack up into second place past the collapsed Yancey, it was not a very good Open for golf's so-called Big Three. Gary Player, the other member, started with a 76 and closed his performance by falling into a creek on the 10th hole and swimming to a 73. Palmer and Player were bypassed by hordes of strange competitors. Not the least of them were Steve Spray, who shot a final-round 65, which included a record-tying 30 on the back nine, to tie for fifth, and two club pros, Don Bies, who tied Spray for fifth, and Jerry Pittman, who tied for seventh. Inasmuch as Pittman is the pro at USGA Executive Director Joe Dey's club in Locust Valley, N.Y. the possibility of a Pittman victory made the mind envision a glorious headline: JOEY DEY'S PRO WINS OPEN.

Nor was this year's Open an especially good one for the other past champions in the field. Billy Casper came to Rochester as the favorite, winner of four tournaments and more than $100,000. But after a 75 on the first round, during which he strained his back, he was never really in contention. Julius Boros, curiously, had a 71 on each of the first three days, just as he had at Oak Hill in the 1956 Open, when he tied for second. But on the final round he shot a 75 instead of a 69 and finished in a tie for 16th. And Ken Venturi, the winner at Congressional in 1964, did not even make the cut.

As for Palmer, he did nothing right except begin the tournament with a birdie. He drove badly, hit irons sideways, recovered miserably, putted atrociously, and, worst of all, gave up. On one particular day he had five putters on the practice green, and seemed to be asking everyone, including itinerant concession salesmen, what to do about his ills. Anyone who saw Palmer with his five putters and happened to read the Rochester *Democrat and Chronicle* the next day must have been confused. There, prominently displayed, was one of those syndicated instruction articles by Arnold Palmer with a headline that said: YOU'RE ON FAST GREEN? 'TAP' METHOD'S BEST.

DeVicenzo managed to win the "play-off" for the Masters by outscoring Goalby, by 70 to 73, but Goalby was mad about the pairing before they ever teed off. "I walk on the first tee and I get two claps," he said. "What do people expect of me? Roberto and I have played together maybe a hundred

times in our lives, and people got to make something out of
this. I won under the rules of golf, that's all I know. Anyhow,
it's not so good to win if you got to spend all your time at
department stores. My game's going sour with appearances."

The first day of an Open, much of it, at least, is nearly
always dominated by players who seem like brand-new guys.
They have names like John Felus, or Steve Spray, or Ronnie
Reif. There are, after all, 150 men in the field who begin teeing off at 7:30 a.m. So up until a point well into the afternoon, the leader boards at Oak Hill looked like the
Rochester yellow pages—classification, plumbing fixtures. All
sorts of unlikely souls were in red figures (for below par) at
least briefly, while the big names shadowboxed the course.
None, however, trudged along under the gray clouds and
through the chill winds of Thursday quite so dramatically as
John Felus.

He was a little man from somewhere in Pennsylvania,
scarcely five feet tall, who wore the color scheme of any
unknown. Light blue cap, uncertain, semi-lost expression. In
the scant gallery that he drew, he was called "foul-us" and
"fool-us" and "fail-us." No one knew which was he in his
pairing with Billy Farrell and Jim Dolan; who could? It was
only after he hit a short iron into the 13th green to within
one foot of the pin and sank it to go two under par that people knew. The standard-bearer put a red 2 beside Felus, the
guy who made the birdie. Felus was the little guy dressed like
your neighbor in the yard; not the two tall guys with golf
swings. So he went to the 14th tee with the red 2.

Felus took a bit cut at the ball on the 14th tee and drove
down the middle, about an eight-iron from the green. He
mis-hit the approach altogether but it bounced between two
silica bunkers and miraculously rolled up to 2½ feet of the
cup. His putt never even hit the cup because John Feluses are
not supposed to be two-under in the Open, much less three.
Unsteady pars on the next two holes sent Thursday's early
hero to the 17th tee with the U.S. Open lead in his tiny
hands and only Yancey, Trevino and Al Balding behind him
in red figures. Was John Felus going to lead this Open? Could
John Felus *win* the Open? The questions were soon answered.
Felus drove off of the 17th tee like Uncle Andrew in the

onion patch—or like a man leading the Open. He sliced. He sliced about 100 yards into the rough of another fairway, behind trees, bushes, TV trucks and telephone company equipment. He got a free drop, which was lucky. But he then hit a fairway wood into a hot-dog stand to the right of the 17th green.

A lot of journalists had rushed out on the course now to find John Felus. When they reached the hot-dog stand, they wanted a beer and a frank and, for a moment, some of them thought all of these people standing around the refreshment area, including the little man in the green shirt and gold sweater, were waiting in line for mustard. Presently Felus got another free drop, scraped a chip shot and got out of his dilemma with a bogey. He was still one-under and still leading. But he promptly hit another high, raging slice off the 18th tee, and everybody left him. John Felus had come and gone in the 1968 Open, and it was time to turn to Bert Yancey.

For three rounds Yancey played about as well as a man can play. He practically made a joke of Oak Hill with his carefully laced tee shots, his crisp irons and a putter that is known as the best on the pro tour. He came along a few holes behind John Felus the first day to rap in birdies on the 16th and 18th holes for a three-under-par 67, and the opening round lead, two strokes ahead of Trevino.

A player of even tempo who walks along slowly, wears a wristwatch, keeps a pencil behind his right ear and always has a white visor on, Yancey was spectacular with his irons. And he had a game plan: shoot for the middle of the greens and don't make a double bogey. When he got into difficulty with a couple of erring tee shots the second day, he wisely chipped out, then played up and relied on his smooth putting stroke to rescue him. It did. He turned a 74 into a 68, and his total of 135 tied the U.S. Open record for 36 holes, a record set in 1960 at Cherry Hills by Mike Souchak. Trevino, with his own 68, remained in second, two strokes behind.

A rather colorless fellow who casts the image that he's only plugging along out there, Yancey took a moment out on Friday to worry about the public. After an interview he went up to Doc Giffin, the press secretary for Arnold Palmer, and asked, "How was I? Did I sound better? Did I sound O.K?"

Well, he wasn't Don Rickles, of course. Most of Bert Yancey's color is in a beautiful swing—and in his background. He is a deep, moody-looking, often vague fellow who once had a nervous breakdown while he was enrolled at West Point. All he remembers is that one day he blacked out and wound up in a hospital for nine months and finally got a medical discharge. He was all right. During the next three years he went back to college at Florida State, took a club job, got married, had a kid, and went on the tour. Once out there, all he gave a cleat for, said his best friends, was winning a major championship—a Masters or an Open.

"He used to withdraw when he realized he couldn't win a tournament," said Frank Beard, one of his pals. "Bert's a superconcentrator. In bridge games he'll drive you crazy. You sit there waiting for him to bid and finally he'll say, 'You know, that one-iron on the seventh today went sideways.' He really studies himself, and his game."

The third round also belonged to Yancey, although Trevino gained a stroke with a 69. Bert played steadily for a par 70 and his 54-hole total broke an Open record. His 205 was one stroke lower than the 206 Tommy Jacobs had shot at Congressional in 1964. In that third round Yancey and Trevino were paired together, and it already seemed that they were playing one tournament while the rest of the field was playing another. All day long Yancey was seven strokes or more ahead of Jack Nicklaus. Only Trevino was close to him in score, or in person. If you removed those two from the field, the Open looked like an Open should—Nicklaus tied for the lead, with everybody at least two over par. Thus, the thick, cultivated rough, and the silica sand, and the subtle contours of well-prepared Oak Hill were whipping the field. An Open course is supposed to whip the field, as everybody with good sense knows. But it wasn't. It wasn't whipping Yancey and Trevino.

Until the last day when the putter deserted him, along with most every other club, Yancey looked like the complete golfer. And the only logic you could work out was that a good golfer was having a good week on a well-groomed course. A player who had proved he could win on all types of greens—rye at Azalea, Bermuda at Memphis, *Poa annua* at Portland—Yancey was now proving he could win on the bent at Oak Hill in Rochester. He was always right around the cup, or in it, as he primarily destroyed the par-4 holes, birdieing nine of them through the three rounds.

Trevino seemed to be hanging in there only because no one else was, and he figured it might as well be he. Nor was he playing the kind of golf Yancey was. On Friday, for example, Trevino drove eight times into the rough, but his putter kept saving him. Lee would walk down the fairways, hollering at friends and strangers alike, saying, "What am I doin' wrong? I don't know if I'm gonna hook it or slice it." But then he would scramble to the green and get the ball down and stay close enough to Yancey to make it a contest.

When they were paired together for Saturday's third round, the Open sort of became an old-fashioned PGA Championship. Match play was reborn. Yancey went through the first nine in 34 and at one point held a five-stroke lead on the field, including Trevino. But Lee got three birdies on the back while Bert slipped on one hole, and Trevino had charged back into contention. But no one felt it could last.

Any competitor in the locker room who was asked about it said that on Sunday when Yancey and Trevino were going out there head to head again—match play again—it would be Yancey who would play all the golf. Only Nicklaus, they said, had a chance to throw up a 67 or 66 right in front of them, scare them and win.

It was Dave Marr who said, "You know Yancey can play, and you know how badly he wants to win a big one. You just don't know anything about the jumping bean."

You do now. All the gringos do.

There's Never Been An Open Like It

BY DAN JENKINS

THE 1960 U.S. OPEN, PLAYED AT CHERRY HILLS COUNTRY CLUB IN DENVER, MARKED A WATERSHED IN THE HISTORY OF THE GAME. IN THE COURSE OF ONE ROUND, WRITES DAN JENKINS, "WE WITNESSED THE ARRIVAL OF NICKLAUS, THE CORONATION OF PALMER AND THE END OF HOGAN."

They were the most astonishing four hours in golf since Mary, Queen of Scots found out what dormie meant and invented the back nine. And now, given 18 years of reflection, they still seem as significant to the game as, for instance, the day Arnold Palmer began hitching up his trousers, or the moment Jack Nicklaus decided to thin down and let his hair fluff, or that interlude in the pro shop when Ben Hogan selected his first white cap.

Small wonder that no sportswriter was capable of outlining it against a bright blue summer sky and letting the four adjectives ride again: it was too big, too wildly exciting, too crazily suspenseful, too suffocatingly dramatic. What exactly happened? Oh, not much. Just a routine collision of three decades at one historical intersection.

On that afternoon, in the span of just 18 holes, we witnessed the arrival of Nicklaus, the coronation of Palmer and the end of Hogan. Nicklaus was a 20-year-old amateur who would own the 1970s. Palmer was a 30-year-old pro who would dominate the 1960s. Hogan was a 47-year-old immortal who had overwhelmed the 1950s. While they had a fine supporting cast, it was primarily these three men who waged war for the U.S. Open championship on that Saturday of June 18, 1960. The battle was continuous, under a steaming Colorado sun at Cherry Hills Country Club in Denver. Things happened *to* the three of them and *around* them—all over the place—from about 1:45 until the shadows began to lengthen over the same elms and cottonwoods, the same wandering creek, and the same yawning lake that will be revisited this week as Cherry Hills again is host to our grandest championship.

In those days there was something in sport known as Open Saturday. It is no longer a part of golf, thanks to television—no thanks, actually. But it was a day like no other; a day on which the best golfers in the world were required to play 36 holes because it had always seemed to the USGA that a pro-longed test of physical and mental stamina should go into the earning of the game's most important title. Thus, Open Saturday lent itself to wondrous comebacks and horrendous collapses, and it provided a full day's ration of every emotion familiar to the athlete competing under pressure for a prize so important as to be beyond the comprehension of most people.

Open Saturday had been an institution with the USGA since its fourth annual championship in 1898. There had been thrillers before 1960, Saturdays that had tested the Bobby Joneses, Walter Hagens, Gene Sarazens, Harry Vardons, Francis Ouimets, Byron Nelsons, Sam Sneads—and, of course, the Ben Hogans—not to forget the occasional unknowns like John L. Black, Roland Hancock and Lee Mackey, all of them performing in wonderfully predictable and unexpectedly horrible ways, and so writing the history of the game in that one event, the National Open.

But any serious scholar of the sport, or anyone fortunate enough to have been there at Cherry Hills, is aware that the Open Saturday of Arnold, Ben and Jack was something very special—a U.S. Open that in meaning for the game continues to dwarf all of the others.

The casual fan will remember 1960 as the year old Arnie won when he shot a 65 in the last round and became the *real* Arnold Palmer. Threw his visor in the air, smoked a bunch of cigarettes, chipped in, drove a ball through a tree trunk, tucked in his shirttail, and lived happily ever after with Winnie and President Eisenhower.

And that is pretty much what happened. But there is a constant truth about tournament golf: other men have to lose a championship before one man can win it. And never has the final 18 of an Open produced as many losers as Cherry Hills did in 1960. When it was over, there were as many stretcher cases as there were shouts of "Whoo-ha, go get 'em, Arnie!" And that stood to reason after you considered that in those insane four hours Palmer came from seven strokes off the lead and from 15th place to grab a championship he had never even been in contention for.

Naturally, Palmer had arrived in Denver as the favorite. Two months earlier he had taken his second Masters with what was beginning to be known to the wire services as a "charge." He had almost been confirmed as The Player of the New Era, though not quite. But as late as noon on Open Saturday, after three rounds of competition, you would hardly have heard his name mentioned in Denver. A list of the leaders through 54 holes shows how hopeless his position seemed.

The scoreboard read:

Mike Souchak	68-67-73—208
Julius Boros	73-69-68—210
Dow Finsterwald	71-69-70—210
Jerry Barber	69-71-70—210
Ben Hogan	75-67-69—211
Jack Nicklaus	71-71-69—211
Jack Fleck	70-70-72—212
Johnny Pott	75-68-69—212
Don Cherry	70-71-71—212
Gary Player	70-72-71—213
Sam Snead	72-69-73—214
Billy Casper	71-70-73—214
Dutch Harrison	74-70-70—214

| Bob Shave | 72-71-71—214 |
| Arnold Palmer | 72-71-72—215 |

Through Thursday's opening round, Friday's second round, and right up until the last hole of the first 18 on Saturday, this Open had belonged exclusively to Mike Souchak, a long-hitting, highly popular pro who seldom allowed his career to get in the way of a social engagement. His blazing total of 135 after 36 holes was an Open record. And as he stood on the 18th tee of Saturday's morning round, he needed only a par four for a 71 and a four-stroke lead on the field.

Then came an incident that gave everyone a foreboding about the afternoon. On Souchak's backswing, a camera clicked loudly. Souchak's drive soared out of bounds, and he took a double-bogey 6 for a 73. He never really recovered from the jolt. While the lead would remain his well into the afternoon—long after Arnold had begun his sprint—you could see Souchak painfully allowing the tournament to slip away from him. He was headed for the slow death of a finishing 75 and another near miss, like the one he had experienced the previous year in the Open at Winged Foot.

Much has been written about Arnold Palmer in the locker room at Cherry Hills between rounds on Open Saturday. It has become a part of golfing lore. However, there could hardly be a more appropriate occasion for the retelling of it than now. As it happened, I was there, one of four people with Arnold. Two of the others were golfers—Ken Venturi and Bob Rosburg, who were even farther out of the tournament than Palmer—and the fourth was Bob Drum, a writer then with the *Pittsburgh Press*. It was a position that allowed Drum to enjoy the same close relationship with Palmer that *The Atlanta Journal's* O.B. Keeler once had with Bobby Jones.

Everybody had cheeseburgers and iced tea. We bathed our faces and arms with cold towels. It was too hot to believe that you could actually see snowcaps on the Rockies on the skyline.

As Palmer, Venturi and Rosburg sat on the locker room benches, there was no talk at all of who might win, only of how short and inviting the course was playing, of how Mike Souchak, with the start he had, would probably shoot

269 if the tournament were a Pensacola Classic instead of
the Open.

Arnold was cursing the first hole at Cherry Hills, a 346-
yard par four with an elevated tee. Three times he had just
missed driving the green. As he left the group to join Paul
Harney for their 1:42 starting time on the final 18, the thing
on his mind was trying to drive that first green. It would be
his one Cherry Hills accomplishment.

"If I drive the green and get a birdie or an eagle, I might
shoot 65," Palmer said. "What'll that do?"

Drum said, "Nothing. You're too far back."

"It would give me 280," Palmer said. "Doesn't 280 always
win the Open?"

"Yeah, when Hogan shoots it," Drum said, laughing heartily
at his own wit. Drum was a large Irishman with a P.A. system
for a voice and a gag-writer's knowledge of diplomacy.

Arnold lingered at the doorway, looking at us as if he were
waiting for a better exit line.

"Go on, boy," Drum said. "Get out of here. Go make your
seven or eight birdies and shoot 73. I'll see you later."

Bob Drum had been writing Palmer stories since Palmer
was the West Pennsylvania amateur champion. On a Fort
Worth newspaper, I had been writing Ben Hogan stories for
10 years, but I had also become a friend of Palmer's because I
was a friend of Drum's.

Palmer left the room but we didn't, for the simple reason
that Mike Souchak, the leader, would not be starting his last
round for another 15 or 20 minutes. But the fun began before
that. It started for us when word drifted back to the locker
room that Palmer had indeed driven the first green and two-
putted for a birdie. He had not carried the ball 346 yards in
the air, but he had nailed it good enough for it to burn a path
through the high weeds the USGA had nurtured in front of
the green to prevent just such a thing from happening. Palmer
had in fact barely missed his eagle putt from 20 feet.

Frankly, we thought nothing of it. Nor did we think much
of the news that Arnold had chipped in from 35 feet for a
birdie at the second. What *did* get Bob Drum's attention was
the distant thunder that signaled that Arnold had birdied the
3rd hole. He had wedged to within a foot of the cup.

We were standing near the putting green by the clubhouse, and we had just decided to meander out toward Souchak when Drum said:

"Care to join me at the 4th hole?"

I said, "He's still not in the golf tournament."

"He will be," Drum said.

And rather instinctively we broke into a downhill canter.

As we arrived at the green, Palmer was in the process of drilling an 18-foot birdie putt into the cup. He was now four under through 4, two under for the championship, only three strokes behind Souchak, and there were a lot of holes left to play.

We stooped under the ropes at the 5th tee, as our armbands entitled us to, and awaited Arnold's entrance. He came in hitching up the pants and gazed down the fairway. Spotting us, he strolled over.

"Fancy seeing you here," he said with a touch of slyness.

Then he drank the rest of my Coke, smoked one of my cigarettes, and failed to birdie the hole, a par 5. On the other hand, he more than made up for it by sinking a curving 25-footer for a birdie at the par-3 6th. At the 7th, he hit another splendid wedge to within six feet of the flag. He made the putt. And the cheers that followed told everybody on the golf course that Arnold Palmer had birdied six of the first seven holes.

It was history book stuff. And yet for all of those heroics it was absolutely unreal to look up at a scoreboard out on the course and learn that Arnold Palmer still wasn't leading the Open. Some kid named Jack Nicklaus was. That beefy guy from Columbus paired with Hogan, playing two groups ahead of Palmer. The amateur. Out in 32. Five under now for the tournament.

Bob Drum sized up the scoreboard for everyone around him.

"The fat kid's five under and the whole world's four under," he said.

That was true one minute and not true the next. By the whole world, Drum meant Palmer, Hogan, Souchak, Boros, Fleck, Finsterwald, Barber, Cherry, etc. It was roughly 3:30 then, and for the next half hour it was impossible to know who was actually leading, coming on, falling back, or what. Palmer further complicated things by taking a bogey at the 8th. He parred the 9th and was out in a stinging 30, five under on the round. But in harsh truth, as I suggested to Bob Drum at the time, he was still only three under for the tournament and two strokes off the pace of Nicklaus or Boros or Souchak—possibly all three. And God knows, I said, what Hogan, Fleck and Cherry—not to mention Dutch Harrison, or even Ted Kroll—were doing while we were standing there talking.

Dutch Harrison, for example, had gone out very early and was working on a 69 and 283. And way back behind even Palmer was Ted Kroll, who had begun the round at 216, one stroke worse off than Palmer. Kroll and Jack Fleck had put almost the same kind of torch to Cherry Hills' front nine holes that Palmer had. Kroll had birdied five of the first seven holes, with one bogey included. Fleck had birdied five of the first six, also with a bogey included. Kroll was going to wind up firing the second-best round of the day, a 67, which would pull him into what later would look like a 200-way tie for third place at the popular figure of 283. One last footnote: Don Cherry, the other amateur in contention, was the last man on the course with a chance. There was this moment in the press tent when everyone was talking about Palmer's victory, and somebody calculated that Don Cherry could shoot 33 on the back nine and win. Cherry was due to finish shortly after dark. He quickly made a couple of bogeys, however, and that was that. But, meanwhile, we were out on the course thinking about Palmer's chances in all of this when Drum made his big pronouncement of the day.

"My man's knocked 'em all out," he said. "They just haven't felt the shock waves yet."

History has settled for Bob Drum's analysis, and perhaps that is the truth of the matter after all. The story of the 1960 Open has been compressed into one sentence: Arnold Palmer birdied six of the first seven holes and won.

But condensations kill. What is missing is everything that happened after 4 o'clock. The part about Mike Souchak losing the lead for the first time only after he bogeyed the 9th hole. The part about Nicklaus blowing the lead he held all by himself when he took three ghastly putts from only 10 feet at the 13th. This was the first real indication that they were all coming back to Palmer now, for Nicklaus' bogey dropped him into a four-way tie with Palmer, Boros and Fleck.

But so much more is still missing from the condensation. Nicklaus' woeful inexperience as a young amateur cost him another three-putt bogey at the 14th hole, and so, as suddenly as he had grabbed the lead, he was out of it. Then it was around 4:45 and Palmer was sharing the lead with Hogan and Fleck, each of them four under. But like Nicklaus, Fleck would leave it on the greens. Boros had started leaving it on the greens and in the bunkers somewhat earlier. He was trapped at the 14th and 18th, for instance, and in between he blew a three-footer. In the midst of all this, Palmer was playing a steady back side of one birdie and eight pars on the way to completing his 65. And until the last two holes of the championship, the only man who had performed more steadily than Palmer, or seemed to be enduring the Open stress with as much steel as he, was—no surprise—Ben Hogan.

It was getting close to 5:30 when Hogan and Palmer were alone at four under par in the championship, and the two of them, along with everybody else—literally everyone on the golf course—had somehow wound up on the 17th hole, the 71st of the tournament.

The 17th at Cherry Hills is still a long, straightaway par five, 548 yards, with a green fronted by an evil pond. In 1960 it was a drive, a layup and a pitch. And there they all were. Hogan and Nicklaus contemplating their pitch shots as the twosome of Boros and Player waited to hit their second shots, while the twosome of Palmer and Paul Harney stood back on the tee.

Hogan was faced with a delicate shot of about 50 yards to a pin sitting altogether too close to the water to try anything risky. Ben had hit 34 straight greens in regulation that Saturday. He needed only a par-par finish for a 69, which would have been his third consecutive subpar round in the tournament. He had to think this might be his last real chance to capture another Open. And nobody understood better than Hogan what it meant to reach the clubhouse first with a good score in a major championship.

Armed with all of this expertise as I knelt in the rough and watched Hogan address the shot, I brilliantly whispered to Drum:

"He probably thinks he needs another birdie with Arnold behind him, but I'll guarantee you one thing. Ben'll be over the water."

At which point Hogan hit the ball in the water.

He made a bogey 6. And in trying to erase that blunder on the 18th with a huge drive, which might conceivably produce a birdie, he hooked his tee shot into the lake and suffered a triple-bogey 7. Sadly, only 30 minutes after he had been a co-leader with just two holes to go, Hogan finished in a tie for ninth place, four strokes away.

Second place then was left to the 20-year-old with the crew cut, and Nicklaus' score of 282 remains the lowest total ever posted by an amateur in the Open.

All in all, these were tremendous performances by an aging Hogan and a young Nicklaus. The two of them had come the closest to surviving Palmer's shock waves.

It was later on, back in the locker room, long after Palmer had slung his visor in the air for the photographers, that Ben Hogan said the truest thing of all about the day. Ben would know best.

He said, "I guess they'll say I lost it. Well, one more foot and the wedge on 17 would have been perfect. But I'll tell you something. I played 36 holes today with a kid who should have won this Open by 10 shots."

Jack Nicklaus would start winning major titles soon enough as a pro, of course. But wasn't it nice to have Arnold around first?

Day of Glory for A Golden Oldie

B Y   R I C K   R E I L L Y

THOUGH HE CAME TO AUGUSTA IN 1986 WITH 19 MAJOR TITLES UNDER HIS BELT, JACK NICKLAUS HADN'T WON ONE IN SIX YEARS. NOR AT THE AGE OF 46 DID HE SEEM LIKELY TO. BUT AS RICK REILLY RECOUNTS, THE BEAR OF OLD HAD NOT DEPARTED. HE HAD JUST BEEN HIBERNATING.

That arm. Who could forget that arm? In the roar of roars at the 18th green, from behind a Masters scoreboard glittering with names of golf's power brokers—BALLESTEROS and WATSON and LANGER and KITE—under the sign that said No. 18, beside the huge black letters that read NICKLAUS, next to a red 9, came the arm that had put that number there, the arm that seconds before had placed a red 8 next to NORMAN, and that arm was pumping furiously.

No head, no body, no shoulder, just an arm belonging to the leader-board man, pumping and pumping for pure, wallowing joy. To hell with employee objectivity. Jack Nicklaus had just won the Masters, once again, and that arm just couldn't help itself. If it was Old St. Nick who had delivered the goodies; if it was the Ancient One who had posted that birdie at 17, then parred 18, while Greg Norman had taken out his Fore!-iron and mailed the gallery a souvenir on the same hole; if it was the Olden Bear who had mystically come from five shots and a couple of decades back to hijack the Masters golf tournament, then it was that arm behind the scoreboard that was telling us what it meant.

Can't you see? That red 9 set off an avalanche of history. Jack Nicklaus, a 46-year-old antique, had won his 20th major golf championship, his first green jacket in 11 years, his sixth over three decades and all in this, the 50th, and arguably the best, Masters.

How complete, how whole this was for Nicklaus. Hadn't he been duped out of that 20th long ago? Hadn't Tom Watson's chip taken the U.S. Open from him at Pebble Beach in 1982 and broken his spirit? How many times had he led a major only to have his pocket picked at the end? Now the spikes were on the other foot. Here was Nicklaus, in one swell swoop, reaching down from another era and snatching a major championship from the reigning czars of this one. It is a trick no other golf god has pulled, not Palmer or Hogan or Snead or Sarazen. Nicklaus had beaten young men at a young man's game on young men's greens and beaten them when they were at their youthful best. As Tom Kite, destiny's orphan, put it, "I hit nearly every shot the way I dreamed about today. But that's the strange thing about golf. You don't have any control about what your opponent does."

And just in the Nicklaus of time, too. Who else but Jack could save us from the woeful, doleful bowl full of American Express (do-you-know-me?) golf winners of late? And who else could play John Wayne, riding in to rescue the Yanks from golf's rampaging foreign legion: the dashingly handsome Seve Ballesteros of Spain; the stone-faced Bernhard Langer of West Germany; Australia's Norman, he of the colossal swing and larger-still reputation, more unfulfilled now than ever; and Zimbabwean–South African–Floridian Nick Price, who on Saturday broke the course record that had gone unsurpassed for 46 years, then on Sunday recoiled in the giant shadow of what he had done.

Here had come Nicklaus, an American legend still under warranty, armed with a putter the size of a Hoover attachment, denting the back of Augusta's holes with 25-foot putts at an age when most guys are afraid to take the putter back. Here had come Nicklaus, sending such a deluge of decibels into the Georgia air that lakes rippled and azaleas blushed; starting such a ruckus that grown men climbed trees, children rode on shoulders, concession-stand operators abandoned their posts, all just to tear off a swatch of history. Was that Jack in the checked pants and yellow shirt? Hmmmm. Yellow goes nice with green, doesn't it, Jack? You devil.

Maybe that was it. Maybe Nicklaus had drawn up a contract with Lucifer for one last major, for that slippery 20th that had eluded him since 1980, for a sixth green blazer. In exchange, Nicklaus would do pro-ams in Hades the rest of his days.

What else could explain it? How else to explain the guy in 160th place on the money list, just one spot behind Don Halldorson, winning the Masters? How else to explain a man who hadn't won in two years charging back the last day, going seven under for the final 10 holes, sculpting a 30 that tied the Masters record for the back nine—winding up with a sporty 65 as he roared past eight players and won? This is a guy who missed the cut at the Honda, for the love of Hogan. In fact, Nicklaus missed the cut in three of seven tournaments this year and withdrew from a fourth. Of the ones he finished, his most impressive showing was a tie for 39th at the Hawaiian Open, which didn't exactly throw a scare into Corey Pavin, who won. The $144,000 for winning the Masters means he's up to $148,404 for the year. Nicklaus goes through more than that in limo tips.

The man is older than Pete Rose, for crying out loud. He has played in more Masters (28) than Pavin has lived years (26). When Nicklaus won his first Masters, in 1963, Norman was eight years old, Ballesteros and Langer five. Nicklaus either signed his soul away or is angling for an endorsement contract with Efferdent.

"I read in the Atlanta paper this week that 46-year-olds don't win Masters," said Nicklaus. "I kind of agreed. I got to thinking. Hmmm. Done, through, washed up. And I sizzled for a while. But I said to myself, I'm not going to quit now, playing the way I'm playing. I've played too well, too long to let a shorter period of bad golf be my last."

More remarkable in all this comeback talk was the fact that rumors were flying that Nicklaus had been missing some serious greens, and not just the kind you take a Toro to. "My company was a mess," Nicklaus says.

In an effort to improve the fortunes of his own company, Golden Bear International, Nicklaus let the contract of his chief executive officer, Chuck Perry, lapse seven months ago and assumed day-to-day control of the business himself. "Chuck worked very hard for me," says Nicklaus, "but he wanted to build an empire. He was sending out p.r. releases talking about a $300 million empire and all that stuff. But I don't want an empire. What am I going to do with an empire? I've got five kids, a beautiful wife and I'm hoping on some grandkids. That's what I care about."

Nicklaus admits that he has been distracted by business worries, in particular about a couple of his many golf-course and real-estate deals. But he says he is not in a financial crunch, which makes it just a coincidence that he recently signed as a spokesman for Nabisco Brands and is in negotiation with ABC-TV to appear on golf specials for five years. "The ABC contract is with the lawyers right now," Nicklaus says.

With his business dealings weighing heavily on his shoulders, to say nothing of his checkbook, it was no wonder he was floundering on the golf course. His irons and woods were still Jack Be Nimble, but his putter had been pure Tip O'Neill. Take Thursday's opening round, for instance. He had 11 putts inside 15 feet and made one. On Sunday's front nine he missed two four-footers. "If I could just putt," he said Friday, "I might just scare somebody. Maybe me."

But that seemed fanciful, and it wasn't just newspaper writers typing him off. CBS analyst Ken Venturi told *USA Today*, "Jack's got to start thinking about when it is time to retire."

After all, who could take Nicklaus seriously after his opening rounds of 74 and 71? Besides, by Saturday, the leader board was doubly stocked with people you had actually heard of. One was a certain swashbuckling Spaniard who has been out of work much of this year, what with his father's recent death and his sword-fighting with PGA Tour commissioner Deane Beman. Coming into the Masters, Ballesteros had played only nine competitive rounds in all and had made precious little money. "Ninety dollars," he joked. "All on practice-round bets with [Ben] Crenshaw and [Gary] Player."

Still, Ballesteros's rapier hardly looked rusty, and when he opened with a convincing 71–68 and a one-shot lead, nobody could make him less than the favorite for his third coat. "They ought to name this place after him," said Price. "He hits it so long and so high and draws it so well and is so imaginative around the greens that I don't think he'll ever finish out of the top five here."

Price's game isn't all that ill-fitting, either. On a windless Saturday that Watson said left the course as "defenseless as I've ever seen it," Price's 63 was a course record, a Jackson Pollock splash of birdies—nine in a series of 12 holes—that broke the course record of 64, set in 1940 by Lloyd Mangrum and equaled by Nicklaus and four others. That left him at five under, and when Seve got heavy on Saturday, turning a one-shot lead at 17 into a one-shot deficit by the time he hit the clubhouse, Price found himself tied with Ballesteros, Langer and Donnie Hammond, one shot behind Norman.

Everybody genuflect. It's Sunday morning in the cathedral of golf, and the high priests are all here. Norman leading, with Price, Langer, Ballesteros, Watson, Tommy Nakajima of Japan and Kite all within two shots, not to mention an altar boy, Hammond. Nicklaus, with a Saturday 69 ("The first time I've broken 70 since I can't remember when," he said), was looking surprised but quite harmless at four back.

"My son Steve called me at the house we're renting this morning," Nicklaus said, "and he asked me, 'Well, Pop, what's it going to take?' And I said, 'Sixty-six will tie and 65 will win.' And he said, 'Well, go ahead and do it.'"

But as Sunday's round began, Nicklaus looked as if he was going to keep on doing what he had been doing, which was knocking the ball tight and putting loose. He missed four-footers at the 4th and the 6th, and when he got to the 9th tee, he was right where he started—two under. He was also five shots behind Norman.

Then, suddenly, all heaven broke loose.

Playing two groups ahead of Ballesteros and Kite, four

ahead of Price and Norman, Nicklaus finally got a birdie putt to drop, an 11-footer. Four shots back.

At the 10th, he birdied from 25 feet, which should have put him three back, except for an odd set of goings-on at No. 8, where both Kite and Ballesteros had left the hole without ever pulling their putters. Kite had holed a wedge from 81 yards for an eagle, followed by Ballesteros from 40 for another eagle. Not only did that speed up play considerably, but it also kept Nicklaus four back of the leader, now Ballesteros.

But when Ballesteros bogeyed No. 9 and Nicklaus answered with a birdie at the portal to Amen Corner, No. 11, Augusta National began to overheat like a $99 Impala. Two back.

Then Nicklaus did something that got him cooking. He made a bogey 4 at the 12th hole. Three back.

"I don't know why, but it really got me going," he said. "I knew I couldn't play defensive with the rest of the course. I knew I needed to be aggressive coming in."

On the par-5 13th, the Curtis Strange Memorial Hole, where the Masters is often lost and rarely won and where Nicklaus bent a three-wood so precariously close to the woods that his part-time caddie and full-time son, Jackie, thought he had put it in the creek on the left-hand side. "Shots like that are a little too much for a 24-year-old heart, Dad," he told him. Dad hit a 210-yard three-iron over Rae's Creek and to within 30 feet, then two-putted for birdie. Two back.

Now it was Ballesteros's turn at 13, only he did it better, letting a six-iron drift lazily in left to right and sinking an eight-footer, his second eagle of the day and third of the tournament. At this rate, with the par-5 15th still to come, the Spaniard looked as if he could radio ahead with his sleeve length. Nicklaus now was four behind him, two back of Kite. See you at the awards stand, Seve.

Desperate, at the 15th, Nicklaus let loose a mammoth drive, 298 yards, so big it surprised even him. He had changed his swing (less hands) and his diet (more food). He had gone on the Eat to Win Diet and lost. "I was down to 170 pounds and I realized I couldn't play golf at 170," he said. He's up to 190 and hitting it farther than ever. Fat Jack is truly back.

With 202 yards to go at 15 and the tournament in the balance, Nicklaus turned to Jackie and said, "You think a three would go very far here?" To which Jackie said, "Let's see it."

Obligingly, Nicklaus hit his four-iron to 12 feet and made the eagle putt for exactly that—a three. The crowd's yelp was downright frightening. Two back.

As Nicklaus walked from the 15th green to the 16th tee, one had the odd feeling of being indoors at, say, an overtime Kentucky basketball game, yet all the while being outdoors. That's loud.

And wild. Six-figure executives were slapping high fives. Women in $400 dresses were sprinting ahead to get a vantage point. "He's hot! He's hot! He's hot!" one man kept shrieking, perhaps about to ignite himself.

"The noise was deafening," said Nicklaus. "I couldn't hear anything. I mean, nothing! I wasn't trying to think about the leader board. All I knew was that I was putting the ball on the green and making birdies and I was going to keep on doing it."

As Ballesteros was walking up the 15th fairway after a King Kong–like drive, Nicklaus was pulling out a five-iron at the par-3 16th. "I nailed it," he said. But he couldn't see it. "I could hear the gallery at the green starting to rumble and I said, 'Oops, I've hit it close.'"

Oops, he had come within inches of a hole in one, the ball skittering three feet by the pin. The eruption from the gallery may have been the most resounding in Masters history, next to, of course, the one that greeted the putt that came next. One back.

What does one feel like when all around you, a golf course, a state, a country, are coming unglued and you are the only person keeping them from imploding entirely? Ballesteros surely found out as he stood over his four-iron, 200 yards from the 15th green, his ears ringing. What he felt like when he hit it is unknown since he was off the Augusta property within minutes of the finish of his round. But to watch your Masters chances go kerplunk in green-dyed water as his did cannot be good for your est training.

"He had a awkward lie up on a knob, but he hit his last few iron shots heavy," Kite said. "It was a tough situation: the lie, the circumstances, what Nicklaus was doing, the noise. It was so noisy you couldn't even hear each other."

"I wasn't under pressure," Ballesteros said on Monday. "It's just that I hit too easy a swing with a four-iron. I should have hit a hard five. I played very good. Just one bad shot, that's all."

Now Nicklaus had reeled in Ballesteros but not Kite, who would birdie 15. That made it a three-way tie at eight under par. Meanwhile, Norman had quickly recovered from a double bogey at 10 and was sitting two back.

Nicklaus tried to get ready to drive at the par-4 17th but had a small problem. "I kept getting tears in my eyes," he said. "It happened to me once at Baltusrol. But here, it happened four or five times. I had to say to myself, Hey, you've got some golf left to play."

After driving into the left rough he hit a 125-yard pitching wedge to 11 feet. He drained the putt. "Dead center." Nicklaus leads. One up over Ballesteros and Kite.

Moments later, Ballesteros, shaken, three-putted at 17 for bogey, but Kite made par from the back of the green and Norman was stormin', too, making birdies at 15 and 16. Still one up, now over Kite and Norman.

Eighteen surrendered without incident for Nicklaus. He hit onto the front of the tiered green, almost precisely where the pin traditionally has been set for the final round. This year, the green had been redesigned, and the pin was now set on the back level. He nearly holed out from 40 feet, dropped it in for the par, then hugged Jackie.

"I was getting choked up with all the people cheering on every hole. I was so proud of him," Jackie said. "Finally, when he putted out on 18 I told him, 'Dad, I loved seeing you play today. It was the thrill of my lifetime. I mean, that was awesome.'"

Father and son walked arm in arm to the scorer's tent and then to the Bob Jones cabin to wait and see.

What they saw first was Kite at 18 lining up a 12-foot putt for birdie and a tie. Would Kite, so long denied, finally have a chance at a major?

"I made that putt," said Kite. "It just didn't go in. Honest to God ... I made it so many times in the practice rounds—seven or eight times—and it never broke left once." It broke left. Still one up.

Now the only obstacle between Nicklaus and perhaps his most remarkable major of all was Norman.

"We heard the roar [for Nicklaus] on 15 and then another roar and another," Norman recalled. "By that time, Nicky [Price] and I were back there with about 50 people following us. So I said to Nicky, 'Let's do something to wake these people up.'"

Out of an impossible divot lie on 17, Norman somehow made a pitch-and-run shot over a hill that stopped 12 feet from the hole, then sank the putt. Tie. Nine under par.

With pandemonium all around him, Norman chose to hit a three-wood from the 18th tee. The shot was fine and straight, except that it left him holding his four-iron, which in Norman's hands lately works about like a waffle iron. It was the four-iron he had hit into the gallery at 10 to set up the double bogey.

He sliced it this time into the gallery ringing the 18th green, and couldn't get up and down for par, his 16-footer missing left. "I just basically spun out and pushed it to the right," Norman explained. "I was trying to hit it too hard and too high.... I was going for the flag. I was going for the birdie and the win. It was the first time all week I let my ego get the best of me."

Your usual, Jack, 42 regular?

"This," said Nicklaus in triumph, "was maybe as fine a round of golf as I've ever played."

He drove down Magnolia Lane and out the iron gates in green for a preposterous sixth time. He had won at Augusta in 1963, when Sam Snead finished two strokes back, and '65, '66, '72, '75 and now, '86. That's a 23-year span between his first and last fitting. His original jacket was a 44 long. "It fits me like a tent," he said. "I wore [New York Governor] Tom Dewey's jacket for years, and finally I had my own jacket made."

His record of longevity and dominance is unequaled. And that includes his victories in five PGA Championships (1963,

'71, '73, '75, '80), four U.S. Opens ('62, '67, '72, '80), three British Opens ('66, '70, '78) and two U.S. Amateurs ('59 and '61). He has now won three majors in his 40s, which is another first.

All of which says, truly, once and for all, that if there ever was a better golfer than Jack William Nicklaus, then Woody Allen can dunk.

"I finally found that guy I used to know on the golf course," Nicklaus told his wife, Barbara. "It was me."

So welcome back.

The Best Against The Best

BY   FRANK   DEFORD

IT IS A RARE TREAT WHEN TWO SUPERB GOLFERS, EACH AT THE
PEAK OF HIS POWERS, GO HEAD-TO-HEAD WITH A MAJOR TITLE
AT STAKE. JACK NICKLAUS AND TOM WATSON HAVE WON EIGHT
BRITISH OPENS IN THEIR ILLUSTRIOUS CAREERS, BUT NONE PRO-
VIDED AS MANY THRILLS AS THE 1977 OPEN AT TURNBERRY.

As they approached the tee at the 72nd hole, Alfie Fyles, Tom
Watson's caddie, spoke up. "Go for the jugular," he said, and
Watson broke a small grin and nodded his head and asked for
his one-iron. This was it, at last; this would be the final hole
in what, even then, people were calling the greatest golf
match ever. Watson had gone head to head with Jack Nicklaus—the young lion, the challenger of this decade, vs. the
golfer of the ages—in the first British Open ever played on the
Ailsa course at Turnberry, on the Ayrshire coast, by the Firth
of Clyde, off the North Channel of the Irish Sea. It was July
of 1977; Nicklaus was 37, still in his prime, and Watson was
27, the new Masters champion, just coming into his.

On this last hole, Watson's tee shot drifted a bit left, but
still clear of the bunker that sat 260 yards out. It was "awfully
perfect," said Watson, so Nicklaus didn't hesitate.

For the first time on this hole he yanked out his driver and called up his power. It was incredible what he and Watson had done: identical 68–70s the first two days, matching 65s the third day, playing almost stroke for stroke together the final two rounds, pushing each other higher and higher, driving the gallery into a happy frenzy. They were a shot apart coming to the last hole, but still, either one of them could *10*-putt the 18th green and finish runner-up. The winner's 268 would be the best score in British Open history by eight strokes. Two men had never played golf like this before, side by side.

The instant Nicklaus finished his swing he knew he had tried too hard and had hit the ball too full. The 18th fairway bent left just past the bunker Watson had missed, and Nicklaus wanted his drive to drift that way. Unfortunately his drives had been sailing to the right all day, and once again his tee shot flew that way, through the crook in the fairway, into rough as deep as there was anywhere on the course. Nicklaus turned the driver in his hand like a baton, took the offending club end and banged the handle down angrily to the turf as he stomped off the tee. To think it would end like this. It had to finish in glory. Nobody should *lose* this match. He or Watson, either one, O.K., but this was a match one of them had to *win*.

Watson walked over to check on Nicklaus's lie. At first he wasn't sure that the ball was even playable; it was buried deep in tall grass, only inches from a prickly strand of gorse. Would Jack be able to bring a club back, much less muscle the ball out? Watson decided Nicklaus would just be able to negotiate a swing, and he returned to his own ball, which lay perhaps 180 yards from the pin.

"What do you think?" he asked Alfie. The caddie fingered the seven-iron. Watson stared at him quizzically.

"What? You know I can only carry 160–65 with a *six*."

"The way your adrenaline's pumpin', Tom...." was all Alfie said, and his man took the seven. Watson hit it full-blooded to the pin, 30 inches from the cup.

It surely must be over now.

Nicklaus grasped his eight-iron. He took it back right through a branch of the gorse bush, macheted it down with

a superhuman swat and sent the ball and a massive divot flying out. Somehow the ball found the right side of the
green, 32 feet from the flag. It was impossible. Right away
Watson knew—*knew*—that Nicklaus was going to make that
putt for a birdie.

Nicklaus strode off. Barely had he turned heel than the
Scots rushed over and reverently began dropping coins in the
gash in the ground where Nicklaus's ball had lain, bribing the
god of chance for a good putt. Pennies went onto the spot,
twopenny coins, tenpenny pieces, even some old shillings.
The pile began to resemble those cartoons of the pot of gold
at the end of the rainbow.

Watson tried to fight his way through the rabble that
swarmed onto the fairway. People were scrambling, bumping,
tussling. Alfie got knocked down, pitched full forward. At
the last moment he reached out and broke his fall, but he
strained his left wrist, and as Watson broke through the mob,
he looked back and was shocked to see his caddie's wrist
already swelling. Until then, Alfie had been a pretty fair player himself, "a bit of a hustler." But even after the knot went
down, the wrist stayed stiff, and he never again played a hole
of golf. Alfie has carried, all told, for six victorious British
Opens, and no other caddie has won more than half as many.
After being so close to the perfection of those two men those
days at Turnberry, maybe it was meant that no mortal should
himself ever play again.

Nicklaus studied his putt, right to left, down into a dip and
up. It was 32 feet on the 72nd hole of the British Open,
with his rival lying less than a yard from the hole. Watson
turned to Alfie and whispered, "You know, I believe Jack'll
make this." Alfie looked at Watson as if he were mad. "I
expect him to make this," Watson declared.

"Fine, and so you can make yours."

"Mmmm," was all Watson said back. If Nicklaus birdies, 30
inches looks like 30 miles.

Nicklaus struck the ball and started it on its path. Even
before it was halfway, Alfie could see that Watson was right.
Impossibly, incredibly, it was a birdie.

"Good god," Alfie thought. "Tom's dead right. The bloody
ball is going into the hole."

Although the British Open was first played in 1860, only 15 courses have been used in the rotation—what the British call the "rota." Turnberry, the scene of next week's Open, has long been generally recognized as the best links on Scotland's west coast, but not until 1977 had it ever been tapped for the Open. Part of this was circumstance, for Turnberry— Tonbrrry, the Scots say—though only 50 miles from Glasgow, is isolated down the coast, with the only close lodging at the Turnberry Hotel itself. The hotel is a magnificent old building, built on a hill, looking out onto the golf course below and the firth beyond, its long, burnt-red roof visible from almost everywhere on the links except, perhaps, from the depths of the 66 well-like bunkers that are scattered around the course.

Inconvenience aside, Turnberry would surely have entered the rota earlier, except that twice it had to go to battle. In the Great War it served as a flight training station for the Royal Flying Corps and Commonwealth Flying Units, and then in World War II it was all but ripped apart and reassembled as an air base, with 18-inch-deep runways laid down where the Scots had hit second shots out of the fescue and buttercups. After World War II, when the whole useless place—hotel and acreage, the lot of it—could have been had for £10,000, the course was knitted back together. Now only here and there do bits and pieces of tarmac remain alongside the gorse. Otherwise, all that is left of Turnberry's noble other life is the monument on the knoll overlooking the 12th green, on which the names of the brave lads who flew off from the old links, never to return, are listed. Besides the English and the Scots, there were Aussies, South Africans and Canadians.

The Turnberry lighthouse stands just a fairway beyond the monument. By all that is holy in British golf, the courses ordained for the Open must lie by the sea, on sandy soil the land has reclaimed from the god Neptune. These are the undulating links courses, literally linking those two realms of nature that make up God's blue-green earth. Curiously, though, while St. Andrews and Muirfield, Carnoustie and Royal Troon—all fabled Scottish links—reside by the sea, they are folded into the land in such a way that the sense of water can be lost. Turnberry alone is one with the deep. From the 4th hole to the 11th, the course clings to the firth coastline like a wet suit, and from almost everywhere on the course wee boats are visible below the dunes, with whitecaps breaking and winds blowing trenchant and briny.

On the best of days it's possible to see beyond the Mull of Kintyre, all the way to Ulster in Northern Ireland. The greater, looming presence, however, always belongs to Ailsa Craig, 10 miles out at sea and 1,113 feet high. It is a massive rock that stands at the mouth of the firth as if it were the helmet top of a monster Norse warrior god who will, if piqued, finally bestir himself from the sea floor, then stomp across the links and the heather.

The Scots say, "If ye can see Ailsa Craig, it's gaun to rain. If ye canna see it, it's already raining." The Scots also say, "If it's nae rain and it's nae wind, it's nae golf," and while that obtains on any links, Turnberry is the model. On the odd day when there is no wind, without what is known at The Tonbrrry Giant, the course, sans trees and tricks, is defanged. Like some large, toothless animal, it could still box your ears and gum you something fierce, but it could never take a bite as big as an 85 out of Gary Player's hide, as it did at a tournament in 1972 when The Giant blew in. In that tournament, as the wind picked up round by round, Peter Townsend posted a progressively revealing 65-70-75-80. The next year, during the same tournament, a huge hospitality tent was lifted clean off its moorings and blown away. There have been days at Turnberry when rain, hail, sleet and snow have arrived sequentially, each at gale force, and at times The Giant howls so ferociously that fairways cannot be reached with a driver. On most parts of Turnberry the gorse has been tilted over by the prevailing winds, left as if it were cowering in fear.

But the wind lay still in the summer of '77 when Nicklaus and Watson arrived. Everything was askew. The previous two summers had been absurdly hot and dry, and then that winter there had been too little moisture, which further inhibited growth. (The golfers who come to Turnberry next week will find the fairways as narrow as ever—some barely 20 paces across—but the rough will be ever so much more formidable than it was nine Julys ago.) At that time, too, a bizarre Scottish heat wave swept in, discombobulating man and sheep. In the gallery, many of the Scotsmen went without shirts, their unaccustomed bare skin glowing a bright pink. This being the land of wool and cashmere, there literally wasn't a T-shirt to be found, and some of the fans actually stripped to their underwear. Ailsa Craig shimmered like some misplaced Club Med isle.

Into this alien Scotland came Nicklaus, who was posted as the 6–1 favorite even if he was suffering what, for him, had been a regular depression. Although he had been the PGA Player of the Year the past two years, he had actually gone six majors in a row without a victory. To help put an end to this nonsense, Nicklaus eschewed the use of a British caddie and brought with him his American aide, Angelo Argea, an imposing man with silver steel-wool hair and a menacing, mustachioed countenance.

The affable Alfie Fyles came up from near Liverpool to—as his fading ilk still puts it—caddie *to* Watson. Alfie had caddied to Gary Player for more than a decade before shifting his allegiance to the young Watson two years before. It was a fortuitous pairing. Watson had been tagged a choker by captious critics, but though he arrived at Carnoustie in '75 too late for a practice round, he won his first major title there—in a playoff, to boot. Given that Watson was in a strange land, unprepared, accomplishing something he had never managed under the best of circumstances back home, Alfie assumed that he must have played a role of some consequence indeed in the young Yank's triumph.

British caddies have always presumed a more significant, distinguished role than their American counterparts, who, often as not, have been viewed as little more than necessities, on the same order, say, as pinsetters in a bowling alley. British caddies have always had their opinions solicited, and usually valued, even by the grandest and most savvy of golfers. For one thing, the elements are forever shifting in Britain. But much of the status of caddies has to do with the differences between the two societies. In America it's considered beneath oneself to labor as an athletic domestic, yet the British, comfortable with the gentleman-servant relationship, saw that men could make an honorable career out of toting other men's bags. Except for time out as a seaman in the Royal Navy, Alfie has caddied for about half a century.

Alas, there are fewer such stalwarts all the time. Long John, The Wasp, The Lawyer, the one-armed Wingy Eugene, the similarly handicapped Halifax Wingy (who lost his hook in some heavy rough once), Johnny One-Blank (who did have all his limbs but lacked an eye), Mad Mac, Laughing Boy, Yorky Billy have all gone. And disappearing just as rapidly is the caddie's Cockney argot, which featured a rhyming code. A Vera Lynn, for example, meant a gin, a Gregory Peck a check. A beehive was a five (usually used in association with cherry picker, which meant a knicker, which was itself a slang word for pound; thus a caddie with a beehive cherry picker had a £5 note). And St. Louis Blues was shoes, Holy Ghost was toast, and sizzle and strife meant the missus.

But the career boys are a dying breed. "All you've got is your bag-carriers now," Alfie sneers. "All they can do is give the golfer a weather report—not the right club." Nothing sets Alfie's blood to boiling more than the familiar sight of a man who calls himself a caddie throwing grass up in the air to detect the wind direction. In Alfie's view, you might as well have a homing pigeon asking a bobby to show him the way back to the house. "Once it was all eyeball," he explains. Caddying is telling your man to use a seven-iron to carry 180 yards when the most he can hit a six is 165. That is caddying, eyeball.

And in a world today where Americans expect to have a little piece of home wherever they go—the English language and the baseball scores, McDonald's and MasterCard—most American pros bring their caddies over to Scotland for greater security. Watson and Alfie are the exception. And even they had one great falling out, right at the beginning, after Alfie eyeballed Watson to his first major, at Carnoustie in '75. When he went up to the Watsons' room to get his pay, Alfie was so disgusted at the figure Watson gave him that he threw the Gregory Peck down on the floor. "You must need this more than me," he snapped. Linda Watson was furious, and Alfie told Watson to have her leave, that he worked for Tom, not for his wife. But Watson wouldn't budge, so Alfie picked the check off the floor—"before Tom could take me literally"—and left in disgust.

The next summer Watson brought his American caddie over to help him defend his title at Royal Birkdale and he missed the 54-hole cut. Both the Watsons began to seek rapprochement after that, and Alfie was waiting for Watson when the Yank arrived at Turnberry. They've been together every July since then, and Watson has the finest British Open record—five championships—of any American.

In 1977 it wasn't until Friday, the third round—when Nicklaus and Watson were first paired together—that they began to outdistance the field. Indeed, when they started off that midday, both having shot par 70s the morning before, they were a stroke behind Roger Maltbie and there were 16 contenders within four shots of the lead.

But on that third day Nicklaus and Watson would both shoot 65s—six birdies and a bogey apiece—and on Saturday they would move off into a realm by themselves. The pattern was set at the 1st hole, too, when Nicklaus struck a wedge to within three feet and made a birdie. Always, over the last two days, Nicklaus would draw ahead and Watson would fight back. On Friday, Nicklaus was two strokes ahead, playing the 8th hole, called Goat Fell, when the overcast skies turned electric. Both men were on the green, but Watson wanted to take cover immediately.

Nicklaus, the senior, prevailed, though, and Watson reluctantly went along, but as soon as they both putted out, parring, the golfers and their caddies scurried down to find shelter among the rocks on the beach. Only when they were protected by an overhang did it occur to Alfie that water made the best conductor, so back up the cliff they hustled to take refuge in a BBC trailer. Watson and Nicklaus didn't say much to each other, but rarely does either talk on the course. When the storm passed they put on sweaters and proceeded to the forbidding 9th tee, the one stuck out on an overlook, the one that Herbert Warren Wind has described as "out of a Gothic novel."

They both parred there and sank long birdie putts on 10. Nicklaus took his only bogey of the round with a bad putt on 14, and when Watson sank a 20-footer on 15, they were level once again. Nicklaus should have gained a stroke on 17, but he missed an eagle putt and, like Watson, had to endure a mere bird. Both parred 18. Nicklaus 31–34, Watson 33–32. Both: 203 for 54 holes, seven under par.

Curiously, it still wasn't viewed strictly as a duel. There was Ben Crenshaw, of whom great things were expected, only three shots back, at 206. Nicklaus was near the height of his powers, but even if Watson had won at Carnoustie in '75 and had edged Nicklaus at the Masters three months earlier, there remained something unsubstantial about him. In time Watson would tote up eight majors, but the "quitter" charge still lingered then with Watson, as even now he is being written off early, after only two years of struggling. "It has the same flavor," he says, biting off the words. Pause. "The same smell." Then, too, even at his best, Watson was neither awesome nor mysterious, and while he was invariably described as having "a Huck Finn look," Huck's playful, mischievous aspect was missing. Besides, the British had never held it against Nicklaus, the way the Americans did, that he eclipsed Palmer, so there were more cheers for Jack.

Nobody knew then how great a force Watson would become in the British Isles. "Tom's a good thinker," Nicklaus says, "and you have to think well over there to win. You're playing in adverse conditions, and there are just a lot of our guys who can't do that for 72 holes."

Watson would also develop a peculiar facility for playing his best down the stretch against Nicklaus—better even than emotional characters like Trevino and Palmer, who could sway a crowd. In his entire career, Nicklaus says, "my hardest loss" remains the '82 U.S. Open, when Watson beat him straight-up by chipping in from off the 17th at Pebble Beach. Watson never let Nicklaus's majesty intimidate him. Three months before Turnberry, at the Masters, playing in adjacent twosomes, Watson was on the 13th fairway when he saw Nicklaus raise his putter toward him after he sank a birdie on the green ahead, as if to say, *Take this.* In fact, Nicklaus was only exulting, but Watson upbraided him for his seeming hot-dog action as soon as they encountered each other off the last green. Nicklaus, stunned, didn't have the foggiest idea what he was being accused of, and Watson finally backed off, embarrassed but undaunted.

Watson is not an easy man to characterize. Principled and sensitive, he also bears the rap of being a know-it-all. He is one of the few athletes left who still smoke. While most other golfers play out of planned Sunbelt subdivisions, Watson went off to Stanford to school and has returned to his native Kansas City to celebrate his family, the Royals and the seasons. Some days in January or February he's the only person playing at the Kansas City Country Club. "It's cleansing," he says. After that, Turnberry and the other links may not seem quite so beastly.

The fans at Turnberry were jostling for places when the two men teed off in the final pairing late Saturday morning. It was a bright, sunny day, but for the first time all week a brisk wind was coming steadily, broadside off the firth. Nicklaus wore a pale yellow sweater with dark blue slacks, while Watson chose a sea-green sport shirt, which he wore with checked light-green-and-orange trousers and a wide, white belt that was the fashion at that time.

It's funny, looking back. Today, at 36, Watson is nearly the age that Nicklaus was then. Watson now appears, naturally, older than he did in 1977. The Huck Finn business is behind him. Plus, looking back, that wide, white belt locates him firmly in time. On the other hand Nicklaus, a renowned 46 now, looks almost the same as he did in '77. Examining the old pictures, and then studying the men today, one gets the impression that Nicklaus has stood still for a decade while Watson has been catching up.

On this occasion Nicklaus and Watson were playing a final round *together* for the first time, and it almost appeared decided on the 2nd hole, named Mak Siccar, when Nicklaus sank a 10-footer for a birdie and Watson, playing indifferently from off the green, bogeyed. A two-stroke swing. Nicklaus went up three just two holes later, when he rolled in a 20-footer at Woe-be-Tide. But Watson remained foolish enough to think he could still win. "In '82, the time I beat Jack at Pebble Beach, I was lucky," he says. "I was driving the ball all over, but the gallery packed down the rough, and I knew the course. Turnberry was different. It had an element of a Texas summer to it and I was the same way—very calm inside the boiler, so to speak. I could feel the heat, but only as if it were around me."

As for Nicklaus, even if he was three strokes ahead, he wasn't taking anything for granted. "If I'm playing Tom Watson, I know I have to win," he says. "With somebody else against you, maybe you feel they'll lose instead."

And sure enough, Watson steadied and started to fight back. On the 5th, Fin' me Oot, he hit a five-iron to 16 feet and popped it in. Never again would there be a three-stroke margin, although there could have been on the very next hole, Tappie Toorie, a long par-3, for Watson put his three-wood in a bunker. He splashed out to six feet and eyed the putt nervously. Nicklaus had his par assured. Then Watson asked Alfie for his opinion. In all their British Opens together—before and since—this was the only occasion when Watson, one of the finest putters of his era, ever asked Alfie for help on the green.

Shaking, Alfie stood behind his man and allowed that it seemed to him that it would break left at the last. It did just that. "Good line," was all Watson said as they walked off to 7, the 528-yard Roon the Ben. The tee there is elevated, the beach almost straight down, 60 feet below. Both drove to the left, but Nicklaus drove well beyond Watson, leaving himself only a three-iron. Watson pondered his plight. "What do you think, Alfie?" he asked.

"Everything you got, Tom."

"A driver?"

"If you can lift it."

"Yeah, O.K.," Watson said, and he took out the driver, used it on the fairway and put the ball on the green—"my best shot of the day." And it was he, not Nicklaus, who made birdie. He had two of the three strokes back.

On the 8th he got the tie. It was a 20-foot putt, dead center. "It was lucky," Watson says. "It had the line but not the touch. If I had missed at all, it would have gone six, seven feet by."

Except for the wives and girlfriends and accountants of the other golfers, there wasn't a fan on the course who wasn't in the last gallery. They kicked up such a dust cloud chasing down the 9th fairway that Nicklaus fought his way over to Watson and said, "Tom, this is getting out of hand." The junior man agreed, so Nicklaus went to the gallery marshals, and the two players sat down on their bags for several minutes until the crowd was brought to heel. The damn thing was getting like a football match at Wembley.

Maybe the disruption upset the golfers. The picturesque 9th was, in sum, their worst of the 36 holes they played with one another, Watson taking a bogey, Nicklaus only saving par with a 12-foot putt. And then, just like that, when Nicklaus sank a 20-foot birdie putt on 12, under the monument, the great champion was two ahead again, and there were only six holes left.

So, O.K., Watson broke serve right back. On the difficult two-tiered elevated green at the 13th, Tickly Tap, Watson ran in a 12-footer, and now he was only a stroke back and the crowd was beside itself again, reinvigorated, scurrying this way and that down the sides of the 14th fairway, so that Watson, with the honor, had to pause before he hit his drive.

Watson did get a squeak at the hole on 14, but he missed his seven-footer, and they went to 15 with Nicklaus still one stroke ahead. It's the last par-3, 209 yards, Ca Canny, which means Go Very Carefully, bunkered on the left, with a great drop off the right of the green. Predictably, the flag for the final day had been put far right, too, and so Watson played prudently to the left, but his ball drifted too far that way, off the green, between two traps. "Damn," said Watson after the shot. Nicklaus instantly realized he could absolutely, finally, put Watson away, and he went for the stick. He hit right on line, too, with an uphill putt for a reasonable birdie try and a two- or maybe three-stroke lead.

Though he was well off the green, Watson took his putter. He practiced this sort of shot regularly—the old "Texas wedge"—and, in fact, he had also already played a similar easier version off the 12th green. Here, he was a full 60 feet away, but he hit much too hard, about 70 feet's worth. Only the cup got in the way. Slam dunk. Watson jumped high in the air. Somehow, Alfie had the presence of mind to glance over at Nicklaus. He was just reaching down to put his ball back on his mark when Watson's ball swooped in, and

Nicklaus literally rocked back, as if he had been coldcocked. More even than any of the great shots he himself hit at Turnberry, this is the one Nicklaus best remembers to this day. And when he missed his own putt they were tied again.

The Scottish sky would hold the light for hours yet, till 11:00 or so, and just now, late in the afternoon, for the first time was it starting to slant low. Standing on the 16th tee, Watson felt the rays on his freckled face, and he sensed the moment, what he and Nicklaus were doing, and he couldn't help himself. He couldn't help but smile, and when he did, he turned to Nicklaus and he said, "This is what it's all about, isn't it?"

Nicklaus smiled back beatifically, and then they both struck magnificent drives and strode off down the fairway. They both liked it that they were head to head, *mano a mano*, in the manner of most other sports, where your opponent is more flesh and blood and not the turf and the trees. Nicklaus dolefully recalled his second British Open, at Royal Lytham in 1963, when, standing on the 18th tee he could see Phil Rodgers and Bob Charles come off 16, he didn't hear any cheers so he assumed they had both parred and he played it safe on the last hole—only to lose by a stroke to Charles because, in fact, both Charles and Rodgers had birdied 16, but the wind was blowing the other way and had carried the cheers off with it.

Nicklaus and Watson were still tied after 16, Wee Burn. Seventeen, Lang Whang, the short par-5, was an obvious birdie hole, the one where Nicklaus should have had an eagle the day before. As was the pattern, Watson drove straight down the middle while Nicklaus went a bit right. Watson then unloaded a three-iron, which rolled around in a ringlet, ending up only 12 feet away for a chance at an eagle.

And that was when Nicklaus gave way. He was the one who made the kind of shot everybody else in the field had been making all four days. He botched a four-iron. It stayed right and, while it did stop a few yards short of a bunker, it left him in the scarred rough, 50 feet or so to a green that sloped away, five or six feet below. For the first time, Watson arrived at a green as if he were stalking it, and realizing how difficult his rival's plight was, he turned to his caddie and uncharacteristically cracked, "I've put a nail in his coffin now, haven't I, Alfie?"

So Nicklaus promptly played a perfect chip, running the ball out of the rough, down to within four feet of the pin, and then Watson, shaken, missed his eagle try. They were both putting for routine birdies in order to go to the 72nd even.

It was Jack Nicklaus who missed his.

He played it to break, but it went right through the break, a hair to the left.

And that was when Alfie said, "Go for the jugular," and Watson took out his one-iron. At last, after 71 holes, at last he had the lead, and Jack Nicklaus was in his lee.

Minutes later, though, Watson's premonition that Nicklaus would sink his birdie putt at 18 proved to be correct, and the roars of amazement reached a crescendo even before Nicklaus's ball tumbled in for his birdie: 68-70-65-66, 11 under. The nearest competitor besides Watson was Hubert Green at one under; and no one else had ever shot better than four under in 105 other British Opens. Only, of course, if Watson sank his two-and-a-half-footer, if he made his birdie, he would finish 68-70-65-65, 12 under.

Watson did not hesitate. He could not let the crowd rule. "All right, I'm ready to win this thing now," he said to himself, and he sized up the putt as Nicklaus raised his arms to quiet the mob. Still there were, in fact, the odd lingering whistles and sighs when Watson brought his putter forward and tapped the ball firmly. Alfie watched. It was not short. Tom Watson was never short then. It was not straight either.

But it was straight enough.

The ball plunked into the right side of the cup, and the greatest golf battle ever was over. Watson raised his hands to the crowds, putter high, and he was almost dazed when Alfie reached his man and embraced him. Then, there was Nicklaus before him, looking Watson square in the eye and telling him, "I'm tired of giving it my best and not having it be good enough."

Watson was almost too stunned to reply. "Thanks," was all he could manage. Remembering that, still a bit ashamed at how tongue-tied he had been, Watson drew on a Winston and shook his head. "I'm not very good at words in situations like that." But Nicklaus had understood. He put his arm around Watson's shoulders, squeezed him affectionately about his neck and escorted him off the green that way, as if he were the winner and Watson the vanquished.

Then at the ceremony, Nicklaus said in public, so graciously, what he had first said to Watson alone. "I gave you my best shot," the greatest player said, "and it just wasn't good enough. You were better." And then, too, a final, very British understatement: "It was well played." The Mona Lisa was well painted. Hamlet was well written.

A day's work done, Nicklaus went to dinner. His memories of Turnberry are not nearly so vivid as Watson's. "I couldn't take you around that course if I had to," he says. But then, he figures he has played 500 courses. "I just don't remember a whole lot when I lose. But you've got to understand: I don't remember a whole lot about the ones I win, either; only, when I win people keep bringing them up, so I'm not allowed to forget. But what's to say here? I shot a 65–66 and another man shot a 65–65. Well done." It's not Nicklaus but his wife, Barbara, who remembers how touched they were when they came into the dining room a bit later and the whole place, people at every table, rose and applauded him, the runner-up. Well done.

Watson, with Linda and a couple of friends, arrived a few minutes later, and once more the entire dining room rose and applauded. Watson went over to Nicklaus and spoke briefly to him. He came back to his own table and said he had told Nicklaus "what a wonderful speech Jack gave." Linda hurried to assure her husband that he had given a fine speech, too. "No, my speech was awful," Watson said and he shrugged. He had forgotten, perhaps, how eloquent he had been on the 16th tee. That *was* what it was all about, wasn't it?

Then, when dinner was finished, Watson went into a small ballroom where a dance band was playing, and he walked over to the leader and requested a song. "It'll be *Blue Skies*," Linda said. And it was *Blue Skies*. That was his father's favorite song. His father taught Tom to play golf. Tom took Linda in his arms and they danced to his father's song.

It was late, but the light lingered. The manager of the hotel had sent a bottle of champagne to the Watsons' room. They sipped it and talked of the wonders of this day. No matter what else Tom Watson would ever do in golf—and he would do much more—history had embraced him now, for he had beaten the best at his best, best to best.

The Watsons' room was on the top floor, and from there, under the red roof, with the last of the sun's rays falling behind the Mull of Kintyre, they could see down and across Turnberry. It was still below, except that here and there a lone Scotsman or two strolled the links, taking the unusual tropic air. It was as if the universe had been turned upside down, and dark was light and up was down and the people below were like stars sprinkled above in the heavens.

And then downstairs, outside on the promenade, a lone piper began to walk, playing his pipes, the Scottish melodies drifting up to where Tom and Linda sat drinking champagne. And they looked at each other and began to cry.

"I think it was at that time that I really fell in love with the game," Watson said, reminiscing. And now, just like that, just simply remembering, he began to mist up again. For a long time, then, he simply sat there, the tears welling up from the glorious days past into his eyes. He knew he was crying, he was told he was crying, and still he made no effort to brush away the tears.

"I'd always loved golf, but now it was a new type of love I could have," he said, and without disturbing them he let the tears keep rolling down his cheeks so that they could reflect the memories of Turnberry past, tinting them with his pride and joy.

Bank Shot

BY RICK REILLY

AS WELL AS BEING A GAME OF INCHES, GOLF IS A GAME OF
LUCKY OCCURRENCES, SOME OF WHICH MIGHT BEST BE
DESCRIBED AS JUST PLAIN WEIRD. AS RICK REILLY TELLS IT, THE
1992 MASTERS WAS DECIDED BY A SHOT THAT SEEMED TO DEFY
EVERY LAW OF NATURE.

One less drop of rain. One more run of the mower. A cup
less of fertilizer last fall. One more breath from a nearby but-
terfly. A blade of grass with weak knees. An eyelash less luck.
Any of these things could have cost Fred Couples the Masters. But somehow, some way, Couples's golf ball hugged the
steep slope at Augusta National's 12th hole, clung to it the
way a sock clings to a towel fresh out of a hot dryer. The
ball steadfastly refused to fall into the water. Does Maxfli use
Velcro?

Lookee here now, there are laws at the Augusta National
Golf Club, and they will not be trifled with. No tipping. No
women upstairs in the clubhouse locker room. The green
jackets never leave the property, except the one belonging to
the reigning Masters champ. The azaleas are even told when
to blush. And the No. 1 law of the par-3 12th hole, the edict

that never gets broken, is that any spheroid that hits the bank in front of the green rolls back into Rae's Creek, and you're wearing at least a 5, bucko. No exceptions. It was that way for Gene Sarazen. It was that way for Ben Hogan. It was that way for Tom Weiskopf, who spun five balls into that creek, two of them bank jobs, in the first round in 1980.

A ball has about as much chance of stopping on that bank as a marble does of stopping halfway down a drainpipe. Does not happen. This is where Henry Longhurst often used the term *a watery grave*. Said Furman Bisher of the *Atlanta Journal-Constitution*, who has been coming to Augusta since 1950, "In all my years of coming here, I can't remember one staying on that bank."

But on Masters Sunday 1992, on the biggest day of Couples's 32½ years, with Ray Floyd and Corey Pavin breathing hot down his neck and with a brilliant career waiting to bloom, one finally did. "The biggest break, probably, in my life," said Couples.

Well, why not? Why shouldn't all the laws of physics come to a halt? Practically every other precept at staid Augusta was folded, stapled and mutilated last week.

For instance, at Augusta no business is allowed to be conducted on club property. Business is not even to be *discussed*. However, while walking between the 9th and 10th holes during a practice round on April 8, the day before the tournament started, hunky chunk John Daly got a piece of paper stuck in front of his face for the nine millionth time that day. This one, though, wasn't in search of an autograph. It was an envelope. Daly didn't grip it, didn't rip it, didn't even want to look at it. "Hell," said Daly, who ended up tied for 19th in his first Masters, "it could have been a love letter."

It was, sort of. It was a notification that he was being sued for paternity and breach of promise by his ex-girlfriend Bettye Fulford. *Dear John: Your butt is sued. Enjoy the back nine.*

At Augusta no running is allowed. But on Saturday, Ian Baker-Finch and Jeff Sluman, who were a twosome that day, literally ran to their shots on the 17th and 18th holes. Double-parked on Magnolia Lane? No. A three-hour rain delay earlier in the day meant that, to finish before play was called for darkness, Baker-Finch and Sluman had to sprint between shots as fast as their little spikes could take them. At one point Sluman was putting out on number 17 as Baker-Finch was madly planting his tee at 18. They made it.

At Augusta no littering is allowed. However, all tournament long Ray Floyd kept leaving balls lying in cups. You would think that, at five months short of 50, he would know better, but he kept dumping balls into Augusta's holes and then just walking away with that gunslinger strut he has. At 43 Floyd won the U.S. Open and told us it was wonderful because he wasn't sure when he would ever get another chance at a major. At 47 he nearly cried after losing the 1990 Masters in a playoff to Nick Faldo and told us he wasn't sure he would get another chance to win a major.

Now here he was on Saturday night, sixth on the PGA Tour money list, winner of the Doral Ryder Open earlier this year, two shots out of the lead at the Masters and making the world wonder how you can Retin-A a golf swing.

"Do you *feel* 49?" Floyd was asked.

"I don't know what 49 is supposed to feel like," he said with a grin as wide as a bunker rake. "I feel good. If you're supposed to feel real good, then, yeah, I feel 49."

At Augusta "excessive demonstrations by a player or his partisans are not proper because of the possible effect upon other competitors," Bobby Jones wrote. Club officials even print Jones's words on every pairing sheet. Yet each time Couples swung a golf club last week, that dictum took a serious whomping. Couples arrived as the man who could save U.S. golf from the Ians and the Josés and the Bernhards, and the crowd roared with his every fidget. After all, an American hadn't won the Masters since Larry Mize did so in 1987.

With victories at the L.A. Open and the Nestle Invitational earlier this year, Couples arrived at Augusta as the first American ever to rise to No. 1 in the Sony Rankings, which were instituted in 1986, and as the No. 1 money winner on the Tour this year. What's more, since last summer's U.S. Open he had finished among the top six in a chilling 19 of the 24 tournaments he had played and had won five of them. Here, finally, was Chip Hilton in a visor.

All Couples hadn't done was win a major championship. If he could do that, golf might start thinking about giving him

Tom Watson's old locker. If he never did, he would get thrown in the heap over there with Tom Kite and the rest of the very good players who got off the bus one stop short of greatness.

Could Couples overcome the tainted image—great swing, no drive—that had dogged him for so long? This is a man who once said that he does not answer the telephone at home because "there might be someone on the other end." When destiny finally called, would Couples let the answering machine get it?

"He's got one step left," said Floyd more than once during Masters week, "and that's to win the major championships. Believe me, he will win major championships."

Couples looked to be on his way to doing that after shooting 69 and 67 in the first two rounds, which left him one stroke off the lead. "Are you happy with where you stand?" somebody asked Couples during his press conference on Friday night. He gave his usual meandering reply while his wife, Deborah, answered the question out of the corner of her mouth in the back of the room.

"Oh, nooooo," she said. "We thought we should be 13 strokes ahead by now. Having every single person we've seen the last four weeks hollering at Fred, 'Get the green!' hasn't been *any* pressure on Fred at all. No, sir. We should be miles ahead."

Couples's fast start nonetheless prompted his old University of Houston dormmate Jim Nantz, who was anchoring CBS's Masters telecast, to take Couples aside and say, "Shoot your badge number twice more, and you'll be wearing the jacket." The number: 70.

Couples did the badge one better in the third round with a 69, but he was still one shot behind the leader, Australia's Craig (Popeye, for his forearms) Parry. Not enough, Americans fretted. And, in fact, by the third hole on Sunday, Couples was losing ground. He started like a B player in the Elks Club tournament. He smother-hooked drives off numbers 1 and 2 and had to scramble for a par and a bogey. Meanwhile, Parry, his playing partner, had gone par, birdie. Suddenly, Couples was three strokes behind Parry.

But between number 3 and the Miracle at Rae's Creek,

Couples stomped back. He thumped a nine-iron to within the length of a putter grip on number 3 for a birdie. After a bogey at number 5, he sand-saved par on number 7, dunked a 25-foot no-hoper on 8 for a birdie, curled in an 18-footer for birdie on 9 and salvaged par on 10 out of a hideous bunker. By the time he reached the 12th, he had a three-shot lead and was almost taking complete breaths.

However, the 12th at Augusta dines regularly on final-day three-shot leads. (See, especially, Gary Player, 1962.) And the 12th particularly eats up the kind of deadhead shot Couples struck there on Sunday: He aimed straight at the pin near the sloping front of the green instead of shooting at the fat of the green, the way anybody with any sense would have. "I didn't want to [shoot for the pin]," he said later, "but there's this thing in my brain that just shoved the ball over there."

The ball landed halfway up the bank, eight feet from the front of the green, and started to roll back, just as every ball before it had done. Just as first-round leader Lanny Wadkins's ball had done on Saturday. That one rolled back into the water the way all of them had, making Wadkins drop and hit another one into the drink, making Wadkins drop and hit another one, which finally reached the green, making Wadkins finish with an 8, making Wadkins throw the damn ball in the pond to join its treasonous brethren. Wadkins does not have to take that sort of thing from golf balls.

Anyway, as Couples's ball rolled toward its certain bath, perhaps it saw something. Another Maxfli sat in the water not six inches from the bank. Perhaps Couples's ball thought of its future and did not want to end up in a barrel of lake balls in some pro shop, on sale three for a dollar. If the ball had rolled in, Couples would most likely have made a double bogey 5, and his three-shot lead would have been cut to one. Instead, the ball inexplicably stopped about a foot from doom.

When a relieved Couples stepped up to it—gingerly—he hit a simple pitch to within gimme range. This day was Couples's. He made his par.

From there it was a walk in the park—Central Park maybe. He sprayed his tee shots, birdied neither of the par 5s (numbers 13 and 15) and made only one more birdie (on 14) down the homestretch. Parry, though, was nothing to worry about. He unraveled like a cheap sweater. After three-putting three times in a row to finish with a 78, Parry blamed part of his troubles on devilish types in the crowd. "On the third hole," he said, "I heard somebody coughing on my backswing." Hey, Deborah, next time take a Luden's.

Only one man stood in Couples's way now, the very man who had tutored him over the past two years, the man who had taught him that "when you have a lead, get *more* of a lead," the man who had steeled Couples's eye and hardened his heart during a triumphant Ryder Cup pairing—Floyd. Floyd got to within a shot of the lead with a birdie at number 15, but Couples replied with that birdie on number 14. Only when Couples's three-wood on 18 caught a fairway bunker was there the slightest hint of a playoff, but the unrushable Couples swept a seven-iron cleanly out and onto the green.

Happiness is needing only to three-putt to win the Masters. Couples lagged a 25-footer 24 feet, 10 inches. Tap. He earned $270,000, putting himself over $1 million in prize money for the year. And it wasn't even tax day yet.

Couples is now the most dominant phenom since Johnny Miller in the early 1970s, and the proof was evident at Augusta. Watson once said great players "learn that they don't need to play their best golf to win. They only need to shoot the lowest score." That was Couples's week. His floor was the field's ceiling.

In the Butler Cabin, which is near the 10th hole, Nantz waited to conduct the interview of his life. Back in the dorm, he and Couples had lain awake plotting their glories. "Someday," Nantz said, "you'll win the green jacket, and I'll be there to announce it."

So when the moment came—after Couples had shot his badge number on Sunday to finish with a 13-under-par 275—Nantz said, "I'd like to be the first to congratulate you as the 1992 Masters champion." They both cried a little.

Outside, Deborah was crying too. "Dang," she said. "I picked Davis Love."

PLAYERS

◆◆◆

Still Glittering After All These Years

BY FRANK DEFORD

IN 1978 SPORTS ILLUSTRATED CHOSE JACK NICKLAUS AS SPORTS-
MAN OF THE YEAR. IN HIS ESSAY MARKING THE OCCASION,
FRANK DEFORD EXAMINED AN ATHLETE HE PLACED IN THE
EXALTED COMPANY OF RUTH, ALI AND BOBBY JONES: CHAMPI-
ONS WHOSE NAMES ARE SYNONYMOUS WITH THEIR SPORTS.

Surely the closest place to Heaven in all of sport is a golf
course. The prevailing feeling is one of good will. For the
most part, the fans at tournaments are themselves active
golfers, and they suffer for the competitors, shouting encouragement to them and calling out travel advisories to the balls
they strike. Players and spectators troop the same ground,
interacting physically from green to tee, spiritually from tee
to green. On the best of afternoons, those soft, bright, blue
days when God's own weather lives up to the luxuriant landscape that He and man have wrought, the game even verges
on the ethereal. A golfer has to be a different breed of cat.

This is where we come to Jack Nicklaus, the greatest golfer
of all time. Of course he has played better than the rest for
almost 20 years. Of course he has won more often. Of
course he has dominated the game. This is all well documented.

What is of greater significance is the mystic oneness that he has had with the game of golf itself during that long span and with the courses on which it is played. Nicklaus would probably reject the word "mystic." But it may have been part of what Bobby Jones understood about Nicklaus many years ago, when he said, in tribute, "Jack Nicklaus plays a game with which I am not familiar."

How many other champions have become so identified with their sport, with every aspect of it, with the very essence of it, that it is impossible to think of one without the other? Babe Ruth, for sure; Bobby Jones himself; Muhammad Ali. But they are few, very few; in his remarkable career, Nicklaus has achieved that preeminence as much as anyone.

It has long been fashionable to say that Nicklaus wins by overpowering the course. But that misses the point. Jack Nicklaus overpower a golf course? Why, you might as well say that Mozart overpowered music or Rembrandt overpowered a canvas. The ultimate art is to make an accomplice of whatever you are dealing with—melodies, forms, fairways. Over the years, scores of golfers have whipped golf courses—overpowered them. Nicklaus has won *with* golf courses, by driving, putting, attacking, thinking—by playing whatever sort of golf was required of him at that particular moment. The uniqueness of Nicklaus, his definition, is that rarely has he ever fought a golf course, so utterly is he in consonance with his sport, with its substance and spirit.

He has never been what is called a "personality." Palmer is a personality, and Player, too, and Trevino, and a few others. But not Nicklaus, he has never been perceived as anything but a golfer. He has never been the showman. Younger or older, fatter or thinner, despised or admired, his enormous presence has always been the product of the shots he has pulled out of his bag. Yet that is not quite all. In a sport in which longevity is a measure of the performer—as much as speed or strength defines athletes in other sports—Nicklaus has for nearly two decades stood up for the values he considers inherent in the game. He has turned down $1 million to play a Vegas-style TV "challenge match" because he feared it would demean the game of golf. His conduct has been so impeccable it is almost boring. It must be, you see, because, as he explains, "Golf is as clean a sport as there is." Just so: *clean*. His attitude in defeat is always as correct and elegant as that which he displays in triumph.

Nicklaus has even come to build golf courses himself, spreading his own ashes while he lives: vanity, yes, but tempered with love and a sense of where he fits in. "My golf game can only go on so long," he says, "but what I've learned can be put into a piece of ground to last beyond me. I'll always be part of golf because I'll have the courses. Building a golf course is my total expression."

The course lasts. Nicklaus knows that. The Rockies may crumble, Gibraltar may tumble, but St. Andrews isn't going anywhere. There is something at once proper and touching that after two seasons without a major championship, Nicklaus, age 38, won the British Open last summer at St. Andrews, age 500; the preeminent man and the preeminent course coming together. It seems apt, then, that this year Jack Nicklaus is SPORTS ILLUSTRATED'S Sportsman of the Year. He has had better years; nearly all of his years have been so very good. Indeed, they have been 20 years of surpassing excellence. And that is why we are naming him now.

In the last twelvemonth, a lot has happened in sports, and most of it predictable. The Red Sox collapsed. The Yankees beat the Dodgers in the World Series. We had another Triple Crown champion. What Borg did not win, Connors did; on the distaff side it was mostly Evert. And moving further down Déjà Vu Lane: the Canadiens won; the Cowboys, too; Kentucky in college basketball, Notre Dame in college football. But for the fact that pro basketball went on and on and on until hardly anybody was watching, we could say for certain that the Celtics won that. One of the Unsers came in first again at Indy. Ali regained his title once more. Bill Rodgers won another Boston Marathon. SWIMMING MARKS FALL. Billy Martin got fired again. And so forth and so on.

However, if you missed any of this, Jack Nicklaus can bring you up to date. One of the reasons Nicklaus has himself in such perfect golf perspective is that he's got most of the rest of the world of sports down pat. He can do such things as quote, verbatim, football tips from Bear Bryant.

When not practicing on the golf course, he devotes himself to every conceivable athletic activity: tennis, skiing, basketball, hunting, bicycling, fishing (he reeled in a 1,358-pound black marlin off Australia last month as a prelude to winning the Australian Open), weight lifting, touch football. You've heard of the girl next door. Jack Nicklaus is the jock next door. His everyday attire is tennis clothes. His closest friend in North Palm Beach, Fla., where he lives, is a high school athletic director and coach; he plans his golf tournaments around the football and basketball schedules of Benjamin High, where his two oldest boys are football and basketball stars. Mom is the scorekeeper for the basketball team, partly because that way she doesn't have to sit next to Dad, who has been known to get excited. Wow, is Dad some kind of bore on the subject of Benjamin High's athletic fortunes. He goes to all the practices; he even knows all the damn plays. Say Barbara Nicklaus, "We have to get to the games 45 minutes early so Jack can get taped."

Nicklaus (cradling a pigskin, to son Steve): You ought to run more play-action stuff.

Steve: We don't have any of those.

Nicklaus (sharply): Whaddya mean? You got 36 and 37.

Steve: Oh, yeah.

Jack Nicklaus, the champion, is forever the son of the father, Charlie Nicklaus, who was the same sort of athletic mentor for him when he was growing up in Columbus in the '50s. Sports would have been Nicklaus' way of life even if he had not become the best in history at this one particular athletic endeavor. Indeed, Jack's estate on the northern shore of Lake Worth, Fla. is a contained sporting paradise, with the air not so much of having been built as wished for, in the manner of a child addressing Santa Claus: "... and I'd like a swimming pool, and two grass tennis courts, and a weight room, and a trampoline, and a basketball court, and a football field, and three boats, and a ..."

The house is large but not ostentatious. The climate is controlled. The rooms are attractive, and so perfectly stylized that they appear to be sets for a situation-comedy family, an athletic Brady Bunch. Some rooms possess an almost Pompeian stillness, while others, around the TV and the kitchen, have just the proper amount of lived-in disarray. The TV set appears to be on permanently, so that Lucy Ricardo or *Hogan's Heroes* are a part of the decor in the same way as, say, the furnishings in the breakfast nook. There are, all told, five children, the middle one a girl. Plus friends dropping by, and a golden retriever. The school drawings of the youngest child are taped on the refrigerator door, just as they would be in the house of an insurance salesman in the suburbs of Columbus, Ohio.

The home is ruled over by the former Barbara Bash, who entertains her friends in the kitchen. The Nicklauses met, if you can stand this, their first week at Ohio State. They were instant sweethearts, wedded after their junior year, and, despite the long odds against the survival of a teen-age marriage parlayed by a traveling husband, they remain hopelessly happily married.

People help Nicklaus run his businesses. People advise him. All right. But what is crucial to understanding Nicklaus and his success is that the former Barbara Bash is his only partner. More than that, she is really the only lasting contemporary in his life. His best Columbus friends, his early business associates, were all older. He never formed a close friendship on tour. He was devoted to his father as a friend, and he still goes back to his one and only golf coach, Jack Grout, who first instructed him at the age of 10.

But Nicklaus, the champion, at this moment in his life that he describes as "somewhere in the prime of my career," is a growing, fuller man. More and more he has assumed control of his business affairs. He has certified his ascension from the Buckeye middle class by learning about wines. He has developed a sense of humor that can be sharp and biting. He is short with those who fawn over him. And for all his balance, he can be something of a know-it-all. "Jack's one problem is that he is an instant expert on everything," says one friend who, with some delight, can't resist citing an afternoon a year or so ago, when, in quick succession, Nicklaus displayed total ignorance of 1) Art Buchwald, 2) Karl Wallenda of The Great Wallendas and 3) Cheryl Tiegs. Granted, a knowledge of this disparate trio does not automatically admit the bearer to the League of Renaissance Men, but the episode does suggest that Nicklaus may not be quite as omniscient about pop culture as he is on wire-service gridiron polls. He can take a joke about himself, though, and sometimes he will take a drink. Oddly, while he never smokes on the course or at home anymore, he will go on a chain-smoking binge at a business meeting or on a fishing trip—and then stop as quickly as he started.

There is, then, a curious blend of the unsophisticated and the mature in Nicklaus; he accounts for it in some measure by invoking his experience in golf. "A kid grows up a lot faster on the golf course; golf teaches you how to behave," he says earnestly. "You start playing with older people, so that a kid who plays golf is different from a lot of these athletes in other sports because he hasn't had his own way. He hasn't been spoiled. He's had to get along with older people, and if he won't play by their rules, he can't play at all. Jiminy Christmas, I've gone through it all, and I still have to keep my place."

But if Nicklaus grouses occasionally at all that is expected of him, he obviously finds comfort in the stability and tradition of his sport. A Teutonic sense of order pervades the man. In another time and place, Nicklaus would have been a farmer, attached to his two anchors, the good land he worked and loved, and the good woman with the large family back at the hearth. Now for him the Masters and the U.S. Open, followed by the British Open and the PGA, are like the march of the seasons of the field; and the home is a place to hie back to, to renew strength and purpose.

The fact that Nicklaus, so in harmony with his sport, is also so devoted to his home, in fact *needs* time at home in order to win on the road—that is surely not just a coincidence. Golf remains the most unchanging of our games. The old values and the old biases endure. Tournaments are distinguished by their male officials, attired in crisp blazers and provided with the energized scepters of power, in these days walkie-talkies and carts. Female volunteers are garbed in less formal clothes, are often obliged to wear beauty-pageant-type streamers diagonally across their fronts and are assigned the unrewarding ambulatory and clerical tasks. The wives in golf, more than in any other sport, are recognized by players, press and fans as *wives*, as worthy support troops.

The most instructive revelation about the Nicklauses and their own strong relationship, and its positive impact upon Jack's career, comes from this exchange, when the name of another golfer was brought up. He is Nicklaus' contemporary and once was presumed to be his likely challenger—or Nicklaus his. But the fellow faded quickly into obscurity.

"Well," says Barbara, "he wasn't married when he was on the tour."

"That's right," says Jack, "he just couldn't get organized." So much for that. As they say, golf is as clean a sport as there is.

Barbara has been ideal in the role of golf wife: ever winsome, ever well groomed, never forgetting a face or a blazer or the name that goes with it. On their honeymoon, he played golf; at one stop, the club was all-male and the bride had to stay in the car. When he was fat, she never brought it up. She heard the boos and the invective aimed at her man when large portions of all the world hated him for slaying the legend of Arnold Palmer, but she never brought it up, waiting for him to. And when he never brought it up, she never brought it up, either.

This is why, although Jack Nicklaus begins his 40th year next month, he and a great many people who know him well have no doubts but that he can keep on winning tournaments into his middle age. The legs go first, don't they? That's what they say. Jack Nicklaus still has all the underpinnings.

Charlie Nicklaus—a druggist, a stout, balding man—joined the Scioto Country Club outside Columbus in order to get exercise to help rehabilitate a broken ankle. He was new to this sort of privilege; his father had been a boilermaker on the Pennsylvania Railroad. It is an article of faith that poor American boys will apply themselves diligently to escape poverty. But for a child, deprivation can be a very relative thing. By the standards of the country club, the druggist's son appeared disadvantaged. So, in one sense, young Jack Nicklaus had the best of both worlds—reasonably comfortable circumstances yet a natural motivation to compete. Jack Grout remembers that of his 50 or so young charges, only the Nicklaus boy would show up to practice in the rain.

He was 10 then. Nicklaus has led a symmetrical sort of life;

he was born at the beginning (January 21) of a neat zero-digit year, 1940, and has proceeded thereafter in decennial cycles: he learned golf in 1950, age 10; he married in 1960 and first came to prominence that year, finishing second to Palmer in the U.S. Open, though still an amateur; in 1970, his first year of being svelte, his father died, and the shock helped dislodge him from the only slump of his career; certainly there must be some special surprise in store for us in 1980.

Charlie Nicklaus introduced his only son to all sports, and Jackie became proficient at many, notably basketball; he only bothered with golf from March to September. The boy was precocious, reaching his full height, 5'11", by age 13. He still wonders whether he might have been inclined to concentrate on basketball or football "if I hadn't been a year ahead of myself in school, if I could have had one more year and become a big high school star."

But inherent in the game of golf were qualities that drew the boy to it. Foremost was the simple fact that he could play it by himself, for hours, whole days at a time. "The thing that sets golf apart from other sports is that it takes self-confidence, an ability to rely totally on yourself," he says. Obviously, this faith came to him at an early age. "When I'm through, what I'll really miss is kicking myself to get it done," he says. "I can live without the week of *playing* the Masters. But the really satisfying time is the three weeks leading up to the Masters when I'm preparing for it."

Golf was right for another reason, too, for, despite his being such a natural athlete, Nicklaus is physically limited in one curious way. "I don't react very well," he says. "In tennis, my best shot is the serve, but I respond terribly when I have to hit a ball *back*. In basketball, I was a really good shot"—not long ago he sank 80 straight free throws on his home court— "but I was poor at passing and at defense." Even today he delights in the most independent—and stationary—aspect of football: he will go out for an hour or more by himself and place-kick—and he can put the ball through the uprights at up to 40 yards. Given all this, there is simply no question but that golf—the game that most requires concentration, introspection, self-assurance, peace—was Nicklaus' destiny.

Also, he could hit the son of a bitch a country mile.

He scored 51 on the first nine holes he ever played; he qualified for the U.S. Open at 17 and birdied the first hole; he won the U.S. Amateur at 19; and at 22, in 1962, he turned pro. There stood Arnold Palmer, and neither man was ever to be the same.

Palmer was not just a beloved hero. That would have been enough. No, Palmer was the very fountainhead of golf. The game had often been maligned as a pastime for rich old men (the more captious critics refused to acknowledge that it was even a sport), but Palmer, the handsome charger, had given the game glamour, expanded its horizons. *He made people proud to be golfers.* And so, to beat Palmer was not just to upset the handsome hero: to beat Palmer was to hurt golf. And onto this stage walked a butterball of an athlete. Nicklaus ballooned as high as 225; he would wear a silly little hat and an $8.95 pair of olive green pants; when, God forbid, he opened his mouth, he spoke in a squeaky cartoon voice.

The business about Palmer is very old hat, of course, but it can never be written off. It is still the only rough edge to Nicklaus' life; more than that, it came near to soiling a very clean game. Arnie's fans booed Nicklaus' good shots; they held up signs in the rough that said HIT IT HERE, JACK; and once someone even hurled a beer bottle at him. It must have hurt so much, but to this day he swears he never noticed, never heard a boo. Can you believe that?

Well, he stands at the 11th tee at the Firestone Country Club in Akron last September. He is playing with Hale Irwin. It is a sharp, clear day, and the wind is blowing in gusts. There is a little sign at the tee, hanging from chains on a pole about eight feet high. It states what hole this is and how many yards longs. As Nicklaus starts to address the ball, the sign starts to creak on its chains. His caddie looks up menacingly at the sign. Irwin looks up at the sign. Irwin's caddie and the scorekeeper look up at the sign. Everybody in the gallery looks up at the sign. By now you can just about hear the necks creaking, making almost as much noise as the sign. Nicklaus never takes his eye off the ball, gripping his club tighter and tighter as he simultaneously brings the club-head closer and closer to the ball resting there upon the tee. And then back away, as if he is winding himself up. At the top of his swing ... the sign catches an even stronger gust, and in the blue-green silence swings now at a regular screech. People grimace, embarrassed that a sign here in Akron is doing this to the great Jack Nicklaus. The clubhead comes down and around in a perfect arc, and the ball flies away, high and handsome.

You know, he never heard that sign.

"What sets Jack apart above all," says Deane Beman, the PGA commissioner and a former golfing contemporary, "is concentration. He has complete control over his emotions, in his game and in his life."

Of course he heard the boos from the fanatics. Of course they hurt. But he never heard when he swung—and what the hell, that was only about 70 times a day.

Maybe the worst of all was at Oakmont, near Palmer's home in Pennsylvania, where the 1962 Open was played. It was not a tournament but a four-day ordination—only the fat kid, who had just turned pro, fouled up everybody's week by tying Palmer over 72 holes. And then he beat him in the playoff, 71–74.

The legend died, right there. It hung around, like Marley's ghost, for many more years, but it was all over that day. Palmer won the British Open later that year, and he won the '64 Masters. He was only 34 then, and he played at the top right through the '60s, but he never won another big one against the fat boy. People talk about the many great years of Nicklaus and Palmer dueling; in fact, that whole era of them both winning championships lasted less than two years.

But make no mistake. If Nicklaus, the golfer, put Palmer away on the course, there is no doubt that the trauma of destroying the legend, of having to overcome the idol of his sport, still inhabits Nicklaus. He will stop and almost obsessively qualify even the most innocent passing reference to Palmer lest it possibly be construed as criticism of his ancient rival. He is at pains to point out their personal differences.

Nicklaus, the golfer, simply cannot comprehend why Palmer hangs on, scuffling each week to make the cut. When Nicklaus can't win at golf, he'll be gone the next day. But Palmer breathes it all in: the cheers, the camaraderie, drinking with the boys, dealing gin rummy, then flying his real-life toy airplane on to the next week's go-round. "Arnold's different from me," Nicklaus says again. "I don't want to tell Arnold what to do," Nicklaus says again. "I won't miss the locker room," Nicklaus says again.

And no matter how badly Nicklaus beat Palmer, he didn't win affection. Esteem, respect, admiration—yes. But affection? It is reminiscent of Willy Loman and his sons talking about their successful cousin Bernard.

Willy: Bernard is not well liked, is he?

Biff: He's liked, but he's not well liked.

It is impossible not to believe that the animus kept Nicklaus fat. He was not fat growing up. His father was a heavy man and Nicklaus was an insatiable eater, and the genes and the appetite finally caught up with him at college, but a man with his discipline, with his incredible powers of concentration could have slimmed down whenever he set his mind to it. In fact, when he finally did decide to lose weight, he called in a tailor from New York, ordering him to measure for clothes still pounds away. "Can you imagine anyone having such confidence in himself?" asks Barbara Nicklaus.

But Nicklaus stayed fat all during the '60s. He knew his appearance fostered more hostility. "If I had looked more like an athlete it wouldn't have been nearly so bad for me," he says. He knew. It was as if he were punishing golf for preferring Palmer's glamour to his skills. Only after Palmer's game had declined, after the hysteria was laid to rest, only then did Nicklaus, the jilted lover, feel secure enough to want to be pretty for himself and his game. Today, down to 180 and less, he is even marginally narcissistic. "There is nothing worse than a reformed slob," his wife says.

Nicklaus' better appearance not only increased his popularity, it also forced his critics to appreciate the full range of his golfing talents. Before, there had been a tendency to write him off as a bully. He not only hit the ball so long, but also so high that it soared over the most time-tested of nature's obstacles. Nicklaus forced the redesign of entire championship courses. Only when he matured and lost 20 yards from his drives did the full, fair recognition begin to come to him. For example, Gene Littler points out, "Jack's the best putter we've had over the past 15 years. He rarely misses from six or eight feet in." Suddenly, now that his drives weren't a furlong past everyone else's, people could notice his exquisite work with irons, his command of strategy, his control of a challenge. And if his short game wasn't as good as the rest of it—although as he points out, he never got a chance to work on his short game because he was always, tediously, on the green—it was suddenly impossible to ignore his complete superiority.

"I never thought anyone would ever put Hogan in the shadows, but he did," says Gene Sarazen. "Nicklaus has the remarkable combination of power and finesse, and he is one of the smartest guys ever to walk the fairways. And he has been an extraordinary leader. What more is there to say? Jack Nicklaus is the greatest competitor of them all."

The same front-runners who booed him a few years ago are now falling all over themselves to adore him. No sooner does Nicklaus strike a drive—and before even he himself can tell whether it is short, long, in the rough or behind a tree—most of the gallery is oohing and aahing and saying "Wow!" "Great shot!" "Way to go, Jack!" And then somebody like Hale Irwin belts one 20 yards longer, to the right place, and silence rolls around the hills.

The fans even defer to Nicklaus' regular caddie, Angelo Argea, fawning over him, seeking his autograph. When two caddies at Akron had to get through a crowd, a blazeperson said, "Hey, let Angelo and the caddie through." The galleries part when Nicklaus moves to the tee, and if he is polite and smiles at someone in his path, the person is most likely to turn away, abashed before his greatness. When he speaks, people just listen to what he says, never noticing the same high-pitched voice they used to mock and laugh at. This is the way it is when at last you are liked.

Since Palmer faded, there has been a succession of challengers to Nicklaus—Player, Trevino, Weiskopf, Miller, Crenshaw, now Watson, with Nicklaus patiently anticipating that Severiano Ballesteros will be trotted out soon. Each has credentials, each has been hot for a time, but looking back across the '70s, one can see that they were mostly dramatic inventions of a press that had to create rivals in order to sustain interest.

The champion always enjoyed the competition—"This is fun," he observed to Weiskopf and Miller in the cauldron of his '75 Masters victory—but in essence, he was only, as ever, competing against himself. "The toughest thing about success is that you've got to keep on being a success," Irving Berlin once noted, but it is typical of Nicklaus that he sees it the other way round. "Winning breeds more winning," he says. "You learn how to win by winning. As long as I'm prepared, I always expect to win."

The slump, so called, of 1976 and '77 would surely not even have attracted attention except that Nicklaus had reached the same age when the legendary Palmer couldn't win the majors anymore. Ergo, neither could Nicklaus. In fact, in 1977 he was tied for the lead in three of the big four with only two holes to play. But early in 1978 he brought the winter tour to its knees, finishing second, first, second, first in four straight tournaments. And in July, at St. Andrews, he won his 17th major championship, which is four more than anyone else has ever won. Even though Nicklaus feels his record will be broken one day, very few agree.

It is Nicklaus' own judgment that he played the 1978 British Open, tee to green, as well as he played any major championship in all his life. His rival at the end was one Simon Owen, a New Zealander of no previous consequence. This detracted somewhat from the drama, but having had two straight previous second places in the British Open and three times been a runner-up in a major tournament since winning the 1975 PGA, it could hardly be said that Nicklaus reached the 16th tee, a stroke back, immune to thoughts of failure. Owen had just chipped in from 25 yards out and was enjoying an unconscious, Fleckful kind of afternoon.

An athlete looks funny putting. Nobody ever said that any golfer *looked* good putting. Hushed and hunched, it is all a man can do not to appear silly. Nicklaus looks no better at it than anyone else. But even all this he understands. It is a verity in the game that the putting touch is the first casualty of middle age. "There is no logical reason for that," he says. "But putting is the least manly thing in golf, and therefore, when a player gets older and he blames it on his putting. He does not want to admit that his power may be leaving him."

Ah, but then the drive. Here is the golfer, here is Nicklaus, rampant. At the 16th at St. Andrews, the Corner of the Dyke, par-4, 382 yards, he took out his three-wood and teed up the ball. Simon Owen, one stroke ahead, watched him. People are usually let down when they first encounter Nicklaus, for he is not nearly as large as they had imagined. But he is genuinely awesome upon the tee. Often as not he will clench and unclench his gloved hand, giving it the threatening appearance of a claw. He never speaks, perhaps with the unconscious knowledge that to reveal his choirboy voice at this stage would spoil the act. Instead, he stands silently behind the ball, his piercing blue eyes scrutinizing it as surely as if it were a bold adversary. Then, Nicklaus raises his head and looks out carefully over the fairway, in every way the captain scanning the sea. The courses he builds are criticized for being too tough, too unyielding, too much in his own image, but they are also marked by one other thing: each hole must either go downhill or give that appearance, so that a man can properly survey his domain.

St. Andrews is distinct from any other course in the world, of course, an unbecoming instrument of the winds that sweep off the North Sea. "Just to see it, it's ugly," Nicklaus says. "The buildings are all ugly—even the old clubhouse—all so gray and stark. There are no trees. But put it all together, it is one of the most gorgeous sites in the world. You see, it is pretty because of what I feel for it."

St. Andrews had restored Nicklaus once before, in 1970, the first major he won after his father died. Now, on the 16th at St. Andrews in 1978, he put the three-wood exactly where he wanted to, 260 yards out, to the left of the Principal's Nose bunkers, and then he strode the fairway. The second shot, 120 yards, a nine-iron, fell barely six feet from the pin. Intimidated, Owen flew his iron over the green, and he bogeyed. Nicklaus drummed home his six-footer, dead on. He makes the six-footers; manhood comes in many-sized packages. And thus in one hole: one down to one up.

"If you look at the PGA figures, you'll see that the guy with the best average is usually less than a stroke under the guy back in 30th place," Nicklaus says. "So you're talking about a fifth of a stroke a day between winning and 30th, and, Jiminy Christmas, you can't tell me there's that much difference in our swings. The difference is something else. I was fortunate in a lot of ways. I was fortunate to have a good father, who helped me get into this. I was fortunate to have a pretty good head. A lot of it's her"—a nod to Barbara—"a gal who's been understanding. There's all that. I know I've won with something besides the shots, but I don't know for sure what that something is."

He parred the 17th, the famous Road Hole, and Owen, obviously pressing now, took another bogey, so that Nicklaus, the old has-been, came to the last hole safe, two up on the field at St. Andrews. A three-wood off the tee and then a seven-iron left him sure upon the green, only 35 feet away; he was a lock now. He gave his caddie the iron, and then, under the lowering sky of a midsummer Scottish day, with 30,000 fans of golf cheering for him, he marched up the fairway. The roars of St. Andrews fell upon him well before he reached the green and, in response, the tears filled up his eyes and began to roll down his face. He had triumphed again, and he smiled as he drew closer. And more: he could look through the mist of his crying and see once again how clean it was all around.

Good Lord
Of Golf

BY SARAH BALLARD

IN 1945 BYRON NELSON DOMINATED THE PGA TOUR AS NO
GOLFER HAS BEFORE OR SINCE, WINNING 18 TOURNAMENTS,
INCLUDING A PGA-RECORD 11 STRAIGHT. BUT AS SARAH BAL-
LARD DISCOVERED, THIS LORD BYRON WAS "EQUAL PART
GOLFER AND FARMER" AND HAPPIEST ON HIS RANCH IN TEXAS.

The Preston Trail Golf Club in Dallas, where the PGA tour
stops this week, is typical of a kind of club that exists in or
near every sizable American city. It is a sporting refuge of
wealthy and powerful men and others who aspire to wealth
and power, a place that carefully straddles the line between
ostentation and invisibility. A member of such a club would
not be the sort to boast of his advantages, but neither would
he care for them to go altogether unnoticed.

Byron Nelson is a lifetime honorary member of Preston
Trail. At 67, a prosperous rancher, a businessman, a sitter on
boards of directors, he would be indistinguishable from other
members of his age and station if it were not for his hands.
Nelson's hands are huge—thick of palm and long of finger,
powerful and weathered. With those hands Nelson won the
life he now leads; because of those hands and the magic he

performed with them almost four decades ago, this week's tournament is named for him. During a professional career that began in Texarkana, Texas in 1932 and came to an end in Portland, Ore. in 1946, Nelson did things that no golfer has done since. For some of those 14 years he was unquestionably the best golfer alive, and for most of them he was a superlative striker of the ball, a player whose long irons were very nearly perfect.

Yet history has treated Nelson somewhat grudgingly. The record of his deeds remains heroic, but his story has never taken on the proportions of a proper legend. The trouble is that Nelson made it all seem so sinfully easy. Legends do not just step up to the plate, take a warmup swing or two and then hit the ball over the centerfield fence. Legends first point to the centerfield fence.

Nelson was never one for histrionics. In his own mind he was always about equal parts golfer and farmer. His body may have been on the road playing golf for most of 14 years, but his soul lived on an imaginary piece of land somewhere in Texas. By the time he retired, at 34, he had found the place of his daydreams, and that is where he has stayed ever since.

Fairway Ranch lies off Route 114 in Roanoke, 22 miles north of Fort Worth—750 acres of rolling pastureland sustaining 68 head of beef cattle. At the end of a long asphalt drive, in an island of shade trees, is a comfortable two-story house of red brick, gray shingles and neat white trim. Flowers bloom, birds chirrup, snow-white guinea hens dart in and out of hedges and gray speckled Plymouth Rocks cluck in a house nearby.

"I just love chickens," said Nelson one late spring day as he surveyed his peaceable kingdom. "There's no creatures alive that's more appreciative of what you do for them. They're as nice as a dog."

The midday temperature that day was rising into the 90s, but inside, the ranch house was dim and cool. Lunch was from the garden that is Nelson's particular personal delight—new potatoes, sweet corn, young greens and strawberries. Nelson sat at the head of the long, gleaming table with his wife, Louise, at his right. He is a big man, 6' 1" tall and about 185 pounds these days. His television persona, the one that grew out of his 10-year role as Chris Schenkel's yellow-jacketed sidekick on ABC's golf coverage, the one with the round, amiable face and mildly self-deprecating manner, is contradicted in his presence by his height, his bearing and the direct gaze of his pale blue eyes. As host at Fairway Ranch, saying grace at his own table over food from his own garden, he is assured and dominant.

There are few indications that an athlete is in residence at the Nelson house—no trophy cases, no room set aside as a shrine to youthful glories. The ranch is all the souvenir Nelson has ever needed. It is his perpetual trophy, a constant reminder of where be began, where he has been and how he got where he is.

The beginnings were in Fort Worth, in the hard '20s, when money and jobs were tight. Living near the Glen Garden golf course, Nelson began caddying for pocket money when he was 12 and soon enough was playing, too, becoming "a pretty fair, funky player," he recalls. At 16, to help make ends meet, he quit high school and went to work as a file clerk at the Fort Worth & Denver City Railway, practicing golf in the mornings as soon as the sky was light and in the evenings until it was too dark to see.

Two years later, with the Great Depression deepening, Nelson was laid off by the railroad, and since there were no jobs for anyone, anywhere, he gravitated to the pro shop and began to work on his game in earnest. He became good enough to qualify locally for the 1931 U.S. Amateur, but after scraping up enough money to get to Chicago on a day coach, he failed to make the field. "I had never seen or heard of a bent-grass green before," he says. "I had played on sand greens and Bermuda, but these were frightening, slick and fast. I three-putted everything."

In 1932 the first Texarkana Open was organized, offering $500 in prize money. On Nov. 20, Byron Nelson said goodby to his parents, got on a bus for the 200-mile ride to Texarkana, paid his $5 entry fee on the tee and became a pro.

"I didn't think of the tour as something glamorous," says Nelson. "I just wanted to play to beat somebody. My parents didn't know much about golf, but they gave me their blessings. They said, 'Be a good man and do right.' " Nelson finished third at Texarkana and won $75. A month later he was on his way to California for the start of the winter tour of 1932-33.

It was customary, and economically necessary, in those days for golf pros to work at a club and teach the game in the warm months. They hit the tournament road only when the clubs had closed down for the winter. The winter tour began in California in November or December, moved east across Texas to Florida and finally north, up the Atlantic Coast, into spring. Summer tournaments such as the U.S. Open and the PGA Championship were played in odd weeks taken from the club jobs.

Nelson's first winter tour was memorable chiefly for its brevity—exactly three tournaments. He had intended to play Pasadena, Los Angeles, Long Beach and Santa Monica, but after Long Beach he was out of money and had to hitch a ride home. Fortunately, the pro's job at the Texarkana Country Club—salary $60 a month—opened up and Nelson got it. He lived in a rented room in town and worked diligently on his game in his ample free time, there being even fewer golfers at Texarkana than there had been at Glen Garden. In July, at the Texarkana Church of Christ Sunday School, he met Louise Shofner, the pretty, dark-haired daughter of a grocery store owner, and the two decided to get married, says Nelson, "as soon as I could get a dime together."

Late in the fall of 1933 Nelson went west again, this time with $600 borrowed from his prospective father-in-law and a Model A roadster—royal blue and cream with wire wheels— that a Texarkana Ford dealer had let him buy on time. He returned with enough money to repay Louise's father and buy Louise an engagement ring before he was broke again.

Broke or not, they were married in June of 1934, and when the Model A next headed west, Louise was along. In the opening round of the San Francisco Match Play Championship that year, Nelson, the unknown Texas kid, upset Lawson Little, winner of the British and U.S. Amateurs, 5 and 4, and a San Francisco newspaper headline read HONEYMOONER DEFEATS LAWSON LITTLE.

"Louise was so embarrassed she wouldn't leave the hotel," Byron remembers.

"We'd been married *seven months!*" Louise protests.

In 1935 Nelson met George Jacobus, who was president of the PGA and head pro at the Ridgewood Country Club in New Jersey. Jacobus invited Nelson to come to Ridgewood as his assistant, where he would be paid $400 a year plus whatever he could make giving lessons.

Nelson spent two seasons with Jacobus, playing few tournaments but working harder than ever on his game. Jacobus was a teacher of the old school, but he was interested in some of Nelson's unorthodox ideas and encouraged him at a crucial time.

When Nelson began playing the game, golf equipment was in a period of transition from hickory to steel. Originally he had used irons with hickory shafts and woods with steel shafts. His flat caddie-yard swing worked all right with the irons, but with his woods he tended to hook the ball. He was unable to figure out why until, in 1930, he acquired his first set of steel-shafted irons and immediately began to hook them too. The problem, he eventually realized, was the difference in the amount of torque, or flex, between a steel and a hickory shaft. The compensation he was making in the roll of his wrists for the flexibility of a wooden shaft was too much for the stiffer steel shafts.

Therefore, gradually, one step at a time, from 1930 on, he had been experimenting, like most players who were not yet too set in their ways. He was looking for consistency and the clue to the hookless golf swing. And finally, in the fall of 1936, he found what he sought. He quit his job at Ridgewood, left Louise in Texarkana with her family, and headed off on a four-tournament tour of the Northwest. He played well in all of them, finishing in the money in Seattle and Portland, second in Victoria, B.C., and tied for first pro money in Vancouver. "I wasn't hooking anymore," he says. "The harder I hit it, the straighter I hit it." He covered his expenses for the trip and had $2,000 left over when he got back to Texas.

"So that's how it all started," Nelson reflects. "From then on I never looked back and never tried to change anything in my swing. I don't mean to boast. I mean I was in contention from then on."

The next spring—baby-faced and 25—Nelson drew national attention for the first time, winning the 1937 Masters. The tournament was then only four years old, but already it had considerable status. Nelson shot a 66 the first day at Augusta, a score that drew attention not only because it was a course record but also because it was accomplished without his sinking a single long putt. But the feat that got a bridge over Rae's Creek named for him was his obliteration on the last day of Ralph Guldahl's four-stroke lead. Guldahl doublebogeyed the par-3 12th hole, and then, gambling to get the lost strokes back, bogeyed the par-5 13th. Nelson, playing just behind, birdied the 12th, then eagled the 13th. He had picked up six strokes in the space of two holes and had a two-stroke lead that he never relinquished.

In Nelson's opinion, 1939 was his best year. It was the year he established himself as the best golfer around by winning the U.S. Open, finishing runner-up in the PGA Championship, winning two of the most important tour events, the Western Open at Medinah and the North and South Open at Pinehurst, and setting a professional scoring record with back-to-back 65s at the Phoenix Open. In light of subsequent events, it is difficult to make an airtight case for 1939 being Nelson's *best* year, but certainly it was vintage.

The 1939 Open, which is more often remembered as the Open Sam Snead lost than the Open Nelson won, was held on the Spring Mill course of the Philadelphia Country Club. Snead approached the last two holes needing only pars to win by two strokes. Nelson, Craig Wood and Denny Shute were tied at 284 for what appeared to be second place. Snead looked a little shaky when he bogeyed the 71st hole, leaving a six-foot putt short, but no one was concerned because the last hole was a relatively easy par-5 and all Snead needed was a par to win. Even if he bogeyed, he wouldn't lose. There would still be an 18-hole playoff. However, Snead got himself into a bunker that he couldn't get out of and took a triplebogey 8.

So the playoff was three-way—Nelson, Shute and Wood. After 18 holes, Wood and Nelson remained tied with 68s, while Shute shot 76 and was eliminated. As the second 18-hole playoff between Nelson and Wood got under way, it became clear that Nelson, who already had rounds of 72, 73, 71, 68, 68 behind him, was now really getting hot. At the 3rd hole he hit a perfect pitch next to the pin for a birdie, and at the 4th he ripped off a low 210-yard one-iron with a bit of a hook on it that buzzed toward the flag, bounced and rolled a short distance past, then drew back and nestled down between the pin and the back of the cup for an eagle. After that, all Nelson had to do was hang on, and he did, finishing with a 70 and winning the playoff by three strokes. Afterward, Wood, a gracious man who had tied for first in three major championships and lost the playoff each time, said of Nelson, "He's one of the greatest golfers I've ever seen, and not because he beat me."

What astounded Wood, and everyone else, too, when they got around to totting things up, was that Nelson had hit the pin six times during the tournament, each time with a different club—in order, a four-iron, a niblick, a wedge, a driver, a six-iron and a one-iron. Nelson was not yet Lord Byron, the Mechanical Man, but he was well on his way. His long-iron play was already becoming legend, especially his mastery of the one-iron, the most difficult club in golf. "Mark my words," said Wood, "Byron is going to come through in a big way. Certainly the stage is set."

Nelson came through, but it took a while. What the stage was really set for was World War II. After 1939 the British Open and the Ryder Cup matches were discontinued. In the eight major championships that were played between 1940 and 1942, Nelson had the best record of any golfer. He won the 1940 PGA and the 1942 Masters, finished second in the 1941 Masters and was runner-up in the 1941 PGA.

In that period Nelson shared the spotlight with Ben Hogan and Sam Snead. Hogan had yet to win a major tournament (in fact, he won no tournament of any kind until the spring of 1940, when he suddenly ignited and took three in a row), but he had the best scoring average and he won the most money in both 1940 and 1941. Snead, who had first emerged as a contender in 1937, was second only to Hogan in earnings for 1941.

In hand-to-hand combat, though, Nelson was the leader. If one counts a 1927 Fort Worth caddie tournament in which

15-year-old Nelson beat 15-year-old Ben Hogan in a playoff, the rivalry between Nelson and Hogan produced five head-to-head meetings. Nelson won four of them. In 1939, when the Ryder Cup matches scheduled for Ponte Vedra Beach, Fla. were canceled because of the war, challenge matches among the American players were held at the Detroit Golf Club. When Hogan and Nelson met there, Hogan won. In 1940, when they met in a playoff for the Texas Open, Nelson won. But the two great encounters were their quarterfinal match in the 1941 PGA Championship at Cherry Hills in Denver and the 18-hole playoff for the 1942 Masters in Augusta.

Sandy Tatum, now the president of the United States Golf Association, was a 20-year-old Stanford golfer on his way home to California after the 1941 NCAA championships at Ohio State. He stopped off in Denver to visit friends and walked the Cherry Hills course every day, watching one good match after another. "But the classic was Hogan and Nelson," Tatum remembers, 38 years later. "Thirty-six holes on a great golf course on a perfect day. Hogan played a truly Hoganesque morning round, and having played such a round, he was one down to Nelson, which says all I can say about the quality of the golf Nelson played that morning.

"In the afternoon they reproduced the round they had played in the morning, 17 virtually flawless holes of golf. They arrived at the 18th hole with Nelson still one-up. Nelson's drive was on the right side of the fairway. Hogan's was in the middle and a few yards in front. Nelson then hit a two-iron that I can only describe as symphonic. Every time I look at that hole I visualize it against the background of what it was that day. I relive seeing that swing and watching that ball against that blue sky."

Nelson's ball came to rest five feet to the right of the pin. Hogan's second shot also landed on the green, but a good 25 feet from the hole. Hogan putted close, then Nelson sank his five-footer for a birdie and the fourth match between the two was over. Nelson had won 2-up.

Nelson's own memory of that PGA is marred by the nightmare the tournament eventually became for him. After Hogan, he beat Gene Sarazen in the semifinals and then, against Vic Ghezzi, a pro who up to that point had never seriously contended for a major title, Nelson was 3-up through 27 holes of the final match. At that point he began to feel the match slipping away from him. "It was awful," he says. "I could feel myself letting down, but there wasn't much I could do about it. It was fatigue, I guess."

Whatever it was, Ghezzi evened the match by the 36th green, and they went to extra holes. They halved the 1st with pars, but then, on the 2nd, they both missed the green and had to chip on. They hit identical shots, a little too strong, and both balls ended up a few feet beyond the hole and very close together. A measuring tape was produced to determine who would putt first, and both balls, it turned out, were exactly 42 inches from the hole. So a coin was flipped. Nelson lost and had to putt first.

The stymie rule was still in effect in 1941, so both balls remained on the green, where they had landed. The only way a ball could be lifted and marked was if it interfered with the stance of the opponent. When Nelson was asked whether Ghezzi's ball would hinder him, inexplicably he said no. Then, in taking his stance over the putt, Nelson inadvertently touched Ghezzi's ball with the toe of his shoe and moved it slightly. Ghezzi should have been awarded the hole and the match on the spot. Instead, Ghezzi announced that he had no intention of winning the match that way, that no penalty should be charged because no damage had been done. Incredibly, the referee's decision, after much discussion and delay, was that if Ghezzi said it was O.K., it was O.K.

"Well, it *wasn't* O.K." says Nelson, shuddering involuntarily at the memory. "After all that, I still had to make a 42-inch putt. There's no way I can win this match this way, I'm thinking. All over the world people will say.... Well, I didn't miss the putt on purpose, but those are the things I was thinking about. Ghezzi won the match fair and square, *twice*. It was the most stupid thing I ever did in a golf tournament. It was terrible. Terrible!"

Hogan and Nelson met for the last time at the 1942 Masters. Hogan, who had been eight strokes off the pace after 36 holes, shot 67 on Saturday and 70 on Sunday to tie Nelson at 280. Ties at Augusta are decided by sudden-death playoffs these days, but in 1942 a tie meant 18 holes on Monday. To watch this particular playoff, between the two best players in the game, many of the other golfers, with no stake in the outcome themselves, stayed on an extra day to see it, an extraordinary tribute.

Nelson spent the night at the Richmond Hotel in downtown Augusta throwing up, a not unusual occurrence. "There were easier people to have a playoff against than Ben Hogan, you know," he says. "I woke up on the morning of the playoff just miserable. Ben found out about it and came down to my room and said, 'If you're sick we'll just postpone the playoff until later.' I answered, 'No, Ben, let's go ahead and play it.'

"Really now, this wasn't as noble of me as you might think. The upset stomach business had happened to me before, and every time I had been in a keyed-up, nervous condition, I had played rather well. So I staggered to the golf course, but even when I got there I wasn't sure I'd make it. I remember Ben asking me again how I felt, and I told him, 'Just awful.' "

Nelson felt even worse when his first tee shot hit a pine tree off the right side of the fairway and lodged under a small fir, from which spot he could only play out lefthanded. He double-bogeyed that hole, bogeyed the 4th and was three shots down to Hogan before he knew what had happened to him.

"But somewhere around the 5th hole," Nelson says, "my adrenaline glands started to going, and pretty soon I felt just as strong as I could be. I had that old spring in my arms and legs." He birdied the 6th and eagled the 8th, taking the lead when Hogan parred it—then birdied 11, 12 and 13 and played 14, 15 and 16 in par. Hogan played the same 11 holes in one under par and lost five strokes. The final score was Nelson 69, Hogan 70.

A year later Hogan was in the Army and Nelson was back at his club job, and the two never again met head to head.

World War II produced some odd sights on American golf courses. Beef cattle roamed at Baltusrol. Augusta National became a turkey farm. Patriotic members of Wykagyl, in New York's Westchester County, plowed up their 1st and 2nd fairways and turned them into victory gardens. Oak Park in Chicago raised its own chickens for the kitchen, and Twin

Brooks in New Jersey strung nets in front of ponds at the 8th and 10th holes to save its dwindling supply of golf balls.

Gas rationing did the greatest damage. When weekend golfers found they could no longer get to the course on a Saturday morning, they abandoned their memberships in droves. Tournament golf was at a virtual standstill. The winter tour, usually made up of some two dozen tournaments, was reduced to two by 1943. Such were the circumstances in which Byron Nelson was reaching the peak of his talent. He was poised to make sports history at a moment when sports, and most of the rest of human endeavor, were being eclipsed by larger events.

From 1940 to 1945, Nelson was the head professional at the Inverness Country Club in Toledo during the summer months, but during most of the war he spent the largest part of his time performing for wartime charities. He and Jug McSpaden, an old pal from the early years on the tour, were both classified 4F, Nelson because of hemophilia, McSpaden for sinusitis. They became a team, and in 1943 alone they played 110 exhibitions on behalf of the PGA at military hospitals, War Bond sales rallies and fund-raising events for the Red Cross and the USO. They crossed and recrossed the continent, usually traveling by train, sleeping in berths when they could get them, sitting in chair cars when they couldn't, standing in endless lines for meals and always—because they were neither soldiers, children, women nor old—being served last. Occasionally they were treated shabbily. Louise Nelson remembers driving through Arizona during gas rationing and having people shake their fists when they saw Nelson's Texas license plates and his young, apparently able and non-uniformed body at the wheel.

Nevertheless, hardly a week passed that a newspaper somewhere did not print a photograph of Nelson, or of Nelson and McSpaden, at a military hospital, demonstrating a golf shot to an attentive semicircle of young men with short haircuts and GI bathrobes. Their only pay was their expenses.

Once, for 19 days and nights, Nelson barnstormed with Bing Crosby, Bob Hope and Johnny Weissmuller. The four would play an exhibition match during the day and then auction off their clubs for charity. In the evenings Hope and

Crosby would entertain at an armory or a civic center, where audiences would buy War Bonds to see the show. Nelson's admiration for his extroverted traveling companions is still boundless. "Hope and Crosby were the two funniest men together I ever saw," he says, "and their part was so much harder than mine. They played golf and *then* they'd entertain. All I had to do was stand around and laugh and applaud."

By 1944 the worst of the war for the Allies was past, and as the end became perceivable, spirits lightened. Fred Corcoran, the PGA tour manager and publicist, was able to schedule 22 tournaments that year. With the luck of the Boston Irish, he also just happened to have a star on hand ready to be reborn. Nelson won seven of Corcoran's 1944 tournaments. Except for a soured putter, he would have won the revived PGA Championship, too, played at the Manito Golf and Country Club in Spokane, Wash., before the largest crowds in the tournament's history. The PGA was won by an unknown, Private Bob Hamilton of Evansville, Ind.

Nelson's scoring average for 84 rounds in 1944 was 69.67, and he won $37,000 in War Bonds, nearly twice as much as Sam Snead's record total in 1938. The Associated Press named Nelson Athlete of the Year, and TIME reported, "The quality of competition in other sports had fallen off, but in golf the steady competition of par was the same as ever. Against that unwavering opponent, John Byron Nelson had proved himself not only the athlete of the year, but one of the greatest golfers ever."

Who could have imagined that 1944 was only a warmup?

Every great athlete has, at the prime of his sporting life, a season or a year that stands out from the rest. It usually arrives in the midst of a series of good years, and a certain amount of time has to pass before its true size can be recognized. Babe Ruth's year was 1927. Bobby Jones' was 1930. Don Budge's was 1938. Ben Hogan's was 1953.

Byron Nelson's year was 1945. He came as close that year as a golfer can to being unbeatable. He set records in 1945 that are still on the books 34 years later and will undoubtedly be there 34 years from now. He played golf that other golfers found almost unbelievable. In that year Corcoran was able to line up 35 tournaments worth about half a million dollars. Nelson won 18, just over half of them.

Eighteen tournaments was 11 more than anyone had won in a calendar year. Eighteen tournaments in a year is five more than any golfer has won since. Furthermore, Nelson finished second seven times in 1945. His prize money, most of it in War Bonds, was $52,000, half again as much as his own record the previous year. (That $52,000 was 10% of the total purse for 1945. Ten percent of this year's total purse on the PGA tour would be $1.3 million.)

It has often been argued that Nelson's record year could have occurred only at a time when the best of the competition was still away at war, but that overlooks Nelson's scoring, which was barely credible. In 120 rounds of tournament golf, Nelson's *average* score for 18 holes was 68.33. It is a record that has never been touched. Snead, with 69.23 in 1950, came closest. Hogan's 69.30 in 1948 is next. Jack Nicklaus' best stroke average was 69.81 in 1973, and that was for only 72 rounds.

During that year, Nelson was also working on another remarkable string. Between 1940 and 1946, he finished in the money in 113 straight tournaments. Jack Nicklaus came closest to that record with 105 between 1970 and 1976. Also, it should be noted, in Nelson's day most tournaments paid only the top 15 places; during Nicklaus' string, 70 places were paid.

But the record for which Nelson will probably be remembered longer than any other is the Streak. Between mid-March and early August, he won 11 tournaments in a row, a feat that is almost beyond comparison. The closest any golfer has come to the record in 34 years was when Nancy Lopez won five in a row in 1978.

Extraordinary feats in golf, rounds such as Johnny Miller's 63 in the 1973 U.S. Open at Oakmont, and Al Geiberger's 59 in the second round of the Memphis Classic in 1977, are so unusual and so far beyond reasonable explanation that they are frequently said to have happened while the golfers were in a "trance" or a "fog," the implication being that the score was more the product of magic than an act of will. Nelson's 1945 "trance" lasted five months and survived some heavy handicaps. Travel, for instance. Travel during World War II, no matter what the vehicle, was like a rush hour that lasted four years. Further, most of Nelson's travel was by train, which, even when things went according to schedule, required days instead of hours to get from one place to another. Nelson also won tournaments while playing benefits at a rate of at least one, more often two, a week wherever he went. He almost never was able to play a practice round.

The Streak began with a victory in the Miami Four-Ball tournament the second week of March. The next week, when he beat Snead in a playoff at Charlotte, N.C., Nelson sensed something unusual was going on. "I became confident," he remembers. "I realized I could do with the golf ball pretty much what I wanted to do."

After six wins, Byron told Louise he wished he could blow up and get it over with. Instead he went to the golf course that day and shot a 66. People could scarcely believe what they were seeing. Tommy Armour, the famous Scottish pro who in the late '20s and early '30s won the U.S. Open, the British Open and the PGA, said, "Nelson plays golf shots like a virtuoso. There is no type of problem he can't handle. High shots, low shots, with the wind or across it, hooks or fades—he has absolute control of them all. He is the finest golfer I have ever seen."

Meanwhile, Nelson was aiming for the PGA Championship in July at the Moraine Country Club in Dayton, Ohio. His loss the year before to Hamilton had been an enormous disappointment and he was determined to redeem himself. But when he found himself two holes down to Mike Turnesa with only four holes to play in the second round, his hopes for redemption seemed about to go down the drain together with the longest winning streak—eight straight tournaments at that point—in the history of the game.

However, one of the characteristics of Nelson's play had always been his ability to produce wondrous finishing bursts at just such moments. He shot birdie, birdie, eagle and par to win the match one-up on the 36th green. Poor Turnesa, who had shot 68, 69—seven under par—only to lose, moaned, "How can you beat a guy like that? I never played better golf in my life, and when I had him 2-up going to the 15th,

I felt confident I was going to win. Then what happened? Why in the next three holes he throws two birdies and an eagle at me!"

The final was an anticlimactic 4 and 3 win over Sam Byrd, the former baseball player. With it, Nelson had won his fifth and last major championship, and the Streak was still alive. The 10th win was the rich All-American Open at Tam O'Shanter in Chicago, and No. 11 was the Canadian Open.

The end finally came the third week of August in Memphis, when Fred Haas Jr., an amateur, won the tournament and Nelson finished fourth. But there were no headlines and no pauses for standing ovations. In fact, hardly anybody noticed, because on Aug. 6 the first atomic bomb was dropped on Hiroshima and on Aug. 14 the Japanese surrendered and World War II came to an end.

One year later Byron Nelson quit tournament golf for good. Why he retired when he did, at 34, and so quickly after his greatest successes, has been a frequent subject of locker-room conjecture. It has been suggested that he retreated rather than face Hogan's inevitable challenge. It has been said that he lost his nerve, that he had a bad stomach and that he had no stomach for competition.

The truth is that Nelson at 34 was old beyond his age and tired beyond endurance. In the fall of 1945, when he went elk hunting in a remote region of Idaho for two weeks, he had had, by Louise Nelson's calculations, exactly 11 days away from golf since the beginning of the war. He dragged himself through the 1946 season, but his heart was on a ranch outside Fort Worth.

At the PGA Championship in Portland, Ore., in August of 1946, he lost to Porky Oliver in the quarterfinals and then announced he was going home to stay. His face was haggard and his long frame was 18 pounds underweight. Though he managed an occasional smile for the gallery, when he returned to the locker room it was gone and his blue eyes were dull. A few weeks later he told a reporter what was going through his mind. "I'm just tired. It has been a long grind," he said. "There were days when I thought I would scream if I had to go to the course. It was week in and week out for years. I tried to give my best to golf. Now I want to realize a dream. I've got 500 pasture acres and 130 more under cultivation. I've got my dad and mother with me and ... well, that's the story."

Louise Nelson put down her fork and glanced across the luncheon table at her husband. "I don't think all the truth has been told," she said, "and maybe now is as good a time as any." Byron, married to the same woman for 45 years, did not need to ask what she was about to say.

Louise began.

"He kept on wanting and wanting a ranch, but I didn't want him to have one because he didn't know anything about ranching and I was afraid he would lose everything he had worked so hard for. But he kept on wanting it. So finally I said, 'All right, but you cannot touch any of our investments. You have to earn every bit of it.' I said, 'I've got both feet in concrete and I'm not changing. We've worked hard and I'm afraid you'll lose it ranching.'

"Looking back on it I realize I was being selfish. But anyway, he got himself busy and he made a lot of money. That was 1945. When he had saved up over $50,000 in cash, he thought he could start looking. But it wasn't enough money, and I said, 'Well, you're just going to have to work another year. You'll have to work through the National Open.' We made a pact we wouldn't tell anyone, and we didn't. He almost won that Open. It was when his caddie stepped on his ball."

The 1946 U.S. Open at Canterbury in Cleveland was the first in five long years, and the galleries were huge. Fairways were not roped off in those days, which meant that 12,000 people raced to get a spot behind each shot as the leaders played their final rounds. At the 13th hole of the morning round (the last two rounds of the Open were both played on the same day, Open Saturday, until 1965) Nelson's caddie, a young man named Eddie Martin, still in uniform and on furlough from the Army, accidentally stepped on Nelson's ball in his effort to get out of the way of the onrushing gallery. The error cost Nelson a penalty stroke.

In spite of the penalty, Nelson reached the 71st hole needing only a par and a bogey to win. Instead he took two bogeys, ending up in a three-way tie with Vic Ghezzi and Lloyd Mangrum, then lost to Mangrum in the second 18-hole playoff the next day; the three had shot identical 72s in the first playoff round. Of those last two holes of regulation play, one newspaper said, "After playing superb golf, perhaps the finest from tee to green ever seen in any championship, Nelson, the great shotmaker, became just another golfer...."

"I cried for a week after that," said Louise. "But I was just selfish enough that I wanted him to go out a real champion and be able to say, 'Well, boys, that's that.' So he went on and played through the PGA in Portland. But he wasn't playing the way he had been."

"I had already quit in my mind," said Nelson quietly.

The last scene of the 14-year adventure that had begun on a bus leaving Fort Worth for Texarkana in 1932 was not the kind a Hollywood writer of the period would have dictated. But the epilogue was. No discharged GI in America was any happier to be going home than Byron Nelson was in 1946. The ranch had cost him all he had, but it was finally his, and the job of transforming it from the dried-up derelict of a place that it was when he first saw it into the tranquil oasis it is today was a labor made sweeter by its long postponement.

Only once more did Nelson play golf for the prize money in it. He had been retired four years, and by then had realized that he was going to need more income than the ranch and his modest investments could produce. At that point he got a call from Jim Shriver, a MacGregor golf-equipment salesman. Shriver suggested a series of exhibition matches in the Pacific Northwest, Shriver's sales territory, for the spring of 1951. Nelson agreed and Shriver set about booking the matches.

But those four years of retirement might as well have been 40, so quickly had Nelson's star descended and Hogan's risen. The memory of Nelson's triumphs had dissipated like mist on a summer morning. Shriver could book only three matches. The whole project seemed doomed until Nelson received an invitation to play in the 1951 Bing Crosby pro-am with Ed Lowery, an old friend from San Francisco.

"I thought to myself," says Nelson, "if I play O.K. I could get a little publicity and maybe I can make those matches."

So he went to work on his game for a month, and when January arrived he went to Pebble Beach. He not only played "O.K.," he *won* the tournament, the first he had played in four years, beating Cary Middlecoff by three strokes.

The $2,000 prize for first place was welcome, but the publicity worked wonders. Within a week, 26 exhibition matches had been booked. Every day except Mondays for a month that spring, at a fee of $300 a stop, Nelson would play an 18-hole match in the morning, attend a luncheon, stage a clinic, make a speech at a dinner, then get into his car and move on to the next town.

The occasional golf of Nelson's retirement years has been some of his best. Lowery recalls a time at the Crosby in the mid-'50s when Nelson shot a 70 in the first round and was close to the pro lead in the tournament. "We were playing the 8th at Cypress on the second day," says Lowery. "Byron's second shot was short of the green in a bunker. I'm on the green, putting for a birdie from six feet. Byron had his caddie pick up his ball, and I said, 'Byron, you're four strokes off the lead!' He said, 'I'm here for fun; I'm not playing for money.' I didn't understand it, but he lived by it. He was just playing for my sake and for Bing Crosby's."

There were also individual shots as memorable as any he hit in the '30s and '40s, and he savors them as any golfer would. "At Colonial in Fort Worth, the 5th fairway slopes into a ravine, a low area with trees overhanging," he says. "I was in a position where I had to hit the ball under the trees but skin over a bank, and the shot had to hook because a straight shot would go into the river. So I took a two-iron and it just missed the bank and landed eight feet from the pin. Sometimes you can get a great kick out of a shot that somebody watching might think wasn't anything special. It gives you a happy feeling when it works."

Tucked away in the closet at the ranch is a cardboard carton filled to overflowing with pictures taken when Byron and Louise were seeing the world for the first time. It is a time capsule in which are distilled all those years when the work was hard and the rewards were meager but when every sight was a new sight. Here are Byron and Jug in front of an eight-foot snowbank at Lake Tahoe. Louise and Eva McSpaden in front of the same snowbank, Eva wearing a fox fur jacket, Louise with a silly little hat tipped over her right eye. Byron standing next to a saguaro cactus four times as tall as he. Horseshoe Falls with a note penciled on the back: "Water is blue as can be and clear as a whistle." Byron and Louise standing ankle-deep in Lake Erie, he with his pants rolled up to his calves, she clutching the hem of her skirt ("It was our first anniversary and I was in the doghouse. I was supposed to take Louise to see Guy Lombardo and I didn't"). Nelson in a pony cart in Aiken, S.C., in a copper mine in Butte, Mont., in a cloud of locusts in Argentina, under the Oakland Bay Bridge, in front of the Miami Biltmore, aboard the *Manhattan* with the 1937 Ryder Cup team on its way to England.

"I look back now and realize how young I was when I quit," said Nelson recently, from the vantage point of his 68th year. "But still with no regrets. I did what I did. I didn't feel I had no more worlds to conquer. I would have liked to win the Open once more, for instance. But I had bought the ranch and I really wanted to leave. When I did, I felt free, a different type of freedom, and I loved it."

Nobody had any trouble keeping Byron down on the farm, but Louise hadn't yet seen Paree. So in 1955, when Byron was 43, the Nelsons went to Paris. They stayed at the Ritz, and while Louise toured, Byron won the French Open at La Boulie. He was the first American to win it since Walter Hagen in 1920. The Nelsons celebrated by going to the Folies-Bergère, and then when it was time to leave, Nelson applied his winner's purse, 10,000 francs, to his hotel bill. By the time he had settled up and had tipped all the people who needed tipping, he had 500 francs left, which is the way he wanted it. Then he and Louise went home to Texas.

Sir Walter

BY RON FIMRITE

WALTER HAGEN WAS 21 WHEN HE WON THE 1914 U.S. OPEN, THE FIRST OF 10 MAJORS HE CAPTURED DURING HIS BRILLIANT CAREER. BUT, AS RON FIMRITE RECOUNTS, HAGEN'S REPUTATION WAS FOUNDED AS MUCH ON THE FLAMBOYANCE OF HIS LARGER-THAN-LIFE PERSONALITY AS ON HIS PRODIGIOUS GOLF SKILLS.

He had such a jaunty manner, such a regal air, such insouciance that he was called Sir Walter or the Haig. Gene Sarazen, a contemporary and a great golf champion himself, recalls what it was like seeing him for the first time: "It was at the U.S. Open in 1920. I was just a kid of 18, and two heroes of mine, Harry Vardon and Ted Ray, had already come into the locker room. And then in he marched, head held high, looking like he was the sultan of someplace or other. But that was Walter Hagen for you. He acted like he was the whole show all the time. I remember once, a few days before the 1921 Open in Chevy Chase, Md., Walter was in the locker room calmly shaving while President Harding waited for him on the first tee. There was Walter, without a care in the world, keeping the president of the United States waiting!"

Actually, Hagen had something of a fetish about tardiness. He was notorious for appearing on the first tee at the last second, sometimes changing on the run from evening clothes to plus fours. On a pre–World War II tour of the Far East, Hagen was two hours late for a date with Prince Fumitaka Konoye of Japan. When advised by a nervous functionary of this possibly irreparable breach of international etiquette, Hagen blithely replied, "Well, the prince wasn't going anywhere, was he?" No, he wasn't. And the two played a convivial round together.

"Walter always had the guts of a burglar," says Henry W. Clune, novelist and newspaperman, now a lively 99. He's an old Hagen friend from the early days in Rochester, N.Y., where Hagen grew up and where this year's U.S. Open will be played from June 15 to 18 at Oak Hill Country Club. "For all of his truncated schooling and catch-as-catch-can upbringing, he was never a bumpkin," adds Clune.

"Walter was not quite six feet tall, but he always looked taller because he walked around a course as if he owned it," says Charles Price, the golf writer and historian. "He was supremely confident, and he knew the virtue of the grand gesture."

But he did not, as was so often reported, instruct the then prince of Wales, later King Edward VIII, to "pull the pin, Eddie," during an exhibition match. What he actually said, according to Price, was, "Pull the pin, caddie," but the prince got there first and did the job himself.

Besides, as Price points out, the prince was known to his friends and family as David, not Eddie, a fact that might well have eluded Hagen who, for all of his vaunted intimacy with the royal family, was constitutionally incapable of remembering anyone's name. Chances are, if Sir Walter had truly wanted his titled pal to do some caddying for him, he would have addressed him as he did most men of his acquaintance and called out, "Pull the pin, junior."

Sarazen, now 87, is saddened that his old friend and foe, once the most famous of golfers, should now be mostly forgotten, along with so many other flamboyant figures of the Roaring '20s. "I think Walter Hagen contributed more to golf than any player today or ever," Sarazen said from his Marco Island, Fla., home. "He took the game all over the world. He popularized it here and everywhere. Walter was at the head of the class. But they'd probably even forget about Bobby Jones if it weren't for the Masters. It's the sad part about getting old, I suppose. Everybody you know is gone. But Walter should not be forgotten. What golf ought to do is build a monument to that man."

If Hagen is remembered much at all now, it is for apocrypha like the prince of Wales story. It was perhaps inevitable that his outsized personality would overwhelm his considerable achievements. So many golfers have had their moments since he, so many years ago, changed the game from a rich man's pastime to a national craze. But make no mistake, the Haig could play golf, play it better than anyone of his time, with the notable exception of Jones, his only serious rival for public affection. And on one all-but-forgotten occasion, Hagen took even that lordly shotmaker to the cleaners.

Hagen won his first major championship, the U.S. Open, in 1914, when he was 21. He won the Open again in 1919. He won four British Opens, in 1922, '24, '28 and '29, an achievement not surpassed by an American until Tom Watson won his fifth in 1983. Hagen won the PGA Championship (which was decided by match play rather than medal until 1958) five times, including a record four in succession, from 1924 through '27. He was captain of the U.S. Ryder Cup team six times. When the Western Open was still considered major, he won it five times: in 1916, '21, '26, '27 and '32.

Between 1916 and 1928, he won 32 of 34 matches, including 22 in a row, in the PGA. It was his boast that in nearly 30 years of championship competition, he never three-putted an 18th green. Altogether, it is estimated that he won some 75 tournaments and played more than 3,000 exhibitions from the start of his professional career in 1912 until he retired in 1939. He was the first golfer to win a million dollars and the first, as the story goes, to spend two million. At the peak of his career he was paid as much as $1,000 per exhibition round, and in those years he might play as many as nine exhibitions a week. On one tour of western Canada, he earned $3,000, good money in the '20s, and then celebrated his good fortune by tossing a party in a Winnipeg hotel that cost him $3,400.

But he never won a British or U.S. Open in which Jones played, and the younger man's mounting popularity in the mid-'20s rankled Hagen mightily.

Price rather cruelly suggests that "Jones was center ring, while Walter was the sideshow." But the spotlight was on both of them early in 1926, when Hagen, then 33, challenged Jones, 23, to a 72-hole, head-to-head match in Florida, 36 holes to be played on a course Jones favored in Sarasota and 36 at a Hagen stronghold in St. Petersburg. It was a mismatch from the start, because, as Price suggests, Jones, the amateur, played between major tournaments about as often as "your average dentist," and Hagen, the pro, played constantly. But Jones, whose ego was much less threatened by this rivalry than Hagen's, agreed to play, primarily because the match would bring publicity to Florida at a time when he was financially involved in the real estate boom there.

Jones must have suspected he was in trouble early, when on one hole he hit a 250-yard drive down the middle of the fairway and Hagen hooked his tee shot into some brush. Jones hit an iron to the edge of the green and Hagen overshot the green entirely, landing the ball in a swamp. Jones chipped to within inches of the cup, and Hagen blasted out of the bog even closer. They halved the hole, and Hagen hadn't even been on the fairway. It was a typical Hagen performance.

He easily won the challenge match, 12 and 11, and earned $7,800, one of the largest purses ever paid a professional at the time, but spent $1,000 of it buying Jones a pair of platinum-and-diamond cuff links. "I bought the kid a little something," he told Sarazen afterward. This victory soothed some of the sting from subsequent losses to Jones.

Hagen was erratic off the tee, but he had few equals when it came to iron play and putting. And in the days before the sand wedge, which Sarazen invented in 1932, Hagen was the very best at playing out of bunkers with a niblick (nine-iron), a useful talent for one so often in difficulty. "He was an attractive player to watch," says Sarazen. "He was never monotonous, as Vardon and even Jones sometimes could be.

Arnold Palmer would be the closest to him in modern times. Walter was a great scrambler. He was always exciting."

Hagen always had an unfailing instinct for the dramatic. In Sarazen's 1950 autobiography, *Thirty Years of Championship Golf*, Sarazen described the finishing charge that Hagen made against Jones in the 1926 British Open: "On the 72nd, a good par 4, he was told that he needed an eagle 2 to equal Jones' total. Hagen had no use for second place. It was first or nothing. He slapped out a long tee-shot. Before playing his second, he walked the rest of the way to the green—about 155 yards—theatrically surveyed the position of the cup, and asked the referee to have the pin removed from the hole. He walked calmly back to the approach he had to hole to tie, and played a really lovely shot that hit the green only two feet from the flagless hole. Had anyone but Hagen requested the flag to be removed in such a spot, it would have been laughable. Coming from Walter, it was Hagen."

He played swiftly, striding with his confident air directly to the ball and, without undue fuss, hitting it with his peculiar lurching stroke. If he wasted any time at all, it was in pondering the easy shots, a ploy designed to disarm or irritate his opponents. The hard shots he just hit. He played shamelessly to the gallery, joking, teasing, even flirting with spectators. In his first U.S. Open win, he arranged a date with a pretty young woman watching him on the 16th fairway, this when the tournament was still in doubt and his nearest competitor, the fine amateur Chick Evans, was still on the course. When he was advised of the threat Evans yet posed, Hagen replied cavalierly, "So what? I've got my score for the day." He wasn't talking about golf.

Hagen had his crude side, and he would certainly never measure up to the spotless moral standards we seem to demand of our public figures today. "Walter broke 11 of the 10 Commandments," the late PGA director Fred Corcoran was fond of saying about him. One of Hagen's favorite drinking and wenching buddies was Babe Ruth, whose appetites were similarly voracious. Once, in 1932, the two were stopped for driving recklessly on the newly opened George Washington Bridge by a policeman who was so startled to find himself in the company of these legendary athletes—as well as a couple of chorus girls—that he sent them on their way without a citation. Hagen made no secret of his fondness for the bottle and the ladies; if anything, he embellished his own reputation. He was fond of boasting that he neither smoked nor drank until he was 26, but made up for those viceless years with a vengeance thereafter. In the early '20s, though, Hagen didn't drink nearly as much as he claimed he did. Sarazen sometimes caught him knocking back "Scotches and water" that were actually iced tea, and it was not uncommon for Hagen, after conspicuously ordering round after round, to dump his own drinks into handy flowerpots. He reveled in his bad-boy image. Price says Hagen sometimes had his valet-chauffeur-caddie, Spec Hammond, roll his tuxedo into a ball in the morning so that Hagen could appear at the course dressed as if he had come directly from an all-night party, when, in fact, he had had a perfectly good night's sleep. Hagen might even play the first hole in his dancing pumps, then switch shoes with Hammond on the second tee. "That man ruined my feet," said Hammond, who was often obliged to walk 17 holes in tight-fitting patent leathers.

But from 1926 on, Hagen no longer needed to fake his carousing. By then he had the money to live in the grand manner, and he did. In 1928 he played a 72-hole challenge match with British golfer Archie Compston before the British Open. Hagen, afflicted with a cosmic hangover, lost by the amazing score of 18 and 17. Afterward, on the drive home, Hagen told his manager, Bob Harlow, "I can beat that sumbitch on his best day." A week later, he did, defeating Compston for the Open title by three strokes.

The British Open generally brought out the best in him, and not only in terms of golf, for it was in this event more than any other that he liberated the lowly professional golfer from a kind of social bondage. When Hagen first started playing the game, golf was dominated on both sides of the Atlantic by gifted amateurs—in England by aristocrats, in the U.S. by the socially prominent. Clubhouses were sanctuaries for the members and strictly off-limits to the club professionals. The pro in those days was little more than a servant, an instructor to the rich, a craftsman who fashioned clubs in the quiet of his own quarters, far removed from the social whirl of the clubhouse.

And then along came Sir Walter. "Bumptious," as Price has written, "sparkling with wisecracks, dressed in bandbox clothes, Hagen played the game with the aplomb of a man who held the mortgage on the club." Such a man bristled at the ridiculous notion that he wasn't good enough to be seen inside a clubhouse. He met snobbery head-on at his very first British Open, in 1920, at Deal, England. He arrived with 12 color-coordinated golf outfits. He set up headquarters at the Ritz in London and hired an Austro-Daimler limousine and a footman. Disdaining the makeshift accommodations provided for the players, Hagen repaired to his limo and had the footman ostentatiously serve him lunch, with appropriate wines, inside the great machine. At another Open, he grandly hired an airplane and had himself flown 40 miles away to a fashionable inn where, he noisily proclaimed, the strawberries were infinitely superior to those served in the clubhouse. These adventures in one-upmanship were duly reported back home in the U.S. press.

Hagen's boldness, bolstered by his mastery of the British Open, eventually carried the day. An incorrigible social climber, he somehow succeeded in charming the British upper crust, most notably the glamorous young prince of Wales himself. In the '20s, the prince had become something of a golf groupie, and Hagen was his personal favorite. On one golf outing the prince invited Hagen and Sarazen in for lunch at the Royal St. George's clubhouse. They were ready to order when an embarrassed steward begged his Highness's attention. The rules of the club, he whispered, prohibit golf professionals from invading the dining area, even those in the company of such a distinguished guest. The future king of England glared indignantly at the steward and said, in a voice that could be heard clearly by everyone inside, "You stop this nonsense or I'll take the Royal out of St. George's." Hagen and Sarazen were royally entertained.

Hagen was not in any way intimidated by the aristocracy. Fresh from the course and still wearing plus fours and a flashy plaid jacket, he once crashed a high tea at Trent Park, Sir Philip Sassoon's 1,000-acre estate outside London, where the women guests wore long dresses and the men cut-away coats. Introduced there to Ernestine Schumann-Heink, the acclaimed Wagnerian contralto, he stared unashamedly at the diva's mountainous bosom and confided to her, "My dear, did you ever stop to think what a lovely bunker you would make?"

American country clubs had long taken their social cues from the British, and because Hagen seemed to be such a hit abroad, clubhouse doors here were finally opened to the golf pros. His colleagues had only to ride his gaudy coattails to respectability. "He lit a flame that transformed the world of professional golf," said none other than Donald Smith, an officer of the Royal & Ancient Golf Club of St. Andrews. "When we look back on it, Walter Hagen did more for professional golf than anyone else."

Hagen himself was made an honorary member of the Royal & Ancient, but not until 1968, a year before his death. And it wasn't until 1960 that he finally became a member— the only non-dues-paying lifetime member—of the Country Club of Rochester, where he had started as a caddie nearly 60 years earlier. Actually, Hagen's reputation as a social liberator may have been exaggerated. It was years after his star descended before some of the fancier clubs accepted pros into their inner sanctuaries.

And now, in an era when professionals are the true aristocrats of golf, Hagen's triumph—if that is what is was—seems far less significant. In fact, he made a much more important contribution to the game: He made it popular with the general public. He brought golf into the mainstream of the Golden Age of Sports. He was as colorful and popular as many of the other legends of the time—Ruth, Grange, Dempsey, Tilden. It is no accident that with his emergence—and a bit later with Jones's—golf became not merely a rich man's game but everyman's game. And on his world tours Hagen took it to people who didn't know a mashie from a machete. "You get 200 people together anywhere," says Price, "and Walter would play."

And he had a helluva time doing it.

Walter Hagen was born on Dec. 21, 1892, in Rochester, the second of five children of William and Louise Hagen. His father was a blacksmith who worked, for $18 a week, in various auto body shops in East Rochester. Hagen grew up in the Corbett's Glen neighborhood of suburban Brighton, half a mile from the Country Club of Rochester, which had been organized in 1895 by members of the posh Genesee Valley Club in town. He began caddying at the club when he was not quite 10 years old, earning the princely sum of 10 cents a round with an occasional nickel tip. A natural athlete, he learned the game by watching such expert club players as Irving Robeson, Walter Powers, Gurney T. Curtis and J.C. Bonbright and from the club professionals, Al Ricketts and Andy Christie. He learned more than golf from these proper gentlemen, for he studied their mannerisms, their speech and their bearing. Years later Hagen would write: "Whatever sportsmanship through the years I have acquired definitely belongs to these great men." Hagen reasoned that the country club was giving him all the education he would require, so he quit school at 12 to devote more time to it, supplementing his sparse income with part-time jobs as a piano finisher, a taxidermist, an apprentice to a mandolin maker and as a garage mechanic. At the club he advanced from caddie to Christie's assistant. Then, in 1913, he became the club professional, succeeding Christie, who had moved on to another job in Vermont. Hagen's responsibilities also included teaching ice skating and tennis, two sports where charm more than skill carried him over the rough spots.

In 1912 Hagen entered his first tournament, the Canadian Open, and finished 11th. It was with some embarrassment then that he beseeched the Green Committee, chaired by Powers and Beekman C. Little, for four days off so that he might compete in the 1913 U.S. Open in Brookline, Mass. His request was granted only grudgingly. But he finished tied for fourth behind Brookline's own Francis Ouimet and the famous British players Vardon and Ray.

By then, though barely out of his teens, Hagen was building a reputation as a golf fashion plate. His sartorial model was an older player named Tom Anderson Jr., who affected a red bandanna, silk shirts, white flannel trousers and white shoes. In 1914 Hagen entered his second U.S. Open, this time under the sponsorship of a wealthy Rochester gentleman, E.R. Willard, who paid for his trip to the Midlothian Country Club outside Chicago. The night before the opening round Hagen, already honing a taste for high living, dined on lobster at a Chicago restaurant. He was violently ill the next morning and would have dropped out of the tournament before it started had he not felt an obligation to the generous Mr. Willard. So, green-faced and red-bandannaed, he bravely teed off on schedule. He shot a 68 (to Ouimet's 69), one of the few rounds under 70 to that point in U.S. Open history. Those were the days of hickory shafts, carelessly mowed fairways and infrequently watered greens, so a 68 then would be more like a 62 now. Hagen led from the first round to the last and bought himself a car with the $300 prize money.

He returned home a champion, but "he was hardly canonized by the Country Club of Rochester members," as his friend Clune recalls. "It was a pretty stuffy place then. There was a very strict social hierarchy there, and Walter was still thought of as just a glorified servant, a kid to fetch and carry." In his memoirs, Clune wrote, "Hagen returned to Rochester with little more panache than a factory hand punching a time clock."

The young Hagen was a handsome devil, black-haired and green-eyed, sturdily built and, at 5'11", tall for the time. He was a clean liver in those days but already a terror with the ladies. Not long after his Open victory, he met a lively and attractive young Rochester woman named Margaret Johnson, whose father, George W. Johnson, owned the Clinton Hotel on South Avenue. Margaret and her brother, George, had finished third in a dance contest staged by Vernon and Irene Castle, the premier popular dancers of the time. "Margaret was a thin, graceful girl then," says Clune. "She dressed like Irene Castle, and she was far wittier and more sophisticated than Walter. Margaret regarded him as a country boy. She wanted him to be a Fancy Dan, a gentleman sportsman. She would have preferred him to be an amateur golfer with a classy job as a stockbroker. She wanted him to take advantage of his new fame."

Hagen wasn't even certain that he wanted to continue with golf. In 1914, he had a tryout with the Philadelphia Phillies.

He had been an ambidextrous pitcher in semipro ball in Rochester, so when Phillies manager-to-be Pat Moran asked him to throw a few, Hagen inquired of a dumbfounded Moran, "With which arm?" Moran was impressed, but he told Hagen he would have a better future as an outfielder and advised him to come back the next season for another tryout. Hagen decided golf was his game.

He and Margaret were married in 1917, and the country club set them up in a cottage on the premises. It irritated the socially ambitious Mrs. Hagen, however, that neither she nor Walter had clubhouse privileges. And Walter himself had begun to think with some trepidation of horizons beyond the place where he had spent his youth. In January of 1918, Margaret gave birth to Hagen's only child, Walter Jr., and soon after Hagen asked Clune to join him at the Pompeian Room of the Seneca, then Rochester's most popular hotel.

"Henry, they want me out in Detroit to work at a new millionaire's club there, Oakland Hills. They say I'll be just like a member. What do you think?"

"Well, you're going, aren't you?"

"Jeez, I don't know. I was born here. I've always lived in Rochester. You know how it is. When I walk down the street, everybody knows me. Out there ... I don't know...."

But Margaret would have none of these doubts. Hagen took the job. And his life changed. By coincidence Clune himself got a job as a newspaperman in Detroit a few months later, and he observed firsthand what he calls the metamorphosis of his friend. "In Detroit any aspect of the yokel disappeared," Clune says. "Margaret may have aspired to the high life, but Walter far surpassed her in living it." The golf course at Oakland Hills was not yet complete, so Hagen had ample time to knock back a few with the millionaire automobile crowd downtown at the Detroit Athletic Club. He began coming home later and later in the evening. One night, when he showed up two hours late for dinner and still had the cheek to complain about the menu, Margaret snapped at him, "Shut up, you. I can remember when, if you had ham on the table, you'd have thought it was your birthday."

"I'm afraid," wrote Clune, "Walter was as ill-suited for the restraints and ordinances of the conjugal state as a pirate."

In 1919 Hagen represented Oakland Hills at the U.S. Open at Brae Burn Country Club, in West Newton, Mass., the first Open after a two-year interruption caused by World War I. He shot a 78 in the opening round and was five strokes behind the leader, Mike Brady, entering the final 18. But he nibbled away at that lead, and he needed only to sink an eight-foot putt on the last green to tie Brady and force a play-off. Hagen insisted that Brady be brought out from the locker room to witness this dramatic event. Reluctantly Brady showed up, and Hagen, grinning broadly, knocked the ball in the hole.

That night, with the playoff to begin the next day, Hagen threw himself a "victory" party at the hotel. When one of the guests suggested long past midnight that maybe Walter should think about getting some sleep, Brady having already been in bed for hours, Hagen replied, "He may be in bed, but he ain't asleep." Hagen beat Brady by a stroke in the playoff. And when he returned to Detroit for a banquet in his honor at Oakland Hills, Brady, unaccountably, was with him. At the banquet Hagen rose to accept the club's congratulations, and then he shocked the members by announcing that he was resigning on the spot to become golf's first unattached, full-time touring professional. "But," he said, "I've got just the fellow to replace me. He's here tonight—Mike Brady."

Hagen never turned back. The Scotch and champagne flowed and there were women everywhere. His marriage collapsed. In April 1923 he married again, but as the second Mrs. Hagen, Edna, complained in her divorce action, Hagen deserted her as early as 1926. She was, she said, a "golf widow. The only place I can find him is on the sports pages." He did make some token appearances, though. Once, as he prepared for bed in the hotel room where they were staying, Edna observed that her husband was not wearing the underwear he began the day with. When she remarked on this phenomenon, Hagen glanced down, slapped his naked buttocks and cried out, "My god, I've been robbed!"

He was the ultimate good-time Charlie, the big spender who bought drinks for the house, the storyteller who kept everybody in the speakeasy or bar up till closing time. Somehow in all the excitement, he did remain close to his son,

Walter Jr. He took the boy on some of his trips, and he played with him in exhibition matches. In time Walter Jr. became a fine amateur golfer, but he was no match for his father either on or off the course. When someone would be insensitive enough to ask the younger Hagen, "How come you can't play golf like your father?" he would reply coldly, "Now, you tell me who in hell can."

For all of the affection Hagen lavished on the boy, he was still an absentee and often hilariously absentminded father. He probably never did know exactly how old his son was. On Walter Jr.'s 14th birthday, Hagen proudly gave him an Auburn sedan, unaware apparently that the boy was too young to drive in most places. And when Walter Jr. was a student at Notre Dame University he received a six-foot-long cablegram sent by his father from Rangoon, wishing him a happy 21st birthday, with a heartfelt fatherly message about the responsibilities of manhood. The message was not lost on Walter Jr., but the birthday was only his 20th.

Hagen was having a wonderful time taking his show on the road, often in the company of the trick-shot artist Joe Kirkwood. "Never hurry and don't worry," Hagen was fond of saying. "You're here for just a short visit, so don't forget to stop and smell the flowers." The money he won in major tournaments represented only a small portion—perhaps 15%—of an income that was swelled by exhibitions and occasional stints as a pro in residence to more than $100,000 a year, an astronomical figure for the '20s and certainly for the Depression years. Ruth's highest annual salary, by comparison, was only $80,000. But Hagen spent it as fast as he made it, or at least spent what he could find, because his manager, Harlow, was clever enough to deposit much of Hagen's earnings in banks the golfer didn't know about.

The Haig was no longer a phony drinker, but a prodigious one, and he was smoking 2½ packs of cigarettes a day. Still he remained faithful, for the most part, to the lessons on deportment he learned from the swells at the Country Club of Rochester. He never swore, while Jones, the Harvard-educated Southern gentleman, could cuss like a sailor. And Hagen never revealed any of the details of his amatory adventures. "He was a womanizer who put women on a pedestal," says Price. "He treated them all the same, with courtliness, whether they were movie stars or cocktail waitresses."

His skills, though, were fast eroding. He won the British Open in 1929 and the Western Open in '32, and at age 42 he finished third in the U.S. Open in 1935, but he was no longer much of a threat. "If I win another big one," he told San Francisco *Examiner* columnist Prescott Sullivan in the late '30s, "it will be dumb luck."

And yet he still had his moments, some of them vicarious. He was playing with Sarazen in the final round of the 1935 Masters when golfing history was made on the par-5, 485-yard 15th hole. Sarazen and Hagen were the last two out that day, and Hagen was growing impatient. The leader, Craig Wood, was in the clubhouse, and Sarazen, three strokes back, was struggling to catch him. Sarazen's drive was 265 yards down the middle of the fairway. As Sarazen debated what club to use for the second shot, Hagen, noting the late hour, called out to him, "Hurry it up, will you, Gene. I've got a big date tonight." Sarazen obliged him, hitting a spoon (three-wood) shot 220 yards into the hole for the most famous double eagle ever. He tied Wood and beat him the next day in a 36-hole playoff for the championship.

But there were also sad times by then. Hagen had just shot back-to-back 72s in the first two rounds of the St. Paul Open in July of 1934 when, returning from the course to his hotel, his car struck a six-year-old boy, Laurence Johnson, who had darted out onto the street. The boy was then run over by an oncoming streetcar. Hagen leapt from his car and ran to the fallen youngster. "Don't tell me you're dead, sonny," he cried out. "Come on, speak to me." But the boy had been killed. The police determined that the accident was "unavoidable," but Hagen was badly shaken, and from then on the onetime lover of fast cars rarely drove. "He hated driving," says Price, who tried unsuccessfully in the early 1950s to collaborate with Hagen on an autobiography. "I'd drive for him, but if I ever went faster than 45, he'd have a fit. 'What's your hurry?' he'd say, as cars whizzed by all around us. I never knew about the incident."

As the years passed, Hagen retreated more and more to the Michigan backwoods he had grown to love since his days as the Oakland Hills pro. Price spent a year with him at Lake Cadillac trying to get him to concentrate on his autobiography, but it was no use. "He was content to just horse around. He'd get up in the morning at six and have a beer in his hands at seven. Then maybe he'd give me a lesson. I learned a lot about golf, but after a year I realized nothing was going to happen with the book." The autobiography, now long out of print, was completed with another writer several years later.

Hagen would still show up at his old haunt, the Detroit Athletic Club, but beyond that his public appearances were few. He refused to appear on a television show, *Shell's Wonderful World of Golf*, that Sarazen hosted in the 1960s. "I think he was worried he'd look too fat on TV," Sarazen says now. And he moved farther north still, to a cottage overlooking Long Lake outside Traverse City, Mich. In the mid-1960s he was staggered by yet another tragedy, the death of his grandson in a shooting accident. His social life was confined mostly to bumper pool sessions at the Little Bohemia bar downtown. When he turned 69 he quipped, "That's the easiest 69 I ever made."

In 1964 he was diagnosed as having throat cancer. In July 1965, Price, then living in New York, was asked by Walter Jr. to help get his father checked into St. Vincent's Hospital in New York City, where he was to have his larynx removed. One of the world's great talkers was about to lose his voice. But getting him into the hospital was no easy chore. "We must've gone to 10 bars on the way to St. Vincent's," says Price. "He was fairly loaded by the time we got him inside, but I'll be damned if he didn't make a pass at a nurse on the way.

"I was with him the night before the operation, and he wasn't the least bit concerned," says Price. "And after the operation he had virtually no voice, but you still couldn't shut him up. He'd just get mad when you couldn't understand him."

His friends in the PGA held a testimonial in Traverse City a couple of years later, and Arnold Palmer said, "If it were not for you, Walter, this dinner would be downstairs in the pro shop and not in the ballroom."

Walter Hagen died of cancer on Oct. 6, 1969. He was 76, an age he had not had the slightest intention of reaching. At his funeral, Edwin A. Schroeder, the pastor of Our Lady of Refuge Roman Catholic Church in Lake Orion, Mich., reaching for the appropriate metaphor, said, "His biggest game is over. He putted out."

It's difficult to say if the Haig would have appreciated that kind of 19th-hole eulogy. It seems more likely he would have liked a couple of the items on exhibit at the World Golf Hall of Fame in Pinehurst, N.C., better. One is a Willard Mullin cartoon showing a young and vigorous Hagen striding down a fairway in white tie and tails, holding aloft a glass of champagne, trailed by a smiling caddie towing a fresh supply of bubbly. That is Sir Walter as he would have liked to be remembered, the real "Lochinvar of the Links."

The other item is a scroll from the Michigan section of the PGA, which reads: "He drew the attention of the common man to golf ... wrote new pages in the record books in all lands ... while folks of all races marvelled at his game, they remember him best as a jolly good fellow."

Golf has yet to build a monument to Walter Hagen. But that'll do.

Sweet Redemption

BY RICK REILLY

NO ONE KNEW WHAT TO MAKE OF JOHN DALY WHEN HE CAME FROM NOWHERE TO WIN THE 1991 PGA CHAMPIONSHIP. THE HUSKY BLOND COULD DRIVE THE BALL A MILE. BUT UNBE-KNOWNST TO ALL BUT HIS CLOSEST FRIENDS, DALY WAS WAG-ING A BATTLE WITH ALCOHOL AND LOSING BADLY.

Bertrand Russell once called drunkenness "temporary sui-cide." But with John Daly, you were never quite sure. Was he just trying to kill himself or everybody else? Take inter-sections, for instance. One night, with about a dozen Jack Daniel's riding shotgun, he got mad and mobile and went fly-ing through 17 straight red lights. Is that the standing record for failed suicide attempts? In the next seat his buddy swal-lowed hard and tried to keep from cutting into the dash with his fingernails.

You want to hurt me? Wrong. I'll hurt myself first.

Daly's wife, Bettye, remembers one afternoon last year when he'd played lousy. She was in the car with their new baby, Shynah. John was brooding and stepping on it. They came to a fairly busy intersection. He wasn't slowing down. She looked at him. He didn't look back. She warned him about the red. He saw it. He never let up on the gas. Bettye screamed. They made it through. "If that's not depressed," says Bettye, "what is?"

Was it the drinking that brought out all the anger, or was it the anger that brought out all the drinking? One night in a bar in St. Augustine, Fla., the glass Daly was holding suddenly shattered from the sheer ferocity of his grip. What was inside him that he wouldn't let out? Sober, John Daly was one of the quietest, nicest guys you ever met. He wouldn't say boo to you if you walked up and spit in his face. Only alcohol let you know how much rage was inside.

So you had to make double bogey at 18? So you had to gain weight? So your first marriage failed. Take that.

He once ripped the seat out of a friend's van in a blurry fit. Once snapped the rearview mirror out of a van and threw it out the window, and then put his fist through a side-view mirror. He filled two towels with blood that night and *still* wouldn't let anyone take him to the hospital. One thing about people who smash mirrors: They usually don't like what they're seeing. All you have to do is look at Daly's hands to see who he has punished the most. His fists are as scarred as a rose gardener's.

But what has never made sense is how those same wounded hands could also be two of the most buttery-soft in the game of golf. Even when he was still high from the previous night's carousing, Daly could play golf like an angel. Come to think of it, that was half the problem.

You think golf is hard? Try it seeing three balls instead of one. Try it with a buzz on. Try it waking up right before your tee time in a rental car in the clubhouse parking lot, wearing the same eau de Jack Daniel's you wore yesterday. Try it with cotton mouth and the whiskey shakes. Daly could play golf all these ways and more. He once played fresh from a hospital where a nurse had told him she'd never seen a .27% blood-alcohol count before.

Bad news, Mr. Daly. Some blood accidentally got into your alcoholstream.

Hard? John Daly did everything hard. Played in an alcohol fog plenty of times on the mini-tours and still kicked butt. Had a beer before he teed off at last year's Honda Classic;

still made the cut. Fractured his right pinkie punching out a hotel room after the first round of a tournament in South Africa; still shot 21 under par and won the tournament. "Christ," he says, "most people'd be drunk two days on what I'd have before dinner."

And every time Daly went out to play while he was still drunk from the night before, Rick Ross, his teacher, would say to himself, "Lord, let him shoot 85." Instead Daly would shoot around 67.

Maybe that's why the sight of a sober John Daly is giving a lot of green-eyed Tour players the shakes these days. If this haystack of a kid could win the 1991 PGA Championship out of the trunk of his car and set a new record for rookie money winnings and be named Rookie of the Year and the next year win the B.C. Open by six shots, all while he was up to eyeballs in Michelob, how unbeatable would he be sober? If he was the No. 1 draw in golf as Troubled Youth, how much would the people love him as Courageous Recovering Alcoholic?

"I know there's a lot of guys would love to see me fail," Daly says. "Well, good. Let 'em. I'm glad."

Already this season, only 150-plus days into sobriety, there are signs of how scary-good Daly can be: a 66 on the sidewalk-narrow fairways of The Players Championship. Third at the Masters. Starting to actually read putts. And only 27 years old. Good gracious. What has rehab wrought?

And what a strange rehab it is. Typical Daly—he's trying it without a net. It is April, and he is sitting in, of all places, a giant country and western bar in New Orleans called Mudbug's. The dance floor is your basic par-5. Two of his friends, Blake Allison and Sean Pacetti, sit on adjacent stools. Daly's heavy-metal haircut is a little long, and he's getting seriously undertall for his weight, owing to the six-pack of peanut M&M's he puts away every couple of hours to calm his sugar cravings. Yeah, you drink an average of 16 beers a day for months and suddenly stop, sugar cravings aren't uncommon. Daly's caddie, Greg Rita, reports somewhat mournfully, "The other day in a Shoot-out, he ate six bags in a hole and a half."

Daly stacks three packs of Marlboros in front of him neatly. He takes out a stack of bills from his money clip and sets them in front of him, also neatly. Allison has rum, Pacetti has a Bud, but Daly has a Diet Coke. Lord, does the man have Diet Coke. So far today he has had 14 cans of it. For the first bill, $7.25, he gives the waitress a 20 and pushes the change back at her. "Just keep 'em comin', he says. You drink hard ever since you were in high school, you want to keep your hands *busy*.

Hard? John Daly still does everything the hard way. *O.K., you think you're going to make it? Let's see you not drink in the biggest bar in Louisiana.* He loves the challenge. He is a reformed pickpocket at a baggy-suit convention. He sits on his stool and never gets up, slugging down DC's and burning down those Marlboros, just one frosty mug away from trouble. The war inside Daly carries on.

You think you can make it hard on me? Not as hard as I make it on myself.

"Seems I used to do everything like I was on a mission," he says. "If it was alcohol, I wanted to drink till I couldn't see straight. If it was golf, I wanted to beat everybody's brains out. If it was driving, I can get there faster'n you can. It's not anybody's fault, I guess. I was stubborn as hell. I had no direction."

Since his wham-bang three-week drive-thru rehab in Tucson in January, Daly hasn't been to an Alcoholics Anonymous meeting and has no plans to attend one. "How long can you sit and listen to somebody else's problems?" he says. "Can you see me all pumped up to play golf the next day in a tournament, and then some guy starts talking about how he got drunk and killed his best friend? I'd be too depressed to pick up a club. I've got my own program."

The Daly Program seems to be, Trust yourself. Failing that, Trust your friends. Like Allison, Daly's extra-large ex–drinkin' buddy, who owns a liquor store in Morrilton, Ark. He was Daly's roommate when Daly was at his worst, fresh off the failure of his first marriage, depressed about his golf, getting outside some serious Jack. "Hell, now that John's quit drinkin'," Allison says, "business hasn't been worth a damn."

Bettye isn't so sure about having old cronies like Allison around John, but she shouldn't fret. The other day John, in a moment of weakness, said, "God, Blake, I *really* need a beer."

Allison looked up from a cold one and said, "If you do it, I'll kill you."

"Good," said Daly, sinking back in his chair. "Kill me. Go ahead and kill me. 'Cause in five years, I'd be dead anyway."

Hell, that wouldn't be much of a surprise. The surprise is that he isn't dead already.

Hard? Hard is having fans treat you like Mount Rushmore, like you don't have ears.

At the Masters, in Augusta, a fan not six feet from where Daly is putting is heard to say, "What'd Daly get busted for, alcohol or drugs?"

"A li'l bit of everythin', I reckon," says another fan.

At TPC, in Ponte Vedra, Fla., Daly is about to step up to an impossible shot when a fan is heard to say, "Right about now, he's wishin' he had a Scotch in his bag."

"Yeah," says another. "Or a wife to punch."

At a Tour stop in New Orleans, a plastered fan is heard to holler, "C'mon, John! We're going to Pat O'Brien's!"

"We're on your tab!" says another.

This is the hard part now: trying to make it. Not caring what they think. Being 27, suddenly rich and trying to figure out a way to get off the roller coaster without getting killed.

In his rented home in Augusta, Daly rises out of his Barca-lounger like a doomed man, takes another handful of the hated peanut M&M's and smushes them into the top of a piece of double-chocolate cake. He plops down again, disgusted with himself. "If I don't stop eating these goddam things, I'm going to look like the Goodyear blimp," he says. "Seriously, I'll bet you any amount of money I never eat another peanut M&M ... after this." Upon which he shoves a chunk of the cake into his face.

"Bg gddm ft slb," he says.

Lord have mercy on the most human man in golf. He hits big, succeeds big and fails big. The only things as big as his heart are his weaknesses. But he is trying to lick them, one demon at a time.

"Make sure you write one thing," he says, washing down a monster glob of cake with a river of Diet Coke. "These people who write me to tell me to stop smoking—by god, I quit drinking. I ain't gonna quit smoking, too. This is hard enough."

On the living room big screen Daly's idol, Jack Nicklaus, is being interviewed about his opening-round 67 in the Masters, which tied him for the lead.

Jack, how can you possibly do this at 53?

"Well," Nicklaus says, "I realized that I had to get in better shape. Today's players are hitting the gym after every round, doing push-ups, sit-ups, working out, eating the right foods."

"That's right, Jack!" Daly hollers from the side of his mouth that's not gripping the Marlboro. "That's very true. Here I am sitting with my 104th Diet Coke and my fifth goddam bag of peanut M&M's, looking like a big bag of —. Yeah, Jack, let me light up another cigarette on that."

And yet inside Daly is a man with perhaps more Nicklaus-like potential than anybody else in the game. As a spectacle, he's already there. Daly is the only man on the PGA Tour who commands bigger galleries than Nicklaus. Tournament directors agree that Daly guarantees an extra 30,000 fans at the gate.

Hard? You have no earthly idea *how* hard Daly hits a golf ball until you have witnessed it. Yes, it's true that his 287.6 yards per drive this season leads all other players by *10 yards*. (The year before Daly arrived on the Tour, the leader won by .2 of a yard.) And yes, it's true that Daly's drives are easily the longest in the 14 years the Tour has kept track. But what's more mind-bending than the length of his drives is their *height*. They go so high that the ball seems to vaporize. And if you're thinking about numbers, consider that Daly gets very little roll off his drives. Most players get at least a 20-yard roll. Daly's drives carry so high that they come down like hailstones and roll almost nowhere.

Daly is Shaquille O'Neal to the rest of golf's Will Perdue. The other day at the Greater Greensboro Open, Daly suddenly turned sideways on the tee of the par-5 13th hole, a dogleg left around a lake, and hit a moon shot that not only carried the 320 yards over the lake but also ended up going about 360. Daly eagled the hole. Nobody remembers anybody else even trying that shot before.

Daly's monsterism is so famed that three or four times a

year Japanese photographers ask his caddie to take the head cover off Daly's Killer Whale driver so they can shoot the legendary beast. *Watch your fingers, boys. It's nearly feeding time*

In an $80,000, winner-take-all, long-drive showdown between Daly and the Senior tour's longest driver, Jim Dent, in April at the Woodlands in Houston, each player had the option to declare his first drive a mulligan. Dent went first. He hit a screamer 318 yards, right down the middle.

"Would you like us to count that one, Mr. Dent?" the moderator asked.

"Oh, yeah," said Dent excitedly. "Count it."

Now it was Daly's turn. He put in orbit a projectile that finally came down 321 yards later, with no roll. The crowd gasped.

"Would you like us to count that one, Mr. Daly?" the moderator asked.

"Nahhhh," said Daly.

The competition was effectively over. Daly went on to average 337 yards, Dent 313.

There is nothing mysterious about it. Daly just plain takes the biggest lick in history. No other player on the planet takes the club back as far as Daly. He has been told by teachers at every level that his grip is too strong, his backswing too big and the end of his career too near. Nobody has been right yet. One of the most commonly heard backswing criticisms is "You're taking it past parallel." Where Daly takes it, parallel is a toll call away. He takes it back and back and back into no-man's land, where double and triple bogeys lurk. He takes it back until the club head nearly touches the ball. Then, and only then, does he begin his cyclonic downswing. Small children have been carried a few feet in the clubsuck.

Everything Daly does on a course is fast and big. *Golf* magazine recently measured the time it took Tour players to hit drives, irons and putts. Daly was found to be fastest overall. Over putts he averaged only 21.1 seconds, about half the Tour average. Over irons, only 15.6 seconds. Over drives, 18.7. It makes his caddie crazy. "He's actually getting better," says Rita. "I used to be in the middle of getting his yardage when he'd hit. Now at least he waits to hear how far he's got."

If Nick Faldo is the game's greatest mechanical player, the

practice-until-you-bleed type, then Daly is the anti-Faldo. He
is all feel and no mechanics, all emotion and no reserve. But
it is not only all that—the feel for the game, the speed with
which he plays, the Rand McNally distances that he hits the
ball—that makes Daly so wildly popular. It's also his chubby
face and sad blue eyes, the kind that mothers love and fathers
counsel. Indeed, Daly's public troubles have only made the
fans love him more. "He just looks," one fan is heard to say,
"like he needs some guidance."

Hard? Daly has done *life* the hard way. The youngest of
three children born to Jim and Lou Daly, John had an overwhelming need to be perfect. Maybe it was because his dad,
a nuclear engineer, was often gone, working on the road,
working nights, sleeping all day. It's hard to get a lot of
approval from an empty chair at the dinner table. If John
stayed around the house during the day, he had to keep quiet
lest he disturb his father's sleep. "We weren't the kind of
family that talked about our problems," he recalls. "We were
a close family, in a kind of faraway way. It wasn't a being-
with-each-other kind of close. We all went our own ways."

Because of Jim's work, the Dalys moved from town to
town—from Sacramento, where John was born; to Dardanelle,
Ark.; to Locust Grove, Va.; to Zachary, La.; to Jefferson
City, Mo. The place to be for a pudgy new kid on the block
was out on the golf course, practicing a game that didn't
require buddies or teammates. Daly would slog through
ponds to find golf balls, take them to a nearby baseball dia-
mond and try to hit them over the backstops. He never had
a junior set of clubs, only an adult set of Jack Nicklaus
McGregors. If you're seven years old and trying to make a
waterlogged ball go over a backstop with a driver as big as
you, you learn to take a serious lash at it.

Daly rarely played with other kids. He took on the men at
Lake of the Woods Country Club in Fredericksburg, Va.
When he won the men's championship there at 12, the rules
were changed so kids couldn't play in it anymore. Daly was
mad about it, but he said nothing. Instead, he kept it inside
and just hit the little white ball a little harder. "Seemed like
the harder I swung, the better I hit it," he recalls.

The booze came early too. Daly tried his first beer at 10, his first mason jar of his parents' homemade wine at 12. Jim was a big Jack Daniel's man, so John became one too. "It was always, 'Let's see what Dad has in the cupboard,' " he says.

When John was a high school senior, his parents moved to New Hampshire and let him and his big brother Jamie live together back in Dardanelle by themselves. John had always made A's and B's, but after that, with so much partying and golfing to do, schoolwork didn't make the cut.

Daly's golf talent got him a half-ride scholarship to the University of Arkansas. There, his coach, Steve Loy, constantly rode him about his weight. He was 230, and Loy wanted him down to 170. For Daly it was like trying to pass under a door. He would qualify for road trips by beating everybody else on the team, only to have Loy take him back to the 1st tee and say, "If you hit this one in the rough, you're not going." Burning inside, Daly purposely would hit the ball in the rough. *You want to hurt me? Wrong. I'll hurt myself first.* He would get left home. And yet not say a word to Loy. "Basically I was scared of him," he recalls. "I hated him."

Loy put Daly on a strict diet. But Daly wanted to play golf more than breathe, so he pretty much stopped eating altogether. His four basic food groups became Jack Daniel's, Diet Coke, black coffee and Marlboros. "No doctor anywhere would put somebody on a diet like that," Daly says now. Still, he wasn't about to say a word to Loy. You grow up being quiet around the house when your dad's sleeping, and you don't say much. You grow up as the chubby new kid on the block, and you take care not to make enemies.

"I was always the one asking everybody *else* if they were O.K.," Daly says. "I never talked about my problems. I didn't want to admit I had problems. I just let 'em build up. I didn't want anybody to know I was hurtin'. I didn't want anybody mad at me." But where do things unsaid go?

The sober Daly became Mr. Whatever You Want. Mr. No Problem. Forever the new kid on the block, trying to make some friends. "If he was down to his last $100, he'd give it to you," says his old Hogan tour buddy Pacetti. If the check came, Daly would pick it up—even if it meant needing to win the next day to pay the Visa bill. Even today Daly is overly generous. He pays Rita a salary, not a percentage of winnings, which is how most other caddies are paid, and the salary is generous. Of the $230,000 Daly earned for his storybook PGA win, he gave $30,000 to the family of a fan killed by lightning during the tournament and another $20,000 to Pacetti's junior golf charity.

But there was a funny thing about the diet he had adopted. For a while it worked. "Everybody told me to stop drinking beer," says Daly. "So what else is there? Whiskey." One thing about Jack Daniel's—it doesn't add much weight, not like beer. Suddenly, Daly *did* lose pounds. No more chubby new kid. People started calling him Skinny. His self-esteem was riding high. A dangerous connection had been made: Jack Daniel's became Daly's very good friend.

At 21 he married Dale Crafton, daughter of one of the fanciest families in Blytheville, Ark. She wanted to live in Blytheville. He didn't. He felt out of place. He did it anyway. The wedding was huge. Daly hated it. The marriage lasted two years. "I did it to please her," he says. "I wanted to make her happy. Her grandparents gave us a house to live in, but I felt like a cheap person. I didn't want anybody giving me anything." The day of his divorce, Daly was playing on the South Africa tour. Drunk and depressed, he went ballistic in his hotel room. He won the tournament with a fractured right pinkie.

When he got depressed, he would drink. When he played bad, he would drink. When he felt himself swallowing his anger, he would drink. Some nights he would sleep in the clubhouse parking lot so as not to miss his tee time. Only trouble was, he would drink so much that he would still be inebriated the next morning. Of the three balls he would sometimes see, he learned to guess which was the real one.

There was the time in Falmouth, Maine, in '90, when he'd been so depressed nobody was sure what to do. He was driving along with a friend, Brent Everson, and said, without blinking, without smiling, "Do you ever think about just running off the road and straight into a tree?" A few nights later he stuck a loaded bottle into his mouth and nearly killed himself with alcohol. He'd been with a buddy, Roger Rowland, who'd been drinking pretty good himself that night. When Daly passed out and Rowland couldn't get him revived, he threw him in the car. Rowland got so scared that he pulled over a cop to ask him directions to the hospital. At the hospital, doctors realized Daly had fallen into a coma and couldn't be revived. "I really thought he was going to die," says Rowland. Daly played well the next day.

Through it all Daly's golf kept improving. He won a Hogan tour event in 1990 and qualified for the PGA Tour that fall. And when he was the last alternate added to the '91 PGA field at Crooked Stick Golf Club, in Carmel, Ind., and won without ever having seen the course before, Daly went from utter darkness to white-light celebrity in the space of 96 hours.

What really slew Daly was how his fame had changed *him* less than everybody else. When he was trying to get his career going, he would ask people for money, for sponsorships and get nothing. Then after he became Long John Daly, American legend, he says, "those same people would come up to me and say, 'We knew you could do it. We always said that, didn't we, hon? Say, do you think you could do us a favor? We could use some tickets.' " And, warring inside, he would get them.

So he escaped to the land of the ever-flowing tap, where the rage would come flooding out in cars and hotel rooms and bars. "Other guys were there socially," Daly says. "I was there professionally." Only now there was as much money as there was booze; one night, after Daly drank from 5 p.m. till 4 a.m., the bar tab came to $1,200. And now people knew exactly who that was nearly passed out in the corner. Rumors flew. Pressures grew. Life got *way* past parallel.

Daly's parents asked him to quit drinking. "He'd have a bad round and get so depressed," remembers his mom. "We just felt he needed professional help."

His friends asked him to quit. "It wasn't relaxing to be around him," says Allison. "You never knew what crazy thing he was going to do to himself next."

Bettye tried to pull him away from temptation. He'd met her in April 1990, when she was a hotel executive in Macon, Ga. She had him play golf all day, tennis all night. Wear him out. But it didn't help. He resented her efforts. They were on again, they were off again. She had told him she was 29 and divorced. She was actually 37 and still married (she didn't get divorced until September 1991). She bore him a daughter. They parted. She sued for palimony and support of the child with no less than Marvin Mitchelson on her side. Daly went back to her. She dropped the suit and married him. Even love, Daly did the hard way.

"Everything we've been through is just a test," says Daly.

The biggest test was still to come.

To escape the old, wild and angry days, they moved to the peaceful quiet of Castle Pines Golf Club in Castle Rock, Colo. Only problem was, the wild and the angry and the drinking came right along with them. On Dec. 19, 1992, the Dalys had a few friends over to the new house. Dan Hampton, the former lineman of the Chicago Bears, was there as a houseguest, along with his girlfriend, Julie. Daly's brother Jamie was there, along with his date, and a few others. Everybody was drinking, playing pool, living it up. All day Bettye had the feeling that Julie was trying to "hit on" her husband. She didn't like the way she had been draping herself on him. When Bettye came down, a little tipsy herself, she finally told Hampton to control his girlfriend and then told Julie, "This is *my* house!" Julie ran upstairs with Hampton.

Daly blew. According to police reports, he pushed her against a wall and pulled her hair. The Dalys say he never touched her. "Slow down here!" John says he screamed. "We're all havin' a good time!" She didn't think so. Two guests left. Hampton and Julie stayed in their room. Daly went double ballistic. He smashed a hole in the wall. He smashed a window. He smashed a picture, cutting his hand badly. He smashed two built-in trophy cases full of crystal. He smashed the glass-encased set of golf clubs he used to win the PGA. *You want to hurt me? I'll hurt myself first.* He smashed a 57-inch television set. He took out food from the refrigerator and smashed it. "Remember when Richard Pryor said he killed his car?" Daly recalls. "Well, I killed my house." There was blood spattered on one wall. As usual, it was all his.

Bettye went upstairs with Shynah and hid in the closet. "I was scared for our safety," she says.

The Dalys still don't know who called the police, but late

that night, after John had already packed up and started driving to Arkansas to cool down, the cops came. Bettye refused to press charges, but under Colorado state law, police are forced to press them at nearly every scene of domestic violence. They did.

Daly had one last drink with Allison at a Hooters in Little Rock on Dec. 21, 1992, at 11:30 p.m., then drove back to Colorado, where he pleaded innocent to misdemeanor charges of battery and harassment. After the story hit the papers, PGA Tour commissioner Deane Beman called Daly and said if he didn't check into alcohol rehab, he would probably be suspended. Daly flew to Tucson to see if he could be helped to end, once and for all, the war inside himself.

John Daly was at it again, beating holy hell out of the furniture, screaming from way inside, the rage and the tears flowing out.

Only this time he was a patient at Sierra Tucson, an addiction treatment center, and the furniture was a huge, compressed block of foam, against which Daly was swinging a *bataka*, a giant, three-inch-thick tennis-racket-shaped foam club.

Where do things unsaid go? Outside, if you've got the tools to expel them. At Sierra, Daly was taught ways to get the rage out without abusing alcohol, mirrors or furniture. If he feels like destroying something now, he'll wet a towel and beat sense into a mattress until he crumples from exhaustion.

He learned that he might occasionally be angry at someone besides himself. If he feels used by somebody from the past, he'll set the memory of that person down in an empty chair and let fly: "Hey, where in the hell were you when I needed you? I mean, you didn't give a —— about me when I had nothin', so what do you want from me *now?*"

Now Daly wants to puke every time he smells liquor on somebody's breath. Maybe this is not one of the Twelve Steps, but it has got to be a good sign. His dad got scared enough to give up drinking too. "I'm proud as hell of him," says John. Jim and Lou even went down to the clinic in Tucson and found out they needed to do a lot of talking themselves.

Remarkably, Daly lost none of his friends. "I put their lives in jeopardy," he says. "I nearly *killed* them. And they still love me like I'm their brother or something. That's amazing."

Mirrors are fairly safe again. Daly sort of likes what he sees. Fire-tested, he believes he and Bettye will last forever. "It *has* to be true love that we're still together," he says. "There's no way I could love anybody as much as I love her."

Yeah, he can be moody now and he can still get depressed, and he's a long way from over it. The other day at the Kemper Open, he shot 77 the first day and failed to sign his scorecard, disqualifying himself from the tournament. "I'm sorry about that," he said. "I made a mistake. I shouldn't have been playing. My mind wasn't on the tournament. My mind was going 500 different ways." What was on his mind were the Castle Pines charges scheduled for court five days later. Daly flew to Colorado, plea-bargained to a charge of misdemeanor harassment and accepted a two-year probation. To prove to the court that he is in *some* kind of program, he has agreed to work with former Dallas Cowboy Thomas (Hollywood) Henderson on addiction recovery.

But now at least, among all the other things broiling inside him, there's a little peace, too. He is selling his house in Colorado, where he couldn't practice for three months a year, and moved to Orlando, just down the block from Shaquille O'Neal, a man who is to backboards what Daly used to be to vans. "The number one reason we moved is to help my recovery," Daly says. "I can be outside more. Back there I just sat around drinking."

He's even stopping at all the reds.

"Parents kind of go on too much sometimes, but when I tell Shynah I've been there, that I've been through it, I think she'll believe me," he says. "I'll never have alcohol in my house. Maybe I shouldn't say this, but there have been a lot of alcoholics in my family. I want the chain stopped."

The kid without direction has one now: forward.

"Nobody can know what's in my heart," he says, staring down a New Orleans sunset. "Nobody can know what I'm thinking. I know what I've got to do. If I take another drink, I'm history. It's a lot easier knowing you *can't* do something than knowing you *shouldn't*. I *can't*. I've got a rule: I don't drink while I'm sober."

Sadly, during our visit it happened.

Looking back on it, the surprise should've been that it took so long. After all, most of Daly's friends and family were doing it right in front of his nose. He told them to go ahead, that *he* was the one with the problem, not they. And yet as he watched them, he ached. It had been *so* long. Worse, it was sitting right there, in the middle of the kitchen table. His willpower was so skimpy that he had asked them all to watch him closely, but they were busy in conversation. They wouldn't see in time. Like somebody breaking free of shackles, he suddenly lurched for it. In an instant, it was gone. The bag of peanut M&M's.

"Gddmn ths thgs," he said.

COURSES

◆ ◆ ◆

Jones, Hogan And the Rest

BY   DAN   JENKINS

GREAT HONOR ACCRUES TO ANY COUNTRY CLUB THAT HOSTS THE U.S. OPEN. VERY FEW HAVE BEEN FORTUNATE ENOUGH TO HOST MORE THAN ONE. IN 1971 DAN JENKINS VISITED "SHORT, ELEGANT AND CEREBRAL" MERION, ON PHILADELPHIA'S MAIN LINE, WHICH THAT YEAR HOSTED ITS THIRD OPEN.

"Nobody wins the Open. It wins you." These are old words, coming back to us from some forlorn contender groping for daylight from beneath the matted elephant grass of Olympic, or gurgling from under the ponds of Oakland Hills or stranded in the furrowed bunkers of Oakmont. The words tell us of the pressure and the torment, the glory and the glitter, of this thing called the Open Championship of the United States Golf Association—the National Open, as it is known to pedestrians without striped ties, blue coats or armbands. And after next week there will be more evidence of how indecently the human spirit can be wrenched and twisted by a mere game and a mere trophy. For now we go to Merion again, and even on this hallowed ground the Open will go to the man who loses it the least.

One of the things that makes the U.S. Open so fascinating

is that it moves around, from year to year, like a carnival. It goes from the ancient golf world to the new, and back again. This time we find it shifting from the farmlands of Minnesota to the Main Line of Philadelphia. Neither Hazeltine nor Merion would know what to think of one another, for varying reasons, but they share the same history. An Open course gains a distinction that stays with it forever. To stage one Open is enough to turn a country club into a golfing shrine. Merion now joins a select group of clubs—Baltusrol, Oakmont, Oakland Hills, Inverness, Chicago Golf and the Myopia Hunt—that have held the Open three times. And much of next week's suspense will revolve around the hallowed ground itself. Can old Merion stand the test of time? Will the big hitters rip apart this museum of memories?

Not to wish any of the Arnies or Jacks bad luck, of course, but everyone who is familiar with Merion will be rooting for those lovely 127 acres near Philadelphia. They will be cheering for Merion's par of 70 to stand up for all four rounds and hurl the 150-man field into the 280s. Why? Because Merion is a classic course in the old-fashioned sense.

In brief, Merion is short, elegant and cerebral. Compared with Hazeltine, where Tony Jacklin won a year ago, most of Merion's holes will seem like pitch-and-putt. Its length (only 6,550 yards) and excellent condition make it highly vulnerable for the player who can keep it straight off the tee. There are par-4 holes that the Nicklauses can almost drive. And the greens they reach, though speedy, will putt as smoothly and honestly as any in the land.

This will provide the opportunity for a few sizzling low rounds, and maybe Merion will get beaten down the way Baltusrol, Olympic and Oak Hill were—down into the 270s. But this famous old course, underdog though it is, has weapons to fight back with. Quite aside from the usual USGA doctoring— the six-inch rough and narrow, target-shaped fairways—there is the curious pace of Merion itself. It simply isn't like any other course. Starting long and finishing long, with almost all of the birdie chances in between, Merion should play evil games with the modern competitor's tempo. It will put to a full and unique test the golfer's ability to adjust—three times in one round—his rhythm and his thinking.

Merion begins with both of its par-5s crowded into the first four holes, and the 5th is a long, sloping, narrow par-4. After that, for the next 10 holes the course shortens and becomes more and more inviting. But then come the famed quarry holes, the 16th through the 18th, where great length is demanded as well as accuracy for a 4-3-4 finish.

Merion got tapped a few times when the last Open was played there in 1950. A fellow named Lee Mackey Jr. sped around in 64 on opening day, and a better-known fellow named Johnny Bulla carved out a 66 the second day. There were 11 other rounds under par. But when everything was finished the lowest score (there was a three-way tie) was 287—seven over par—and Ben Hogan, who would win the playoff over Lloyd Mangrum and George Fazio, had to hit his fairy-tale one-iron on the last hole to get a piece of it.

History says it was a brilliant shot. Hogan doesn't. "I was 40 feet from the pin," Ben has recalled. "I probably should have hit a four-wood."

Hogan's most vivid recollection of Merion is the glass-slick greens. "If they're like they were in 1950," Ben says, "nothing will hold out of the rough, not even a wedge. I can remember being afraid at times to place the putter behind the ball because it might move."

Not everyone adores Merion. Julius Boros, who will be among the few in the field who know the course at all (he finished ninth in 1950), claims it is simply too short now. Lloyd Mangrum says it was too short two decades ago when he almost won.

"Even before '50 I'd always heard of Merion," Lloyd says. "Bobby Jones and all that. But all I did was hit a bunch of three-irons off the tee. What's so great about a golf course that keeps a three-iron in your hand off the tee?"

Mangrum was exaggerating, of course. Merion makes one reach for the three-iron when one gets sick of the rough that the driver keeps putting one in. The gamble is there on virtually every tee. Which again points up the charm of the place.

Whatever the mystique is, it even affects those manicuring the premises. Only the other day a Merion member stopped to observe a young man taking extreme care as he mowed one of the sacred putting surfaces. The member asked if the young man got any satisfaction out of helping prepare the course.

"I sure do," said the young man. "In fact, I'd do it for nothing."

Such is the lure of history and elegance. Such is Merion.

Playing
Ancient Games

B Y   S A R A H   B A L L A R D

IN THE YEARS SINCE THE LEGENDARY GIANT FINN MacCOOL
CREATED SOME OF THE BEST-KNOWN FEATURES OF THE IRISH
LANDSCAPE, THE PEOPLE OF IRELAND HAVE BUILT SOME OF THE
MOST MEMORABLE GOLF COURSES IN THE WORLD. SARAH BAL-
LARD LOOKS AT SIX GLORIOUS EXAMPLES.

From Dublin's bay around to the mouth of the Shannon, from
sea to shining sea by the coastal route, this is Irish golf. Before
you are six of the most glorious seaside golf courses that ever
nature and man conspired to create. They rank alongside the
best in the world, yet they are virtually unknown to golfers
outside the British Isles. They were laid out at the end of the
last century, with Scottish courses as their models, on the same
terrain that first shaped the ancient game.

The roots of golf lie in Scottish linksland, sandy wastes
beside the sea where only low-lying vegetation survives and
where the wind carves wavelike shapes in the dunes. Over
the last century the game has strayed far from its sandy ori-
gins, but a tribal memory persists in golfers and draws them
back to their ancestral turf. Every year by the tens of thou-
sands these pilgrims descend on Scotland to play the game the

way it was meant to be played, in solitary communion with the wind and the sea.

Lately, however, the communion has turned into a revival meeting. In St. Andrews, where until only a few years ago the tourist season ended in September, tee times on the Old Course are booked through Christmas. By contrast, a golfer with a strong urge to push his electric cart into a nearby artificial lake and get back to basics will find Irish courses both empty and inviting.

Each of these courses—Royal County Down and Royal Portrush in Northern Ireland, County Sligo, Lahinch and Ballybunion in the west of the Irish Republic and Portmarnock in the east, on the edge of the Irish Sea near Dublin—is separately and distinctly memorable, and each is a test of skill and character when a spell of Irish weather sets in. In Ireland, foul weather gear is essential, but umbrellas are useless. The rain blows sideways. And wind, of course, is at the very heart of linksland golf.

The only way to travel among these six courses is by car; the distances are short, the sights along the way rare, and the traffic in most places four-legged. On a one-lane road that runs along the rim of the Irish world in the northeast corner of County Antrim, where the Atlantic Ocean is a thousand feet below, and where it seems that on a clear day you could skip a rock across to Scotland, the only things moving in the opposite direction are a flock of sheep and the man and dog herding them. You pause to let them pass, your car becomes a metallic island in a sea of wool, the man touches the brim of his cap, and you move on.

Ireland is made of memorable moments, not all of them on golf courses. Take an early morning stroll on the outskirts of Ennis, a lovely town on the River Fergus in County Clare, not far from Lahinch, and you'll be passed by schoolboys riding their clunky bikes toward town. As each of them passes, you hear a soft sound that seems to be "gluck." At first you're puzzled, but then it becomes clear. How can anyone resist a country where children wish a stranger "g'luck" when the day has barely begun?

ROYAL PORTRUSH
The British Open has been held only once in Ireland, over

the Dunluce links at Royal Portrush in 1951. Bent clad sand hills roll and heave across the Portrush landscape on the northern coast of County Antrim, but sand bunkers are few. Only two of the 18 holes are absolutely straight; the rest bend and curve. More often than not the greens, polished smooth by the wind, are guarded solely by natural mounds and hollows. The only vegetation higher than wild rose, heather and dune grass is a few scrubby trees clumped in depressions between sand hills. One such clump, between the 9th green and the 10th tee, hides a tin-roofed hut, the "Refreashment House." If a flag is flying above the hut, it means the kettle's on, heating water for hot whiskey.

"The Scots drink hot whiskey," says a Portrush player as the bartender combines Bushmills, the whiskey of the north, with boiling water, a slice of lemon and a couple of cloves. "But they call it a toddy and they drink it for medicinal purposes." At Portrush, hot whiskey is fortification against the rigors of the wide open landscape and the winds that blow in from Scotland and points north.

County Antrim is Finn MacCool country. MacCool is Ireland's Paul Bunyan, a giant who once picked up a clod of earth and hurled it into the sea, thus creating the Isle of Man with the clod and Lough Neagh, the largest lake in Ireland, with the hole left behind.

MacCool seems to be tinkering with Portrush lately. Two recent storms combined to suck away 25 feet of the course, including a big grassy hillock just behind the 5th green. The 6th tee is vulnerable to future storms, as is the club's second course, The Valley. Currently, Portrush members are trying to raise £250,000, the cost of a revetment project for the shoreline. "We've tried all the various government concerns, the M.P.s, the European Commission and so on," says RAF Squadron Leader Eric Wainwright, the club secretary. "They all express sympathy but they didn't put the hand in the pockets."

Fourteen years of The Troubles in Northern Ireland, and the frightening publicity, have greatly curtailed tourism there, but a recovery of sorts has been under way in the last few years. If it keeps up, the costly fight to save Royal Portrush may be won. One hopes so. Portrush is a natural beauty, the kind of course that makes you wonder why anyone ever thought golf could be played anywhere except beside the sea.

ROYAL COUNTY DOWN

There is this saying in Newcastle, the resort town on the east coast of Ulster that is the home of Royal County Down: "If you can see the Mourne Mountains, it's going to rain. If you can't, it's raining."

The mountains of Mourne really do "sweep down to the sea," as Percy French wrote, and the beauty of them can make concentrating on the golf shot at hand difficult. Nevertheless, the temptation to lose yourself in the distant landscape should be resisted lest the landscape at hand—course ferns, spiny gorse, wiry, impenetrable heather, thick, pillowy dune grass—claim golfer and golf ball for its own.

While many golf purists prefer the Portrush course to Royal County Down—"No true championship test should have four blind driving holes," sniffs a Portrush player in reference to County Down—the layout at Newcastle is extraordinary, particularly the front nine. The first three holes, a par-5 followed by two 4s, are narrow valleys between ridges of sand hills that run along the edge of Dundrum Bay and its wide sand beach. No matter how many other golfers are on the course, one has a sense of glorious solitude on these valley holes.

At the far northern end of this stretch, the 3rd green is set in a natural amphitheater of mountainous sand hills, and at any one time or another an elderly man in a tweed cap walking his dog across the course from town to beach and back will appear from around the base of a sand hill and pause to watch a shot or two. These discerning gents with their noncommittal gazes can create odd kinks in an otherwise acceptable golf swing.

The climb up to the 4th tee is literally breathtaking, but so is the vista from the tee as the golfer turns back toward the clubhouse, the town and the mountains. Rain clouds cling to the bare, rounded peak of Slieve Donard, the 2,796-foot king of the Mournes, while the westering sun gilds the green of its lower slopes, and the creases between them plunge into purple.

The 9th is perhaps the most spectacular of all the holes at County Down: a long par-4 with a blind shot from a raised tee and a view of the brick Victorian tower of the Slieve Donard Hotel, all seen against the backdrop of the Mournes. The tee shot crosses a rough valley and soars up toward a directional stake at the brow of a hill. If long enough, it will descend to the flat floor of the valley. For the golfer, struggling around the course while buffeted by 30 or 40 knots of wind, the descent is like dropping from Wuthering Heights into Shangri-la.

In Ireland, Royal County Down is considered a stuffy club. Its members, aside from the occasional royal, are lawyers, judges, businessmen and the like from Belfast. Because golf in Ireland, as in Scotland, is an egalitarian game, Irish golfers delight in the legend of the feud between County Down and an English club. The story has it that a team from England arrived in Newcastle for an interclub match and was refused admittance to the clubhouse. Ever since, this sign has been posted in the locker room at the English club: "All visitors welcome except dogs and members of Royal County Down."

BALLYBUNION
There are no secrets in Ireland. It's a small country, its people are gregarious, and things just naturally get around. In 1981 Tom Watson played in Ireland for the first time at Ballybunion in County Kerry, near where the River Shannon empties into the Atlantic. Watson's visit wasn't publicized, in the hope that he'd be able to play as a private citizen. However, on the ferry crossing the Shannon on the way to Ballybunion, it became clear that the cat was out of the bag. Every car was filled with golf fans, all on their way to watch Watson tackle Ballybunion. Several hundred spectators saw him tee off, and eventually the crowd swelled to a thousand or so.

Now the clubhouse wall at Ballybunion is replete with photographs of Watson taken on that atypically balmy summer day, and every clubhouse regular can detail his round, shot by shot, all 72. As one struggles up the last of many, many hills toward the 18th green, dizzy from the relentless battering of the wind off the Atlantic, eyes watering, nose running, feet wet, hands frozen, someone is sure to mention that the Ballybunion Watson played on that tame day wasn't the "real Ballybunion."

The 1st fairway skirts a small stone-fenced graveyard that's thick with Celtic crosses. One can view this as an omen, however morbid, but, in fact, as graveyards go, it has a certain charm. It's also out of bounds. But the real Ballybunion, in all its ferocious beauty, begins at the 448-yard, par-4 7th, on a tee perched high above the Atlantic, a gale blowing from right to left. From there to 18, you hit it—and pray. At Ballybunion, one often drives, as the late Henry Longhurst once wrote, with the certainty "that if your slice carries far enough, there is nothing to stop it pitching on Long Island, U.S.A."

Steel baskets of stones, called gabions, now barricade the bottom of the cliffs below the 7th, 11th, 15th, 16th and 17th holes, but they weren't in place that brutal winter night in 1976 when abnormally high tides destroyed a 600-yard section of the cliffs. "I remember I went down there and I was absolutely certain our course was gone," says Sean Walsh, the secretary. "If you walked off the 15th green you would certainly have walked into four or five feet of water. Off the ladies tee at 16 you'd have drowned. It washed the carcass of a dead pig—this is quite true—right up into the gap of the 16th."

A successful campaign to raise money to save Ballybunion resulted in worldwide publicity and contributions from as far away as Australia, and the cliffs were reinforced.

PORTMARNOCK

Traditional seaside courses, based on the Old Course at St. Andrews, tend to be nine holes out and nine back. Many days a round of golf on such a course can be one long trudge into the teeth of a gale followed by a long nudge home. Portmarnock, laid out in 1894 by two Scottish professionals, could easily have been the same. But these Scots were inspired. On a long narrow peninsula on the northeast edge of Dublin, washed by the Irish Sea and the Baldoyle tidal estuary, Portmarnock unfolds in two vaguely circular loops, something of a figure eight, so that the hole you're playing rarely lies in the same direction as the last.

Portmarnock is a city course. Its members are prosperous Dubliners, many of whom belong to inland clubs as well. In the early days members took a train from Dublin to Baldoyle Junction, then crossed the estuary at low tide by horse cart.

Harry Bradshaw, an Irish institution, retired as Portmarnock's head professional last year, but visits the premises most days. Now 70, Bradshaw is a big man with a tweed cap and jacket, and in his day he won everything that country-man Christy O'Connor did not. Bradshaw is best remem-bered, however, for the way he did *not* win the British Open in 1949. In the final round his ball rolled into a beer bottle. Instead of waiting for a ruling, which would have given him relief, Bradshaw played the ball as it lay, bottle and all, and wasted what turned out to be a crucial stroke. He tied Bobby Locke, then lost to him the next day in a playoff.

The 390-yard par-4 14th is the best hole on the course, although Arnold Palmer once said that the 187-yard 15th was the best par-3 in the world. His three-iron across the wind wound up three feet beyond the hole. He missed the putt, but apparently bore the hole no grudge.

On a Sunday morning at Portmarnock, the faint peal of church bells drifts across from the mainland, and a fleet of small sailboats races around an island called Ireland's Eye. It's heaven.

COUNTY SLIGO

Over the door of a shop that looks like an Irish cottage that has had its thatch blown off is the sign: W.J. MCGONIGLE, PRO-FESSIONAL AND CLUB MAKER. "Any pro in this part of the world must be able to fix and repair and make clubs," says McGonigle, 57, "although the art is dying out here as well as elsewhere." A custom-made McGonigle driver costs about the same as a good Wilson or Ram.

Better known as Rosses Point, Sligo is 360 acres of true linksland on a spit between Sligo and Drumcliffe Bays. The first four holes wend their soothing way uphill along the inland side of the course, away from the guesthouses and car-avan park of the village of Rosses Point. At 5, a 482-yard par-5, the ground drops to a fairway some 100 feet down. Spread below and ahead are the next 11 holes, surrounded by beach and bay and, across the water, Ben Bulben, a flat-topped mountain whose extraordinary profile is visible everywhere. Yeats, who's buried in the Drumcliffe churchyard, wrote his own epitaph in *Under Ben Bulben*.

... On limestone quarried near the spot

By his command these words are cut:
Cast a cold eye
On life, on death.
Horseman, pass by!

The best hole on the course, and surely the strangest, is the 14th, a par-4 with a double dogleg—first left, then right, into the wind. Said an Irish golf writer, "I wouldn't know how to play the hole except badly."

Sligo's most celebrated amateur was Cecil Ewing, who won the West of Ireland at Rosses Point 10 times. Ewing was a huge man with a large head and a profile to match Ben Bulben's. He's generally credited with having invented the half-to-three-quarter swing. Suffering from an infected big toe, Ewing discovered that he could avoid the pain by placing his feet close together, thus reducing the arc of his swing, and using his powerful arms and shoulders to take up the slack.

A large number of Ewing's countrymen seem to have copied his style. Their backswings are short, they play quickly (an Irish foursome rarely takes longer than three hours to play a round), and they keep the ball in play. Only foreigners lose golf balls on Irish courses. Lots of them.

LAHINCH

Mention Lahinch and people will smile. The course is Ireland's sentimental favorite. Furthermore, in a land where a good story is truly appreciated, Lahinch is a national treasure.

First of all, there are the Lahinch goats. The current Lahinch goats, a herd of five, are descendants of goats that belonged to Tommy Walsh, a Lahinch caddy. The goats are reputed to be reliable weather forecasters. If a storm is approaching they quit their grazing out on the course and retire to the protection of the clubhouse walls. Years ago, when the clubhouse barometer broke, someone taped a hand-lettered sign to its face that read, and still reads, SEE GOATS.

Not long ago, George Eberl, managing editor of the USGA's *Golf Journal*, was playing a round at Lahinch on a somewhat dubious-looking day. Keeping an eye on the scattered dark clouds that were blowing in from the west, Eberl had reached the 12th, as far away from the clubhouse as it's possible to be, when he espied the goats, grazing contentedly beside the fairway. Reassured, Eberl played on. At the 15th tee, a gale hit with the force that can make Irish seaside golf a matter of mere survival.

Later, drying out in the clubhouse bar, Eberl groused to the bartender about the unreliable goats who were "lollygagging" on the 12th fairway when they should have been cowering near the clubhouse.

"New goats," said the bartender offhandedly.

Since 1895, Lahinch has been the site of the South of Ireland Amateur, affectionately known as The South. All of the great Irish amateurs have played in The South, including local favorite Mick O'Loughlin, a butcher from the nearby town of Ennistymon who won twice, in 1937 and 1938. O'Loughlin was a burly man with a great jutting jaw who wore an old hat distinctively pulled well down on his big head and baggy tweed plus fours. "Rugged but warmhearted," O'Loughlin was said to be. Once, in the 1938 final, when he was addressing his putt on the 17th, O'Loughlin overheard Austin (Brud) Slattery, who was then a local schoolteacher and who recently retired as club secretary, talking to a friend near the 18th tee. O'Loughlin straightened up and called out, "Will the schoolmaster stop talking?" Later, after O'Loughlin had won the match, Slattery came up to him to apologize for the disturbance. O'Loughlin said, " 'Tis all right, but I am so tense at times like that, I can hear the bees farting."

The original Lahinch was laid out in 1893 by Old Tom Morris, but only one of Morris' holes remains: the famous, if quirky, 6th. Known as The Dell, it's a 156-yard par-3 with a completely blind tee shot. The green is in a little valley entirely surrounded by four large sand hills. A rock, painted white, faces the tee from the brow of the sand hill, and indicates the route to the pin. When the pin is moved, so is the rock.

Novelties such as The Dell were all the rage before the turn of the century, but as golf's sophistication grew, they fell from favor. Today, The Dell is an anachronism, but it's one of the reasons golfers return to Lahinch. Besides, not many golf holes make you giggle.

Unseen Hands on My Game

BY   RICK   REILLY

ROYAL DORNOCH IN THE NORTH OF SCOTLAND MAY BE THE
LEAST RENOWNED OF THE WORLD'S GREAT COURSES. RICK
REILLY WAS LUCKY ENOUGH TO SPEND A WEEK THERE IN THE
COMPANY OF WATER KELPIES, GHOSTS, AND SANDY MATHESON,
CADDIE EXTRAORDINAIRE.

How shall I put this? Right in front of me, right in front of
my disbelieving eyes, on a dark staircase, in an ancient castle, maybe half a dozen fire snorts from the Loch Ness Monster itself, in the remote reaches of Scotland, there was—and
I can just tell you're not going to go for this—an apparition
... a ghost ... a person of the undead persuasion ... a ceased-
to-be individual AWOL from the grave ... a poltergeist on
the wrong side of the television set ... a soul with a serious
case of unrest. I swear on my first communion medal that
this is true.

And, right away, do you know what went through my
head? What went through my head was, Well, they told me
Royal Dornoch is a haunting place, but this is ridiculous.

I suppose this needs some explaining. I mean that the people who told me to come to Dornoch had called it haunting,

as in unforgettably beautiful, which it was—and is. But I
didn't know they also meant haunting, as in a certain real
estate listing in Amityville haunting. Haunting, as in Kathy,
the maid on the fourth floor at the Dornoch Castle Hotel,
where I was staying and where I was now, once feeling
somebody tugging on the back of her sweater and then turning around to find nobody there. Haunting, as in a certain
Andrew MacCormack unexpectedly checking in at the hotel
one night, which was a mite strange, considering that Andy
had been hanged for stealing sheep 150 years before. Not
only that, but while playing one day at the Royal Dornoch
Golf Club—which was the reason I had gone there in the first
place—I five-putted the 4th green, and I'm quite sure mine
weren't the only hands on the putter, if you get my drift.

Then again—and this tells you a lot about Dornoch—I
thought, for the privilege of playing legendary Dornoch, perhaps some things have to be endured, and sharing my lodg-
ings with a few frequent fliers from the 19th century was one
of them.

DAY 1: *Our hero breaks 90 on the planet's 12th-best course and
discovers the restorative powers of Sandy's favorite spirit*

Golf magazine ranks Dornoch as the 12th-best course in the
world, though anyone who has played it knows that that's
low. But what are the people at *Golf* supposed to do, seeing
as hardly anyone has ever heard of it? It's like *W* naming
Mrs. Eva Dalrymple of Cedar Rapids, Iowa, as the best-
dressed woman in the world. She may *be* the best dressed,
but nobody has ever heard of her. So 12th is as good as she's
going to get.

To see the legend for myself, I took part in Dornoch's
highly unfamous Golf Week: six days of competition and
lessons for the world's golfing impaired—or anyone who signs
up and pays the $440 fee. There were 48 men and women
on hand last year for the week, and each day we got lessons
in the morning, and then in the afternoon we played golf on
the third-oldest course in the world (St. Andrews and Leith
being even older). By day, the pro, the long-suffering Willie
Skinner, described my swing as mostly a horror, but it was at

night that things got really scary. That is why I decided to take the problem straight to Sandy.

Sandy Matheson is a caddie at Dornoch, although that's like saying Fawn Hall was in the NSC secretarial pool. Sandy is not just a caddie at Dornoch, he's also the historian, philosopher, part-time bartender, mayor, official greeter, greenskeeper, constable and minister to the sick. He's about 5 ft. 6 in., with a windburned face redder than a red herring. You'll usually find him wearing two or three sweaters, with a "lung starter" (as he calls a cigarette) in the right corner of his mouth, something perpetually funny to say coming out of the other corner and eyes three times too small for his head. In sum, my favorite Scot of all time.

Sandy is 55 years old and has been caddying at Dornoch since he was a kid. Caddying is the most wonderful job in the world if you do it at Dornoch, even if you have to do it for me, which he did (though I did shoot 89 the first day, which, for a 15-handicapper with the wind blowing and who, on the flight over, had to listen to the guy next to him describe his slides from his last trip to Badlands National Monument in South Dakota, was pretty darn good). Sandy spent a lot of time combing through the thorny whins in search of my ball.

"Whatta ya' playin', sir?" he would ask.

"A J. Robert Oppenheimer Allstate Insurance," I would answer.

Sandy wanted me to play well, I suppose, on the theory that the better I played, the better I would tip. So he often tried to school me. When I would get to thinking too much about where my elbow or left knee should be, Sandy would pull me aside and say, "Wee wheels in ya head, sir. You've got to forget those bloody wee wheels, sir."

One time I ignored his advice and went for a par 5 in two, thereby trying to separate the inside of the ball from its cover. Instead, I nearly separated my back from a disk, and the ball flopped to the ground 15 yards ahead like a soggy newspaper. Sandy said, " 'Tis a game of inches, sir, the most important of them being between the two ears."

When I started the day badly, he would say, "Nay worry, sir. Ripe early, rotten early, sir." When I started badly and finished badly, he would mutter, "Some game this, sir."

When I was faced with a delicate putt, he would say, "Now ya must just tickle her, sir." And when I would forget and hit it with all the touch of, say, Marvin Hagler, and roll the ball eight feet past the hole, he would say, "Aye, you had a rush of blood to the head there, you did, sir."

And when I did something really stupid, like the day I five-putted the 4th green, which I still contend was not my fault, I would say something like, "Well, Sandy, that was kind of abominable, wasn't it?" And he would look at the grass and say, "Aye, it's too true, sir."

Through it all, Sandy never uttered complaint one. It was a steady loop and at the end of every day we retired to the bar, and I bought him a medicinal, as he called it. A Macallan malt whisky—"The finest medicinal ever drunk by man or boy," he said—and we toasted our wounds.

You want smooth? Macallan is smooth. Macallan is a Rolls-Royce Silver Shadow with velvet seats and brand-new shocks. That night, Sandy and I sat there making love to our Macallan, and I said to Sandy, "Have you drunk Macallan all your life?"

And Sandy said, "Not yet."

DAY 2: *We broach this business of poltergeists in the local hamlet*

"Is Dornoch haunted?" I asked Sandy after we had gone around in a tidy 95.

He finished his medicinal and ordered another one from Len, the bartender. After a long pause, Sandy told me that at the end of the week he would show me something, but until then, "donna' let it worry ya, sir."

So, naturally, I let it worry me—but only at night. During the day, I was falling in love with Dornoch, which is, if you will, par for the course. Most everybody who has ever played Dornoch has had an incurable crush on it.

Bing Crosby had one. Whenever he was in London, he would helicopter up on Sundays. There's a picture in the clubhouse of Bing with all the women in town, which is to say maybe 12 people.

Before the 1980 British Open at Muirfield, Ben Crenshaw flew up to play. When he returned, somebody asked him how he had liked Dornoch.

"I almost didn't come back," said Crenshaw.

Greg Norman made a special trip up from St. Andrews three years ago, and Tom Watson played the course on a Saturday before the British Open one year. He had so much fun that after dinner he sneaked back out and played another 18. (This isn't strange, because during the Scottish summer the sun lingers long into the night.) That evening the weather turned unruly. At one point, the rain was pelting Watson's face and the wind was bending back the flagsticks. Watson turned to Sandy Tatum, his American partner, and said, "This is the most fun I've ever had playing golf." Which is what one says in good weather, too.

He loved it so much that he played another 18 on Sunday. The crowd following him seemed unusually big for such a remote little town. Midway through the round, Watson turned to Sandy, who was caddying for him, and said, "Doesn't anybody go to church around here?"

And Sandy said, "Well, that would be hard t'day, sir. That's the minister third from the left, sir."

In his book *Following Through,* Herbert Warren Wind of *The New Yorker* wrote that only four courses in Scotland merited the coveted three-thistles award: St. Andrews, Muirfield, the Ailsa course at Turnberry and Royal Dornoch. The first three everybody has heard of, the fourth nobody has heard of. The problem is that Dornoch is 60 miles north of the Loch Ness Monster and 15 miles south of Dunrobin Castle, and most folks don't believe any of the three exists. Indeed, most people who visit Scotland to play golf never get as far north as Dornoch, which is farther north than Moscow. Yet the course is open for play every day, including Christmas.

The starter used to be a man named Mike Fenelon, who died last spring. You could have gotten a game almost anytime if you brought a piece of chocolate to Sam, Fenelon's dog. The trick was to put the chocolate on Sam's nose, where Sam would just let it balance until Mike snapped his fingers. Then, in a fraction of a second, Sam would flip it into the air and gobble it up. One time, somebody put a chocolate on Sam's nose and Mike got called away and forgot all about the chocolate and it sat on poor Sam's nose so long it melted. And Sam never even took a lick.

One thing that has held Dornoch back as a golf mecca is that it has never been host to a British Open, and the reasons for that include the very things that make it so beautiful. Many of the holes border cliffs that plummet to the beach, limiting the size of the galleries. And the rough doesn't allow for many spectators, either, because it's not simply rough. Rather, it's mainly thick, thorny bushes called whins, which, when blooming their bright yellow, are the fairest sight you might ever hope to see. Nonetheless, if you get in that rough, it's the equivalent of sitting on your aunt's sewing basket.

"My favorite spot on the course," says Watson, "is the 3rd tee. You walk up a hill from the 2nd green to the 3rd tee and then, when you turn around, the course reveals itself. You see it, the expanse of it, the ocean, the whins in bloom, and you say to yourself, 'My God, there it is.' "

There it is, indeed. Ahead of you, miles of white beach, blue Dornoch Firth all around, the North Sea beyond and, in front of you, the whins in the wind doing a shimmy-shimmy all over a treasure of a links that has sat mostly undiscovered for 400 years.

The good Bishop Robert Stewart played here in 1542, and the course hasn't changed very much since he last holed out. Dornoch was designed by "God himself," as Sandy says, with a little help from Old Tom Morris, who changed a few holes around in 1886. Other than some slight alterations after World War II, it has remained relatively, and happily, unspoiled.

Dornoch may have influenced American golf more than any course in the world, owing to the fact that the great golf architect Donald Ross grew up there. In 1898 Ross immigrated to America and over the next 50 years designed more than 500 courses, including Pinehurst No. 2, one of the consummate courses in the world.

But even Pinehurst curtsies to Dornoch, whose first hole is "a handshake," as Watson calls it, a straight-ahead par-4. The Dornoch Hotel's rock wall borders the left side, and on the right are the blue sky and the bluer-still Dornoch Firth. The next seven holes play toward the North Sea, with the prevailing wind coming from the west. Everywhere, bordering each tight, crisp fairway, are the yellow-and-green whins, and near the driving areas and bordering the greens are bunkers with layered-sod faces. These bunkers can be so cruel that one day my playing partner, a plump Englishman, took five blows to bat the thing out forward. When he was finally out, he collapsed in a fleshy pile on the edge of the bunker and buried his head in his hands.

When playing Dornoch, it behooves one to bring plenty of dimpled spheroids. Once, Sandy embarked on the day's loop with an American, 24 balls and a fifth of Macallan. On the sixth hole, he was sent back for more balls and more Macallan.

The 7th hole is the only one from which the water is not visible—this was the hole I played the best, being undistracted by the beach and surf, perhaps. On the clearest of days as you look north along the coast to the village of Golspie, you can see, magically, Dunrobin Castle, which is surely the most castle-y looking castle in the world.

At the 9th, the course hears Len calling from the bar and heads for home. The 9th tee is one of the most majestic in golf, with the waves crashing against the rocks to your left, and whins on your right, as you try, hopelessly, to drive straight uphill with a right-to-left wind blowing across your nose. Most of the holes coming in tickle a cliff that plunges down to the fine sandy beach and the sea, but not the 14th, perhaps the finest bunkerless par-4 in the world. The hard green on a high plateau absolutely screams for a punch shot, which I never hit. The 18th is thirstily uphill. From the tee you can almost see Len pouring the Macallan into your glass.

Ross's home track didn't treat Sandy and me so well on this day. I shot 95—including a ghastly 45 putts. This caused Sandy to begin looking askance at my new Dave Pelz putter, the one with three fake balls lined up behind the blade, and caused both of us to retire to more than one Macallan.

Len was reminded of the time a fellow sat down at the bar and said, "Macallan, if you please."

"Water?" Len asked.

"Only if there's room," the gentleman said.

DAY 3: *We come face-to-face with the Mussel Skitter and hear something go bump in the room above*

If you must know, Dornoch is 6,577 yards long, par 70,

though both numbers mean absolutely nothing, seeing as when the wind blows, which is most of the time, a five-iron can go 250 yards or 60. On this day, the winds were fierce enough to turn Quasimodo into a six-footer, which should convey how good my 91 was, though Sandy didn't seem all that impressed. He was especially grumpy about my 36 putts (including three three-putts) and began leering at my newfangled putter as if he were planning to do it harm, though my own confidence in it remained unshaken.

On the 9th hole, with the wind blowing, I was feeling rather good about my drive until Sandy said, "Two more like tha' an' ya' wonna' be far away, sir." This reminded me of something a famous Scottish caddie once said to Henry Longhurst as they approached a long par-4 on a particularly windy day. "It'll take three good ones to be on in two t'day, sir." Exactly.

So windy is it at Dornoch that when Eric Brown, the fine Scottish pro, was asked what was the toughest shot on the course, he answered, "The second to the 2nd."

The 2nd is a par-3.

To play in such wind, you will find Sandy's Mussel Skitter invaluable. The Mussel Skitter is used on days when it is so windy that a lofted iron shot could prove dangerous to you and your playing entourage. Instead, Sandy advised, employ the Mussel Skitter—top a five-iron in the general direction of the hole and watch that sucker run. Funny, all my life I had been playing the Mussel Skitter and never even knew it.

When I got back to the Dornoch Castle Hotel, which is 800 and some years old, I took to researching the disquieting question of spirits (not the liquid kind) in my very quiet room—no telephone, no TV, no radio, and, hardest of all to believe, no Spectravision. The castle was once a public building, and the room that is now the bar was the town court. Scores of people were sentenced to death in that room and, legend has it, there are bloodstains behind the dado.

As I was reading, the sheep began bleating in the pasture behind the hotel. Have you ever heard a sheep bleat? It's not the sort of thing you want to hear around midnight while you're reading about death sentences and bloodstains.

Maybe it was my heightened state of paranoia but, suddenly, just as I got to the part about the death sentences, I heard banging on the ceiling. If a person who is supine can be said to leap, I leapt. The next morning I approached the reception-desk attendant.

"I'm in Room 4," I said, "and there was quite a lot of banging in the room above me last night and I was just wondering if maybe you could tell the person that...."

"I'm sorry, sir," she said. "There's nobody in the room above you."

DAY 4: *We learn anew why golf at Dornoch bears little resemblance to the member-guest tournament at the Ypsilanti Country Club*

The sight of that strange putter in my hand was beginning to give Sandy a facial tic. He thinks it's a dumb American idea that three fake balls behind the blade could help anyone line up putts. And he doesn't see the point of trying to line up four balls when you can't even manage it with one. After the way I had putted—39 more stabs today, including a four-whack and two three-whacks—I was inclined to agree. At one point, I was so mad I was ready to throw my clubs off the cliff and myself after them.

Sandy probably would have approved, because it would have speeded up play. In Scotland, play is very fast. If a round at Dornoch takes more than three hours, the peace-loving locals might be given to rioting. The Scots usually play match golf and generally couldn't give a farthing about their final scores. "What'd ya shoot today?" is as foreign to them as kippered herring for breakfast is to us. Americans are fanatical about finishing every hole, marking every last stroke, even when the hole has already been lost. The final number is everything, too. Scots are just faster, period. There is not a man, woman or child in Scotland who arrives at his ball, sets up, gets his grip *juuuuuuust* right, waggles 10 or 12 times, takes the club back and then lets go his Gene Littler swing—*as practice*—the way Americans maddeningly do. The Scots hit it, find it, and hit it again.

They are simple people that way. Stubborn, too. The people in a place as remote and small as Dornoch are unswayed by the decades. The names stay the same, only the faces change. For instance, the current town doctor took his father's place. For 40 years in Dornoch, if you got sick, a Dr. MacLeod has come to your house. Willie Skinner has been the head pro for almost 30 years. His dad was the secretary of the club for 15 years. Dr. John Grant is club captain. His dad was the head pro and greenskeeper for 50 years.

Dornoch is a club without pretension. Sandy, the caddie, and Dr. Grant, the captain, can sit down and have a Macallan in the clubhouse without anybody's nose getting out of joint. Golf at Dornoch is also cheap, and Sandy is a member. An international membership costs about $95 a year, which is $30 less than it costs to play *one round* at Pebble Beach.

But remember, a Scottish caddie is smarter than you are. A buddy of Sandy's was out on a raw, wet day carrying the bag of a particularly thrifty Englishman who kept taking sips of a restorative from his flask without offering any to the caddie. The man played 36 holes that day, and toward the end of the afternoon the greens were starting to get especially soggy.

As he set up for a wedge shot, the Englishman pulled out his flask again for a swig and said, "Say, caddie, what's the driest spot here?"

And the caddie said, "Well, sir, you could try the back of my throat."

DAY 5: *The newfangled putter doesn't quite make it all the way to Norway, and we learn more scary things than we had wanted to know*

Thirty-six putts today, including three three-putts on the last three holes.

"Holy woollies, sir," Sandy said after the round. "That putter would do ya' betta at the bottom of the sea, if I may say so, sir."

I agreed, so I took the blasted thing to the beach and tried to throw it across the North Sea. "Aye, sir. Let the water kelpies have it, sir," Sandy said.

"Water kelpies?"

"Aye, sir." Water kelpies, it seems, are the spirits of the ocean Scottish kids believe bring about the drowning of wayfarers. "Like your bogeyman, sir."

And I thought, Is Rod Serling on this trip?

In the hotel bar that night, I asked Michael Ketchin, the

proprietor—who runs a splendid place, otherwise—the question flat out. "Tell me," I said, "is your hotel haunted?"

"Oh, yes," he said. "Or so people say."

And with that, he took me on a tour of the haunt, as it were. Indeed, he confirmed that there is a bloodstain behind the dado, and took me to an upstairs room in which there had been a recent sighting.

In 1974 a guest apparently saw a transparent man wearing britches (shorts), padding down the hall and into this very room. He called the proprietor, who came with his dog. They went into the room, but found nothing. The dog, however, refused to enter the room. He stayed at the doorsill and whined. "I sleep here now," said Mr. Ketchin, who must be nuts.

This wasn't the only oddity. In 1890 the sheriff's wife saw a ghost walking right down the middle of the main street. Plus, there was the aforementioned incident with Mr. MacCormack. A priest exorcised the whole place in 1922, but it didn't seem to help. There was the incident with Kathy, the maid, and her sweater and, in 1980, the incident of the live-in chef who heard footsteps in the hallway, yet, when he went to look, found nobody.

As much as I preferred not to, I went with Ketchin to the cellar, where a dungeon has been turned into a wine cellar. (Any way you look at it, the room has seen some serious fermenting.) The door was a foot thick, and the keyhole accommodated a missing giant key, not unlike one you might see hung from the belt of Friar Tuck.

"People are always talking about the secret passageways between here and the cathedral (across the street)," Ketchin said, "but I've run the place for years and I've not found any yet."

Secret passageways? Dungeons? Ghosts?

Whatever Sandy was going to show me the next day, I was quite sure I didn't want to see it.

DAY 6: *We witness a five-putt and learn Sandy's secret, which, all in all, makes for a very lousy night's sleep*

If I hadn't changed putters, I believe Sandy would have

changed players. One of my partners told me that the day before, as I stood over an eight-inch putt, Sandy had turned to him and whispered, "He's got every chance to one-putt from here, sir." But now I had a new putter, purchased at Willie Skinner's shop. Thus I felt rejuvenated for the big final day, when we students were to engage in a medal-play tournament from the very tees Norman and Crenshaw and Watson had played. I immediately went out and birdied the 1st hole, made a 12-footer for bogey on the 2nd and parred the 3rd with a 20-footer. It was clear that Sandy and I and my new putter were going to win this thing, and with it the new graphite driver that was first prize.

And that is when I came to the par-4 4th hole, lying three, some 30 feet from the cup. My first putt was a rush of blood to the head and went eight feet by. My second putt went three feet by. My third putt lipped out. Holy woollies, another four-putt, I thought. At that point, a strange feeling came over me and, for some inexplicable reason, I blacked out and backhanded it *away* from the hole. All those years of buddy golf must have created a tragic habit. On a four-inch putt like that, I was accustomed to batting it away and scooping it up. Now I had a four-footer just to *five*-putt.

Sandy stood there in horror, looking as though I had just gone through the reception line at Buckingham Palace, taken the Queen's hand and put my used Juicy Fruit in it. We both knew immediately that I could forget the driver and would be lucky to win a bag towel. However, I did sink that fifth putt, which has to go down as one of the best-sunk fifth putts in history.

I finished third and won a bag towel.

Sandy comforted me by buying the Macallan afterward. Figuring, What could be worse, I finally asked if he was now going to show me what he had promised to show me at the beginning of the week. "Aye," he said, and, as the sun began to clock out, we headed past the graveyard that guards the drive up to the clubhouse and made for the Struie Course, nine holes used for practice and by beginners. On the 8th hole there was a little wooden house. In the backyard was a stone inscribed 1722.

"What does that mean?" I asked.

It meant, Sandy explained, that at that site, in 1722, the last witch in Scotland had been burned. Her name was Janet Horne, and she had been accused of turning her daughter into a pony and riding her to the witches' meeting place to have her shod by the devil. The most incriminating evidence against her was that on one of her hands two fingers were joined together. That was more than enough to convict, so they fricasseed her in a barrel of tar right there—a six-iron from the tee.

Next to the ominous stone was a tricycle. "Who lives here now?" I asked.

"The greenskeeper and his family," Sandy said.

And before that? Mr. Grant, the longtime pro, and before that, they say, Donald Ross occupied the house. And where does the greenskeeper's wife work? Dornoch Castle. So there it was. The connection. Golf and goblins were inextricably connected. Dornoch and dungeons. Pars and poltergeists. They were all one. And I was here for both. Maybe the knocking was trying to tell me something.

"Tell me, Sandy," I asked. "Kathy, the maid whose sweater was...."

"She married my cousin," said Sandy.

I didn't like the grin on his face.

That night, returning from the final banquet, my bag towel and I were beat, so we came in the back way and up a staircase I had never used. The hallway lights were out, and I was creeping along, searching for stair rails and doorknobs. I opened the door at the top of the stairs, and that's when I saw her.

She was tall and dark and wore white flowing robes that the wind was pressing up against her legs. In the moonlight, I could see that she was staring at me, blank-eyed. I slammed the door shut. Of all the luck. First I five-putt, and now I get an ex-human for a hall monitor. I opened the door again, a crack. She was still standing there in the same position. I searched for a light switch, but found none. She still hadn't moved.

I opened the door and slunk into the room, reminding myself that I was doing exactly what I had yelled at the main characters *not* to do in every horror flick I had ever seen. You know, you say to yourself, Unless you want to wear a blood clot for a face, you better not go in there! Run, you imbecile! And then they go right on in there.

Inch by inch, I nudged closer, barely breathing ... closer ... closer ... until I could get a good look at her face and see ... that she was ... a ... mannequin.

A mannequin! I touched her face. My hair was grayed, my life shortened for a factory-formed dummy stashed in a back room.

The next morning, checking out, I inquired none too politely about the mannequin. The proprietor's wife said that they put her there for no particular reason except, "just to show people what the 1800s were like."

Next time, maybe a snapshot would do as well.

On the flight home, I drifted in and out of sleep. I began to half-dream, half-think. Was Dornoch real at all? Could I have been trapped in a strange three-dimensional, par-70 paradise-hell? Were the people real? Was Sandy real? It occurred to me that I never really did see the pupils of his eyes. Was the castle real? Royal Dornoch? After all, how could a place so glorious, so historic, so gorgeous, be so colossally unknown? And how could I make people believe in Dornoch any more than they believed in the Loch Ness Monster? And even if all those questions could be answered, the most important one still lay ahead.

Can we get a miniseries out of it?

The 12th

BY   RICK   REILLY

FUZZY ZOELLER CALLS IT THE "SPOOKIEST LITTLE PAR-3 WE PLAY." JACK NICKLAUS CONSIDERS IT "THE TOUGHEST TOURNA-MENT HOLE IN GOLF." IN 1990 RICK REILLY TOOK A CLOSER LOOK AT AUGUSTA'S 12TH, THE PRETTY LITTLE HOLE THAT HAS BEDEVILED MORE OF THE GAME'S GREATS THAN ANY OTHER.

Don't give me the 18th at Pebble Beach. Or the 8th at Pine Valley. The 17th at Sawgrass? *Pleeeeease.* Don't tell me about number 1 at Merion. O.K., the pins have baskets instead of flags. Call the weavers' union. You can keep the 16th at Cypress Point, too. I don't know anybody who has made a par at the 16th at Cypress Point in my lifetime, and I won't in the next one, so why discuss it? If that hole is a par-3, how come you have to hit a driver?

No, the *best* hole in the country is a hellacious, wonderful, terrifying, simple, treacherous, impossible, perfect molar-knocker of a par-3. It's a hole you play with a seven-iron, a sand wedge and eight weeks of scuba lessons. The best hole in the country is the 12th at Augusta National. Everything else is the front nine at the Sturgeon Bay Night Links.

Lloyd Mangrum called the 12th "the meanest little hole in

165

the world." Jack Nicklaus calls it "the hardest tournament hole in golf." Fuzzy Zoeller calls it "the spookiest little par-3 we play."

More green jackets have been lost at the 12th than at the Augusta City Dry Cleaners. When the Masters comes to shove next Sunday, you can bet somebody is going to walk away from 12 looking as though he had just heard from the IRS. Or *60 Minutes*. Tom Weiskopf made a 13 there once. He bounced back the next day with a 7. That was the last time anybody saw him with hair.

Sam Snead once made an 8 there and withdrew. Toney Penna hit the flagstick and *still* made 5. Gary Player putted off the green twice—on consecutive days. Twelve could drive a Baptist to drink.

Don't come to the 12th tee with a little fear hidden in your sock. Or a loop at the top. Or the Sunday Masters lead. You'll end up with a wadded acceptance speech and a wet Foot-Joy.

In 1973, J.C. Snead doubled it in the final round and lost by a shot to Tommy Aaron. In 1977, Hubert Green was four under par through 11 holes on Friday when he buried his tee shot in a back bunker, beat his bunker blast across the green and into the creek, dropped another ball in the bunker, chipped out to 20 feet and made it for double bogey. He took himself out of the tournament on that hole, but it was a hell of a nice putt.

Jack Nicklaus might have a green coat for every day of the week right now if he hadn't double-bogeyed 12 on Saturday in 1981. He lost by two shots to Tom Watson. You'll recall that when Nicklaus did win again (1986), his drop-dead 30 on the back nine Sunday included a bogey on 12. If he just makes a par there, he shoots 29 and is immediately given the southeastern quadrant of the United States.

Gary Player had the Masters won in 1962 until he bogeyed 12 on Sunday and fell into a three-way tie. In the 18-hole playoff the next day, he came to 12 with a three-shot lead and bogeyed it *again*. Bye. In 1964, Dave Marr was three back and on a run when he skipped one off the water, onto the bank and back in the water. Glory has a funny way of going glug, glug at 12.

In 1982, Seve Ballesteros bogeyed it Sunday and lost by one.

On the last day in 1984, Larry Nelson came to the 12th nipping at Ben Crenshaw's spikes. Nelson was within one shot, but couldn't decide between a six-iron and a seven-iron. He should've chosen a waffle iron. "I hit it so bad I didn't know whether to tell it to get up or get down," says Nelson. It bisected the creek perfectly. Nelson made a 5 and finished fourth. In 1987, Jodie Mudd bogeyed the hole twice and doubled it once and lost by a shot.

This is a hole that proves you don't need 230 yards, six miles of railroad ties and an island green surrounded by alligator purses to be great. "If holes were cars," says Peter Jacobsen, "the 12th would be a Cadillac and the 17th at Sawgrass would be a Yugo." Says Robert Trent Jones Jr., a golf course architect, "It's the perfect example of less architecture, more golf."

The funny thing is, from the tee it looks like a Twinkie. It's just a friendly little 155-yard par-3 with a babbling brook running in front of the green and a happy grove of pine trees swaying behind it. And it'll rip your lips off. It has broken more men than bad whiskey and the over-under put together.

It's a pampered little par-3. It even has a thermostat. Since its green gets very little sunlight, it can be ruined by a frost. In 1981, they meticulously dug it up, installed water pipes 10 inches underneath the surface and put it back together. Now, if it gets too cold, they run 60° to 80° water through the pipes.

What they ought to do is bronze it. The 12th hole has more history behind it than Helen Hayes. For one thing, the bridge that crosses Rae's Creek is known as the Hogan bridge. A plaque there commemorates Ben Hogan's thrilling 274 in the Masters in 1953. Just try to walk across that thing without getting goose bumps the size of Pinnacles. It was on the tee at the 12th in 1964 that a nervous Nicklaus cold-shanked an eight-iron. Bobby Jones, his idol, was watching.

The green is about as big as the Des Moines phone book—only nine yards deep in some places, and 35 yards wide. There are three bunkers guarding it: two in back and one in front. Better to have died as a young boy than to get stuck in one of those back bunkers. You'll be faced with a downhill blast to a downhill green that is only slighter faster than the roof of the Transamerica building.

Jones, who designed the course with the Scottish architect
Alister MacKenzie, once wrote about the 12th, "Here the distance must be gauged very accurately, and the wind sweeping
down along Rae's Creek is often deceptive to the player standing on the tee about to hit.... Once the tee shot has been
played into the creek, the short pitch to the shallow green is
terrifying indeed."

What's even more terrifying, indeed, is that it's all tucked
back into a nook of pines that makes the wind swirl in, out
and around the hole. As such, it tortures the best golfers in the
world. There are more theories about how to play the wind at
12 than Ping has lawyers. Hogan once said, "Never hit on 12
until you feel the wind on your cheek." Ken Venturi says to
look at the flags on 11 and 12, because they're never up at the
same time. Don't hit when the flag is down at 12, he says.
Player says, "If the flag on 11 is blowing left to right and the
flag on 12 is blowing right to left, pay no attention to what's
happening at 11." Zoeller watches the trees on the far side of
the 13th tee to see where the wind is coming from. Jacobsen
says he looks at everything, including the fans behind him.
Curtis Strange looks at the water and at the flags. And then
there's Green: "They say if the dogwood tree on the right of
the 13th tee is moving, then the wind is blowing over the
12th green, and when the dogwood stops moving, there's no
wind. I don't believe it."

Bob Rosburg, in the days before he had an antenna growing
out of his ear, came to the hole on a windy day and hit a four-
iron. Now, Rosburg was never known as the Arnold
Schwarzenegger of golf. In fact, it was said that nobody hit
more frog hairs in regulation than Rosburg. But on this particular hole, the wind died just as he hit, and Rosburg's ball
didn't just clear the water, it cleared the green, the back
bunkers, the terraces behind the green and the fence behind
the terraces. It ended up on the 9th hole of the bordering
Augusta Country Club. *You got a line on that, Rossi?*

So Rosburg had to retee. The wind came up again. What to
do? Rosburg swallowed hard and kept the very same club in
his hand. This time, his ball landed 15 feet from the pin and
he made the most maddening 5 in the history of golf.

Playing with Rosburg that day was Arnold Palmer, who

could sympathize. The wind at 12 probably cost him the 1959 Masters. Leading the tournament the last day, Palmer hit a shot that the wind knocked into the creek. He dropped, pitched over the creek and the green, chipped back again and two-putted for a 6. Palmer finished third, two shots behind the winner, Art Wall Jr. Cold-blooded little hole, isn't it?

Nicklaus has a rule for the 12th: Don't go for the pin if it's on the right. Hit for the middle of the green, make your par and get out while you can. There is not enough room, and too much wind, sand and water to go for it. "It comes down to whether you want to keep it in play, or go for a 2 and come away with a 5," Nicklaus says. He must know what he's doing. Until he turned 40, his cumulative score on 12 was even par.

Only three men have made a hole in one at 12 in the Masters—probably because everybody is so scared of it—and each ace comes with a story.

In 1947, Claude Harmon was playing with Hogan. Now, to find two more opposite personalities would have taken six engineers and three computers. It would be sort of like pairing Gary McCord with J.C. Snead. On the golf course Hogan had all the personality of magnesium. Harmon, on the other hand, was a prince among club professionals and was renowned as a charming teacher. He taught four presidents—Eisenhower, Kennedy, Nixon and Ford—not to mention King Hassan II of Morocco.

Anyway, Harmon was your basic hail-fellow-well-met. Hogan was not. On that day Harmon had the honor at 12. He stepped up and knocked the ball into the hole for the first-ever ace there during the Masters. Hogan didn't say a word. Not a shake of the hand, not a "well done," zip. Instead, he took one last puff of his unfiltered cigarette, stepped up to the ball and hit it a few feet past the cup.

As the crowd continued to roar for Harmon, Hogan's eyes never wavered. Harmon retrieved his ball from the hole, accepted the plaudits due him, then moved out of the way. Hogan paced around his putt, stared it down, then stroked it in for a birdie.

As the two made their way to the 13th tee, Hogan finally spoke up.

"You know, Claude," Hogan said. "That's the first 2 I've ever made on that hole."

Oddly, the two were close friends.

In 1959, William Hyndman III, an amateur, made the second ace at 12, thanks to the help of his caddie, who went by the name of First Baseman.

"What's it going to take, First Baseman?"

"Six-iron," said the caddie.

"Six-iron? That's too much," said Hyndman.

"Nope. Got to step up and get it all."

And that's exactly what Hyndman did. The ball took one hop past the pin and spun back into the hole. Touch 'em all.

When Curtis Strange came to the tee in 1988, he was lousy a bet to make 1. He had four-putted the unforgivably slick 9th green and was heard to say as he left, "And you people are paying good money to watch this ——." The pin on 12 that day was in the one place where you're not *supposed* to make a hole in one—far right. But Strange was going so bad he needed to make some birdies just to make the cut. He aimed slightly left of the pin—still a dicey idea at best—and let fly. "I pushed it perfectly," Strange remembers. It hit the green and rolled six or seven feet into the hole for an ace.

But that's when Curtis did something strange. He picked up the ball and threw it in the creek. "I don't know why I did it," Strange says. "I just thought, This'll do something for the people. It was spontaneous. I didn't think about it. It had nothing to do with what I'd done the rest of the day."

Some sportswriters thought Strange impudent. "He could've given it to his grandchildren," they said. Says Strange, "I hope I have something better to leave my grandchildren than a golf ball."

Some people think it made perfect sense. "All the gods of golf are down there in that corner anyway," says Zoeller. "If you beat that hole, you *better* give them something."

It was such an odd thing to do—to throw away a museum piece—that people got suspicious. One rumor went that when Strange got the ball out of the hole, he realized he'd been playing the wrong one. *That's* why he threw it in the water. So nobody could tell on him. There was also the story that Strange didn't want the standard golfer-kisses-golf-ball picture in the papers the next day, because he wasn't playing the brand of ball he was paid to play. Bull pucky, says Strange. Go find it yourself, and you'll see.

If you ever get a wild hair and an oxygen tank and decide to go looking for Strange's ball—a Maxfli DDH, he thinks—pick up half a dozen or so of Tom Weiskopf's while you're at it, will you?

The 12th was to Weiskopf what the *Exxon Valdez* was to shrimp. Weiskopf loved the Masters. "Every year, after I open my Christmas presents, I start thinking about the Masters," he used to say. On Thursday in 1980, the pin was, typically, front left, the easiest of all pin placements because you can shoot for it. Better yet, there was no wind. Weiskopf took an eight-iron and sailed it to the front fringe, where it hit, took a little skip-hop forward toward the pin, then spun rapidly and cruelly back into Rae's Creek.

Bad break. Time to drop a ball on the far side of the water and try again, hitting 3. Only Weiskopf didn't lay up next to the creek, he went farther back—about 60 yards from the hole. "I didn't want a little wedge. I wanted a half or three-quarter wedge."

He hit the exact same shot. Fringe. Skip-hop. Spin back into Rae's Creek. Hitting 5. "Now I'm pissed," he recalls.

Weiskopf decided to drop again in the same place—60 yards back. Even Weiskopf is not sure why. "You're embarrassed," he says. "You're in a fog. You're standing in front of the world, and it's like you're playing the hole naked."

This time his drop rolled into a barren spot and his wedge shot did a little Greg Louganis dead into the water. Hitting 7.

Weiskopf wasn't moving an inch. He was determined to drop in the same place, 60 yards from the hole. Who knows what happens to the mind in situations such at these? My theory is that some madness chemical fires in the brain and reason gets cleat marks in its head.

Madness: *We are going to prove to the world that this was the place to drop! I don't care if we blow the tournament and the next six tournaments after this and we have to go back to frying burgers at the Dairy Queen!#!&!*

Reason: *This is crazy. Let's go up and drop right next to the creek like we should have the first time. Whaddya say, fellas?*

Madness: (Cleatstomp.)

Another drop. Another terrible shot. Another sinking feeling. Hitting 9.

There was absolute and funereal silence now. It's quiet at Amen Corner, anyway. The fans are kept about 20 yards behind the 12th tee. But now there was nothing. No groans, no tears, no muttering, no go-get-'ems—just dead, cold silence, the kind you would get in the car for about three miles after your dad blew up.

Weiskopf's forehead was so hot you could stir-fry on it. Drop again. Same spot again. Splash again. Hitting 11.

One person in the crowd began crying. It was Weiskopf's wife, Jeanne. You make big plans, rent a house, bring the kids, hire a nanny, fly to Augusta, go to all the pretournament parties, and then, in one two-minute span of golf, it all goes *splerch*. Standing next to Jeanne was their close friend Tom Culver. Culver hugged her and said, tenderly, "Jeanne ..."

"Yes, Tom?" she said, choking on the heartache.

"You don't suppose he's using new balls, do you?"

Finally, Weiskopf hit his sixth ball to the back edge of the green, where, somehow, it stayed, and he two-putted for a 13, the highest score ever taken on any par-3, or par-4, in the history of the Masters. Tommy Nakajima had a 13 on number 13 in 1978, but at least that hole is a par-5.

If I were Weiskopf, here is how I would handle the obvious question the rest of my days. It's the way Palmer explained a 12 he made in the 1961 L.A. Open.

Q: "Thirteen? How the hell did you make 13 on a par-3?"

A: "Missed a 20-footer for 12."

When Weiskopf came to the hole the next day, he was mostly killing time until his plane left town. He had no choice but to go for the pin and try to make an eagle. He hit his first shot off the bank and into the water, and he chose not even to walk anywhere near the creek. He simply put another tee in the ground and hit again. "I thought my chances were better."

Reason: *"Look, this is...."*

Madness: *"Just shut the hell up."*

He hit another one in the creek, his seventh surly contribution to the Augusta waterway system in two days. He teed it up again. This was now becoming a scientific quest: Could a lofted metal club send a spheroid over an active body of water? This one he knocked on and two-putted for a 7. He finished with a 79. His two-day average for the 12th: 10. If they ever build a memorial to Weiskopf, it had better be waterproof.

If there was one man who allowed himself a slight grin at Weiskopf's 13, it was Dow Finsterwald, who made 11 there in 1951 and has been walking around having to answer for it ever since. Finsterwald was 21 when he washed four balls in Rae's Creek. His playing partner that day, the late Denny Shute, made a birdie 2. As they were walking off the green, Shute said to Finsterwald, "Well, son, we had a good best ball, anyway."

What's to be ashamed of? This hole has taken a mouthful out of some of the most famous hindquarters in golf. Consider: Deane Beman (two 7s), Billy Casper (8), Ray Floyd (two 7s), Bob Murphy (8), Sam Snead (8), Royal and Ancient secretary Michael Bonallack (a 6 and a 7), David Graham (7), Charles Coody (two 7s), Bruce Crampton (7), Ben Crenshaw (7), Lon Hinkle (7), Craig Wood (8), Al Mengert (8), David Edwards (8) and Graham Marsh (8). And you thought you would never see a snowman in Georgia.

Payne Stewart is the latest famous notch 12 has cut in the Hogan bridge. It was 1985, the final round, and Stewart was in contention to win the tournament. He hit an eight-iron on nothing but the sweet spot, and the ball flew into the right back bunker. His bunker shot rolled just past the pin. And just past the green. And just past the fringe, just past the rough, just past the bank and down into Weiskopf's Creek.

Having dropped another ball on the tee side of the creek, Stewart hit a pitch that landed right next to the hole, then spun back into a liquid home. Now he was hitting 6. It was not a good time to ask him if he still felt he had a chance to win the tournament.

"All I could see was that green jacket getting ripped right out of my closet," Stewart remembers. What to do but try it again? This time Stewart was too conscious of the water, and he hit the ball right back to square one—the bunker. He chopped it out of there like a man might chop at a radioactive weed, with more fear than hope. The ball trickled onto the green and stayed, and he two-putted for a 9, more than enough to cost him the championship.

A chip out of that bunker can give you a facial tic. If you don't hit it just tenderly enough, you can easily watch your Titleist do a little 23 skiddoo over the green and into the water. In 1966, Player hit a Thursday tee shot that slammed down so deep into the bank behind the back bunkers that you could barely see the ball. Player considered taking a drop and hitting 3, and he probably should have, but he was no doubt overcome by the madness secretions. He decided to try to slap it out, let it run feebly into the bunker below and hit it again. But Player goofed. He hit too hard, and the ball scooted across the bunker, over the fringe, onto the green and into the cup for a 2. "One hundred percent luck," says Player.

But there have been a whole lot more tears at 12 than laughs. Take what happened to Bobby Mitchell. He lost more than a few balls and a tournament at 12. He might have lost a career.

It was 1972, and Mitchell was a promising 29-year-old on the Tour. He played brilliantly at Augusta that week—17 holes a day. His week at 12 only Stephen King could love: 5-5-5-4, seven over par. Yet he lost the tournament to Nicklaus by only three shots. "I made double bogey every way you could think of," says Mitchell, who is aiming toward a comeback on the Senior tour. "I got stuck up in the honeysuckle one day, hit it into the water the next and got buried in the bunker another day. That dang hole cost me the tournament." He won the Tournament of Champions two weeks later and finished 11th on the money list that year, but after that he never won another tournament and never finished in the top 60 on the money list again.

Twelve has been a thorn in golfers' Sansabelts since the first Masters, in 1934, when Ed Dudley made four 4s there and lost the tournament by three shots. Three years later, Ralph Guldahl was running away with it when he came to 12, plunked his shot into the creek, chipped too far and carded a little 5. That left Byron Nelson to go on such a tear—a 2 on 12 and a 3 on 13—that he not only won the tournament, but also they put up a bridge in honor of his run. It spans Rae's Creek between the 13th tee and the fairway.

Sam Snead never lost a tournament at 12, but he almost did. In 1952, he and Hogan were tied starting the final round. Snead led by one as he came to 12. His tee shot, though, flew dead into the creek. Unluckily, the ball he dropped on the tee side of the creek landed in a depression. He flailed at it and plopped it barely over the water onto the grassy slope short of the green. He was lying 3, and still he wasn't on the green.

In those days, Snead had a caddie named O'Brien, nothing else, just O'Brien. O'Brien caddied for Snead in the Masters he won in 1949 and would again when he won in 1954. But this time victory looked impossible. Snead would make 6 at the 12th, sure as azaleas bloom in March. But that's when O'Brien looked at him and said, "We ain't out of this tournament yet, Sam." At which Snead chipped the ball, only to discover it had a lump of mud on it. Nevertheless, the ball wobbled across the green, mud and all, right into the cup. He went on to birdie 13 and 16, and beat Jackie Burke Jr. by four shots. "That was the best 4 I ever made in my life," Snead says.

But nobody lost and won more at 12 in one year than Venturi and Palmer in 1958. You could say entire careers were at stake.

Venturi was the talk of the Tour. Two years earlier, playing as an amateur in his first Masters, he had led until the final day, when he shot 80 and finished second to Burke. In a lot of ways, Venturi was like Palmer himself—handsome, rugged and preposterously talented. In fact, sportswriters considered Venturi more likely than Palmer to win that year.

On Sunday, Venturi was one shot down to Palmer. His tee shot on 12 landed in the middle of the green and stayed there for what looked like an easy par. Palmer's ball, though, sailed over the green, hit in the grass between the right back bunker and the green and plugged.

When Palmer got to the ball, he told the rules official there, the late Arthur Lacey, that he would be playing the embedded-ball rule and would take a free drop. It had rained the night before and again early in the morning, making the grounds sodden and squishy. A local rule at Augusta National allowed relief from an embedded ball "through the green," which means damn near anywhere you want except the tee, the green and the hazards.

Lacey, wrongheadedly, was having none of it.

"Not at Augusta you don't," Lacey is supposed to have said. Lacey was a fine British golfer from Buckinghamshire who had played on two British Ryder Cup teams.

"I will too," said Palmer from Latrobeshire, getting his fur up. "It's my right."

The two argued a bit more, but neither was to be swayed. Now, here's where things got cloudy. Palmer says he announced then and there to Lacey and anybody else around that he was going to play a second ball and record both scores, to be figured out by somebody bigger than Lacey as the day went on.

Palmer slapped at the embedded ball and moved it only about a foot and a half. Palmer chipped it close but missed the putt and took a 5. Venturi took 3.

Palmer then went back to the scene of the crime—the site of the original embedded ball—and dropped a new ball. Across the green, Venturi sat on his golf bag and whispered to his caddie, "We're going to win this tournament."

This time Palmer chipped it dead stony and made the putt for a 3. So which was it, a 3 or a 5?

Palmer must have thought it was going to be ruled a 5, because he nearly came out of his shoes with his drive on the par-5 13th. In fact, he hit it so far that he was in a position to go for the green in 2. Venturi recalls that as the two walked along the 13th fairway, Palmer said, "I know they're going to give me a 5."

In fact, Venturi says that's why Palmer went for the green with his second shot on 13—to make up ground. He hit a gorgeous three-wood that checked up nicely on the green, and he sank the 18-foot putt for an eagle 3. Venturi made a birdie 4.

As they were playing the 14th, there suddenly were war whoops from the crowd—Armyish whoops. The scoreboard showed that Palmer's 5 on the 12th had been changed to a 3. Now, instead of the two being tied, Palmer led by two. Venturi was so rattled that he three-putted the 14th green, and after Palmer was given official word of the ruling on the 15th fairway, Venturi also three-putted the 15th and 16th. Palmer won by two, 284–286.

Venturi agrees that Lacey blew the call—Palmer *was* allowed a drop there—but he says the balls should have been played concurrently. "Suppose you sink the first ball," says Venturi. "You're not going to go back and play a provisional then, are you? You declare and then you finish with the farthest ball out and work in. If you were on a par-5 and decided to declare a provisional, you wouldn't finish out with the first ball and then walk 350 yards back and play the next one, would you?"

The rule book for 1958 seems to support Venturi. For one thing, you definitely do have to declare *before* playing either ball, as Palmer did. For another, it reads, "When a competitor is doubtful of his rights or procedure, he may play out the hole with the ball in play and, at the same time, complete the play of the hole with a second ball." Oops. Palmer, who seldom involves himself in controversy, didn't want to touch this one with a 40-foot two-iron. He insists that he played everything exactly by the book.

Palmer eventually won eight majors. Venturi never did win the Masters, and his only major victory was the 1964 U.S. Open. Who knows how different things might have been if Palmer had been stuck with 5 at number 12 instead of 3?

Venturi isn't stewing about it. "I like my position in life now," he says, currently in his 23rd year as a CBS golf analyst. "There were a lot of guys who wanted to beat me back then. And now there are even more guys who want my job."

And Palmer isn't exactly destitute, either.

Here's one last story about the 12th. It was 1963, and the late Champagne Tony Lema was having a rocky Sunday. He had missed a short putt on the 10th hole and three-putted the 11th. Now on 12 he hit a good shot, which left him eight feet from the cup, but his putt just missed. Lema couldn't stand it. He let go a string of oaths that would make a Jersey longshoreman blush. Just then he realized that his playing partner, a Nationalist Chinese named Chen Ching-po, was looking at him curiously.

Embarrassed, Lema apologized for using such language "in front of a visitor to our country."

"Is all right," said Chen. "If I knew those words I would use them myself."

Keeper of the Flame

B Y   J O H N   G A R R I T Y

EVER SINCE THE DAYS WHEN ITS MEMBERS MET IN PUBS AND SHARED PREMISES WITH AN ARCHERY CLUB, NO GOLF CLUB HAS BEEN MORE CLOSELY LINKED WITH THE GAME OF GOLF THAN THE ROYAL & ANCIENT GOLF CLUB OF ST. ANDREWS. JOHN GARRITY PAID A RESPECTFUL VISIT IN 1990.

"It's not allowed, is it? To peek into the trophy room?" The two English women glance anxiously at Tom Wallace, the stern-looking hall porter, who watches from his post behind a waist-high desk. The door behind them is one-third open, providing a glimpse of glass cases, ancient golf clubs and storied medals.

"Go ahead!" says Wallace with a gallant wave. The Englishwomen break out in smiles.

A gentleman in a blazer, waiting at the desk, watches the ladies nudge the door open—an inch at a time, as if they still expect to be rebuked—and turns to Wallace.

"Not sacred territory anymore?"

"Ah, nooo," Wallace says. "The public's been in there now. The portraits have all fallen off the walls."

It's not just the Englishwomen. Everyone who visits the

Scottish coastal town of St. Andrews wants a peek into the Royal & Ancient Golf Club of St. Andrews. The building's exterior is so familiar from photographs—the gray stone that looks as if smokers have been breathing on it for centuries, the sturdy gables and chimneys, the whimsical wind vanes, the big round clock, the stark background of sky and sea. But the *interior* ... that is less well known. Tourists may catch a glimpse of chandelier or fireplace through the club's tall bay windows, but only the unusually bold will cup their hands around their eyes and press against the glass.

So when one does venture inside, there is a tendency at first to rush, to seize images and impressions: giant portraits in gilded frames, dark corridors, high ceilings, light the color of limestone falling from tall windows.

"It's a dreamy kind of place," says Grant Spaeth, the president of the U.S. Golf Association (USGA) and a member of the R&A. "You lose track of time."

"There isn't a setting anywhere remotely like it," says another American member, former USGA president Sandy Tatum.

When strangers come—that's how the club refers to outsiders, as strangers—they pad about the rooms, speak in whispers and practically genuflect at the door of the Big Room.

"Oh dear, how can I put it?" says Wallace. "It's awe, I think. And delight to have been allowed in."

The Royal & Ancient Golf Club of St. Andrews is many things. It is a building, a gentlemen's club, a private museum, an international rules-making body, a stager of golf tournaments—most notably the British Open—and a mystique.

It is not, curiously enough, a golf course. The famous Old Course at St. Andrews, over which the Open will be contested next week, is on the R&A's doorstep, but it is operated as a public course by the St. Andrews Links Trust.

Most strangers are surprised to learn that the R&A isn't even the only golf club associated with the Old Course. The St. Andrews Golf Club has its rooms across the 18th green from the R&A, between the Tom Morris Golf Shop and Rusack's Hotel. Another club, the St. Andrews Thistle Club, is nomadic—it meets on the Old Course and at other locations—and a fourth, the St. Andrews Ladies Putting Club, gathers regularly for competitions on the putting green northwest of the Swilcan Burn, the creek that meanders across the Old Course. Finally, halfway down the 18th fairway, there is the New Club, only 88 years old.

"The number of letters I used to get saying, 'I want to play your golf course,' " growls former R&A secretary Keith Mackenzie. "Here we are, the ruling body of golf, and we haven't even got a bloody golf course!"

But then, the R&A doesn't have that many resident golfers, either. The roster lists 1,800 Ordinary Members, but only 40 or 50 live in or near St. Andrews. For most of the year, the R&A is a ghost club, springing to life only during the spring and autumn "meetings," when members flood in from around the world to conduct club business, socialize and compete for various medals and trophies.

"Then it's pandemonium," says Wallace.

Brigadoon? No, the Scottish village in the musical slept for 100 years between appearances. Members of the R&A merely sleep through the after-dinner speeches at the biannual meetings.

Another misconception is that the R&A is the world's oldest golf club. It is not. The Honourable Company of Edinburgh Golfers, est. 1744, has that distinction by a comfortable 10 years. And yet another myth is that the R&A was the first club to be designated "Royal." That honor belongs to the upstart Royal Perth Golfing Society, given the imprimatur by King William IV in 1833. The St. Andrews golfers had to throw a dignified tantrum before the king would relent and honor them similarly a year later.

The facts are these: Golf was played at St. Andrews for hundreds of years before a club of any kind was formed. The original course consisted of 22 holes of linksland, 11 out and 11 back, believed to stretch from near the St. Andrews Cathedral wall west to the Eden Estuary, a distance of 1¾ miles. Although it was privately owned, the noblemen, lairds and gentlemen who golfed shared the course with sheep, cows, rabbits, horseback riders, archers and strolling minstrels.

Chafing at the lack of class distinctions, 22 nobles, lairds and gentlemen joined in 1754 to form the Society of St. Andrews Golfers. (*Laird* is a Scottish word that applied not only to lords but to any man who owned an estate. The founders of the society also included a professor or two from the University of St. Andrews.) Borrowing from the practice of the Honourable Company, the new St. Andrews club started an annual competition and put up a silver golf club as the trophy; the winner was declared captain for a year, and a silver replica of his feather ball was attached to the silver club.

Borrowing further—this time from freemasonry—the club adopted a number of secret rituals, some of which survive today. One ceremony requires new members at the autumn dinner to touch their lips reverently to the golf ball replicas on the silver clubs—a delicate business that actor and R&A member Sean Connery calls "kissing the captains' balls."

Another tradition is the "driving in." For maybe 50 years, the R&A got its captains through competition, but that method produced some very young captains—schoolboys, practically—and eliminated distinguished hackers from consideration. In 1806, the captaincy—then and now a largely ceremonial office—became elective, and skill with a rut iron was no longer necessary. To maintain the prestige of the silver club, a new tradition was established: On the last day of the Autumn Meeting, at 8 a.m., the captain-elect "drives in" by striking a shot from the 1st tee of the Old Course, directly below the bay windows of the R&A clubhouse, accompanied by a blast from a nearby cannon. With this one blow, the new man "wins" the Queen Adelaide Medal and gets to attach a ball with his name on it to the silver club. To add to the pageantry, the club's "honorary professional"—who was once Old Tom Morris, the beloved clubmaker and greenskeeper and winner of four Open titles in the mid-1800s—tees the ball up for the nervous honoree, and a score or so of caddies trot out toward the Swilcan Burn to await the stroke. The caddie who retrieves the ball receives a gold sovereign as a reward.

Fear of foozling has unnerved more than one captain-elect. In 1922, the Prince of Wales, later King Edward VIII, drove in with a shot off the nose of his club that scattered bystanders and struck a fence 50 yards away. Since the caddies were arrayed 150 yards back, it was a clubmaker who pounced on the ball and got the traditional sovereign, worth about $150 today.

"The caddies were livid," says R.A.L. (Bobby) Burnet, historian and librarian to the R&A. "The prince had had a stiffener, as he confessed later, but that was deemed no excuse. In 1930, his brother the Duke of York, later George VI, was driving in, and the caddies had good memories. I think it was [British golf writer] Bernard Darwin who wrote, 'The lieges stood disloyally close.' Of course, the duke then hit it over their heads with a good hard swing, and they had to run back a hundred yards to get the ball."

The rest of the essential history of the R&A can be summed up briefly. The club was nomadic for a century, meeting in various taverns in St. Andrews—Bailie Glass's House and the Black Bull, for certain—before settling in 1835 at the Union Club, sharing those premises with the Archers' Club. (Silverware stamped UNION CLUB is still used in the R&A's dining room.) The current clubhouse was built in 1854 and added to in 1900, the upper two stories being used now for administrative offices.

In 1893, the club purchased the Old Course from the laird who owned the land, one James Cheape of Strathtyrum. The St. Andrews Town Council, worried that townspeople would no longer be able to use the linksland as a public green, appealed to Parliament and had the course made property of the town.

At about the same time, the R&A built the New Course on land leased from the Town Council and adjoining the Old. The New Course, pursuant to the Links Act of 1894, is also held by the town as "public recreation ground." The R&A retains the privilege of reserving every other tee time on the New Course and gets to hold its twice-yearly meetings on the Old in exchange for maintaining those two and the newer, also adjacent, Jubilee and Eden courses.

The R&A has another history, of course—one full of shouts and cannon fire, as the portraits on the walls testify. Members have fired at Napoleon, fallen at Khartoum, marched with the Black Watch, died in trenches at the Somme, flown Spitfires for the RAF and walked on the moon. (Apollo astronaut Neil Armstrong and America's first man in space, Alan Shepard, are R&A members.) Generals and admirals have put their feet up in the Big Room; crowned heads have lunched on

cold ham and tongue in the dining room; and the presidents
of small nations have showered in the basement. ("Somebody
built the best showers in Britain down there," says Spaeth.)

Alistair Cooke, the suave host and page-turner of television's *Masterpiece Theatre* and an R&A member since 1969,
once felt the full weight of the club's illustrious past. Asked
in 1974 to address the U.S. House of Representatives on the
200th anniversary of the First Continental Congress, Cooke
accepted and sent "abject apologies" to the R&A, which
expected him to speak at its Annual Dinner the same day.

Keith Mackenzie wrote back: "It is a pity that you will not
be following in the footsteps of Francis Ouimet and Robert
Tyre Jones. But it is splendid that you should be following in
the footsteps of Lafayette and Churchill. However, a senior
member asks me to remind you that we are 20 years more
ancient than the First Continental Congress, and maybe you
should get your priorities straight."

Duly chastised, Cooke did his turn at St. Andrews a year
later. "It's a very liquid occasion," Cooke says of the Annual
Dinner, which is a black-tie affair. "Guys have a couple of
snorts at their hotels first. Then they meet for drinks at 6:30.
Then it's dinner at 8:00 with good wines, the captain makes
some after-dinner remarks, guests are introduced, a member
gets up and introduces me for half an hour ... It was 10 minutes to midnight before I ever got up! Half of them were
quietly asleep or already keeled over."

The perils of after-dinner speaking, according to Cooke, are
nothing compared with the pressures that accompany the
club competitions. "It's very scary when you play in the
Autumn Medal—especially when you're a freak like me, who
is there solely because he's supposed to be an urbane ...
something. A friend of mine said all these fellows were inside
in their stuffed leather chairs, and someone said, 'Good god!
It's Alistair Cooke! What's *he* doing there? ' And they all
bounded up to the window to watch."

If nothing else, membership in the R&A is a bargain. When
a candidate is approved, he is billed £144 as an entrance fee—
about $245 at current exchange rates. Dues? Home Mem-
bers, meaning residents of the British Isles, pay an "annual

subscription" of £133.20; for Overseas Members, including American, it's a paltry £72.

Certain reduced rates also apply. Forty-year members pay £10 per annum; 50-year members pay £5; and 60-year members pay nil, since they are, by then, mistaken for furniture. Of the 1,800 memberships, 1,050 are reserved for Home Members. Of the 750 Overseas Members, no more than 275 can come from the U.S. The American roster, which is top-heavy with current and former officers of the USGA, also includes golf architects Pete Dye and Robert Trent Jones, golf writers Herbert Warren Wind and George Peper, *Dennis the Menace* artist Hank Ketcham, ABC-TV executive Roone Arledge, Brigadier General Francis Roberts, International Management Group CEO Mark McCormack, amateur golfers Charlie Coe and Jay Sigel, and Prescott Bush Jr., brother of the U.S. President.

No professional golfer can be an Ordinary Member, but the R&A has made Honorary Members of Kel Nagle, Arnold Palmer, Gene Sarazen, Peter Thomson, Roberto DeVicenzo and, most recently, Jack Nicklaus. Tom Watson, with five British Open titles to his name, is apparently deemed too young.

"To become a member, the one thing you don't do is promote yourself," notes George Wilson, the R&A's deputy secretary. "You must be proposed and seconded by existing members of the club, normally from your own nation. Golfing ability, while it is taken into account, is not a great factor. The club looks more for a degree of enthusiasm for golf, as well as a sense of stewardship, since we are the body responsible for husbanding this great game."

As of late, there has been one further requirement: staying power. The waiting period for overseas candidates averages 14 years; for Home Members it's a dismal 20 years.

"It was two or three years ago when we realized there was a membership crisis," says Wilson. "There was a stage where you were just getting old boys around. We wanted an injection of 50-year-olds rather than 80-year-olds, because there's no point in becoming a member when you're too old to enjoy it."

To make room for these youngsters, the R&A created a

new category of membership: Supernumerary. These are Ordinary Members over the age of 60 who retain all the privileges of membership except the right to play in club competitions. Yet another category—House Membership—exists for those poor wretches who live nearby and have been listed in the Candidates Book for a year or more. To soften their purgatory, the R&A extends limited club privileges, although not the right to wear the club tie, club blazer buttons or any item bearing the club crest.

For that, they must wait.

There is a sense, when one tours the R&A, that the most esteemed members are neither the old ones nor the young ones, but rather the dead ones. At least, that's what one gets from a relaxed walk-around with Bobby Burnet. The club librarian, who retired as a teacher and Shakespearean scholar 10 years ago to catalog the R&A's holdings, begins with a warning: "I'm accustomed to talking for anywhere between a quarter of an hour to half an hour on any subject, so please don't think it rude to interrupt at any time and ask to move on."

The tour begins in the ground-floor Trophy Room, also called the South Room, which overlooks a small parking lot and eight wide stone steps leading down to the 18th green of the Old Course. One's eye is drawn first to a display case housing the club's principal medals and trophies, including two of the fabled silver clubs, laden with fruitlike clusters of captains' balls.

"There are a number of these clubs, and the current club is downstairs in a vault," says Burnet. "What we have here is actually one replica and one genuine club. I normally point out that this club, the oldest one, 1754, shows the development of the golf ball. You have a clutch of feather balls, a clutch of gutta-percha balls [made with a tough plastic that is derived from Malaysian latex] and beyond that, the first core-wound ball with a cover.

"The gutta-percha ball made all the difference to golf because the game would have died out if a cheaper ball hadn't come in. The feather ball cost three to five shillings, which made it more expensive than the club. A man could

make only three of them in a day. You made a leather case
and then stuffed more than a top-hatful of feathers into it. It
was a most exhausting process because eventually you were
using a chest brace with a long awl, getting the last feathers
in by pushing against a wall. You were killing yourself two
ways: You were inhaling feathers and you were damaging
your chest case.

"This made the game very expensive, and various clubs
became defunct around 1817. The transition to the gutta-percha ball took place around 1848, and that made golf available
to the Scottish workingman. It had a huge impact in Scotland.
There were 20 golf clubs in 1850 and about 35 by 1864."

Well, you get the idea. To Burnet, the R&A's trophies and
artifacts are more than icons; they are windows on the 18th
and 19th centuries. The Silver Boomerang, the Calcutta Cup,
the Queen Victoria Jubilee Vase, the Canadian Silver Beaver,
the Kangaroo's Paw—"It's also a cigar lighter"—the Bombay
Medal, the Silver Cross of St. Andrew....

Here is the Open Championship Belt, won three times in
succession by Young Tom Morris, son of Old Tom. Here is
the Open Championship Cup, introduced in 1872 and also
won by Young Tom. Here are clubs used by Allan Robertson
(the first great professional golfer but a member of the St.
Andrews Golf Club), British Amateur champion Freddie Tait,
famed clubmaker and Open champion Willie Auchterlonie,
the turn-of-the-century triumvirate of Harry Vardon, J.H.
Taylor and James Braid, Open champions all.... Here are
track irons, water niblicks, baffy spoons. Behold the heavily
grooved mashie-niblick with which Jock Hutchison won the
1921 Open. "He was using that and spinning the ball back
on very, very fast greens," says Burnet. "The notice banning
corrugated and grooved clubs appeared in the *Standard-Citizen*
alongside the results; it was as quick as that."

Some of the exhibits will move next door to the recently
opened British Golf Museum, Burnet says, "but we must
avoid moving anything that has strong R&A associations."

The tour moves on to the Big Room, a high-ceilinged,
chandeliered chamber dotted with leather club chairs and
small round tables. This is the room with the tall bay windows overlooking the 1st tee of the Old Course. Hardwood

lockers make an elegant wainscot beneath the R&A's prize portraits, which lean out from the walls in massive frames.

"Once a year, on St. Andrew's Day, November 30, the general public is let in here," says Burnet. "All kinds of things are put away; it's practically gutted. The place used to be open on sufferance, more or less—'Come in, but don't bother us.' The latest of the three American captains, [former USGA president] Bill Campbell, 1987, made a point of coming into the Big Room and greeting people, saying, 'I'm captain of the club. How do you do?' Very fine man, of course. Now there's a deputation of House committee to be in the room to receive people."

The portraits. Where to begin?

Queen Elizabeth II, patron of the club: "It's considered to be a pretty good painting," Burnet says. "They move it into the Committee Room when they're cleaning around here, and she looks absolutely marvelous at ground level, when you're looking eye-to-eye."

John Whyte-Melville, captain of the club, 1823: "Quite clearly, as a portrait it's absolutely magnificent. The only complaint might be that the man in the portrait is straight and handsome, whereas John Whyte-Melville was short and fat and very ugly. This is an idealized Victorian study of the man."

The Prince of Wales, later Edward VIII: "He is supposed to have said about it, 'It's a very nice picture of a pair of shoes.'" The face on the full-length portrait is largely obscured in shadow.

Old Tom Morris: "Old Tom is supposed to have said, 'He got the checks in the bonnet right.'"

A story behind every portrait. As Burnet moves around the room, the characters practically leap from the frames. Two-time British Amateur champion Freddie Tait, killed in 1900 in the Boer War: "Chivalrous, you might say simple, in his approach," says Burnet. "Playing one round of the Amateur Championship, the other fellow was in a bad lie and complained. So Freddie went across and kicked the ball into a better lie." Sir John Low, a general in the Indian Army: "At age 90, in 1878, he used to ride around on a white pony and dismount to play his shots. He had a caddie to carry his stool for him, and he'd sit on that until it was his turn to putt."

Burnet pauses to look around. Two members chat quietly over coffee by the window; a housekeeper with a tray moves soundlessly past the door.

"Virtually all the time, there's hardly a soul about," he says, sounding apologetic. "Hardly anyone about."

There is no portrait of a Cheape.

One history of the R&A says the club "declined" the gift of a portrait of Morris Cheape just after World War II, but the reason is not given. Merely mention the name Cheape around R&A officials and there is a flaring of nostrils and a rolling of eyes.

The St. Andrews Links Act of 1894 makes five clear provisions "for the protection of James Cheape and his successors, proprietors of the estate of Strathtyrum." The document guarantees the Cheapes the exclusive right to excavate seashells on the Old Course; pledges that no buildings will be allowed on the links, other than small "wooden erections as shelters for golfers"; and grants the Cheape family and their guests the right to play golf on the links "without payment of any rates and in all time coming."

Since the signing of that document, the relationship between the R&A and the Cheapes has often been contentious. When someone at the R&A was tardy in forwarding the late Sander Cheape his tickets for the '70 British Open at St. Andrews, Cheape collared club secretary Mackenzie and threatened to exercise his shell-digging rights on the 16th fairway of the Old Course. At other times, Cheape allegedly threatened to claim unreasonable tee times on the Old Course. "What happens if it's the Open?" Mackenzie fretted. "What if he says, 'I have three chaps I want to play with,' and Nicklaus is about to tee off?"

Another sore point is the famous painting *The Golfers*, which resides at Strathtyrum. According to those who have seen it, the work is badly in need of restoration. The R&A has long coveted the painting by Charles Lees and would like to hang it in the Big Room alongside the club's other heavily insured treasures. Sander Cheape steadfastly refused to let it out of the house and even spurned Mackenzie's offer to have the painting restored at the club's expense.

"He was a very difficult man, not a lovable person," says Burnet.

Cheape's widow, Glades, now in her 80's, lives on at the Cheape mansion, which is set well back behind gates on the main road out of St. Andrews. She has a "friendly relationship" with the R&A, says Michael Bonallack, the current club secretary, but she's very "conscious of the Cheapes' rights under the Links Act."

The secretary's office wasn't always upstairs, says Mackenzie, who held the post from 1967 to 1984. You just *think* nothing has changed. When Brigadier Eric Brickman had the job, from 1952 to '67, his desk wasn't up on that wonderful perch overlooking the Old Course. The secretary toiled below in an old lounge near the locker room.

"Every member who had to spend a penny in the loo said, 'Let's go see Brick.' He couldn't get any work done," says Mackenzie. "He finally said the hell with it."

If you want to know about changes at the R&A, you go to this man. It was Mackenzie who ushered the R&A into the age of television, who rescued the British Open from anachronism, who saw the R&A's role writ larger in the world.

"The whole setup of the R&A, it's very big business now," he says, savoring coffee and a cigarette in the Trophy Room. "When I started, in 1967, we were a very small band. I had a deputy secretary for rules, and an accountant. There were four or five girls in the office." His eyes get big. "And the Open! In my first year, the total crowd for the Open at Hoylake was under 30,000. For the *week!* This year, they're talking a quarter of a million people for St. Andrews."

Meeting Mackenzie, it is hard to picture him as an agent of change. He is a heavy, large-featured man with a gravel-pit voice and a Churchillian glare. Imagine a figure out of P.G. Wodehouse, a retired colonial officer with a gout-ravaged foot raised on a pillow, *The Times* in one hand, claret in the other. Except for the gout, that's Mackenzie.

"Regular Army, I was with the Gurkhas in India (*cough, cough*), retired in '47 (*harrrumph*), 17 years with Burma Shell in India ... found myself in Rhodesia (*harrrumph*)."

But this is the man who saw leader boards for the first time in 1967, at the U.S. Open at Baltusrol, and took the idea back to Scotland. To Mackenzie, the job was almost a lark. He became secretary through an advertisement in *The Times* of London, making the application, as he puts it, "tongue in cheek." To his surprise, he got the job. "And it was the happiest 17 years I ever had."

Mackenzie's international outlook, corporate experience and promotional skill broadened the R&A's influence in the world. He rejects, however, the accusation that the R&A operates like a colonial power. "These obligations and responsibilities, they were all foisted on the R&A," he insists. "We were *asked* to do it." He is right, of course. It was the Honourable Company of Edinburgh Golfers that drew up the first 13 rules of golf for the links at Leith in 1744. But that club showed little cohesion in later years, while the R&A grew in stature. It was to the R&A that the other clubs turned, in 1897, for a uniform code of rules. Ever since, the R&A has been recognized as the governing authority for the rules of golf throughout the world, except in the U.S. and Mexico, which are governed by the USGA.

"There are jealousies," Mackenzie admits. "I'm not saying the R&A is universally admired. There are people in various organizations saying, 'Why in the hell should the R&A have these powers?'"

Implying what? A challenge to the R&A's rule-making authority. A schism? A putsch?

Mackenzie shakes his head. "The lines of communication and trust are so ingrained now. We'd have to do something blatantly stupid."

Besides, the rules aren't written by a few old boys nodding over their toddies in the Big Room. The Rules of Golf Committee consists of 12 R&A members, elected by the club, plus 11 representatives of national golf unions and associations worldwide. Every four years, representatives of the R&A and the USGA meet to review the rules, make changes and adjudicate their differences.

"We don't think we have a divine right to go on as sole arbiter of golf worldwide," says Bonallack. "But somebody's got to make the rules. We are looked on and we see ourselves as the custodians of the game."

Bonallack, a five-time British Amateur champion, is signing documents at one of the long tables in his office above the Big Room.

The work might go easier at a proper desk, he concedes, but six years as secretary have not convinced him that a change is needed. "This is how I found it when I moved in, and I think it's the same as my predecessor found it," Bonallack says. Even the old carpet, with its stomach-turning Victorian pattern, strikes Bonallack as worthy of keeping. "You'd have to be pretty good with words to describe it."

Bonallack is a big man of middle years, unhurried but never ponderous. He dresses for work in a blue blazer, light slacks, a blue tie and a golf-club tie clip. "This is probably the best office in the world," he says.

Apart from the indescribable carpet, he is probably right. The spacious room opens on a canopied balcony overlooking the Old Course and the sea. Overwrought iron and a 19th-century telescope suggest the bridge of a Jules Verne moonship.

"Trouble is," Bonallack says, "you hardly get to look out." That's the CEO in him talking. With 22 full-time employees, not counting domestic staff, the R&A is still a relative minnow—an official of the USGA, which has about 150 employees, once looked at the R&A's organizational chart and asked, "Where's the rest?"—but even those numbers are too many for a sedate old gentlemen's club. The Open Championship staff, numbering eight, works out of a building a short walk away.

The British Open is the R&A's engine these days, the source of its most significant revenues and the most visible celebration of its mission. Unlike the USGA, which stages the U.S. Open through the committees and resources of host clubs, the R&A rents tournament venues outright. The Championship staff sells the tickets, puts up the grandstands, licenses the concessionaires, prints the programs and, when the show is over, keeps the profits.

"The biggest difference is what we do with the money generated by the Open," Bonallack says. "That money cannot go back for the use of the members. It's got to be used for the good of the game."

Typically, the profits go for grants: money to build and staff the British Golf Museum, subsidies for golf unions in developing countries, payment for coaching, interest-free loans for builders of new golf courses and practice grounds. "Czechoslovakia needs clubs and golf balls and shoes. Hungary wants a mower," Bonallack says.

One mower?

"They only have one nine-hole course."

Those who journey to St. Andrews next week for the Open should note this: There will be caps, sweaters, towels and shirts for sale, and all of these will have Open logos or crests on them with the words OLD COURSE ST. ANDREWS printed boldly. But there will be no caps, sweaters, towels or shirts with ROYAL & ANCIENT GOLF CLUB OF ST. ANDREWS on them, not even a discreet R&A on a visor or sleeve.

It isn't done.

Nor will the Open itself be sold to the highest bidder. "It will never be the So-and-So British Open Championship," vows Bonallack. "There will never be a sponsor's name attached to it."

The clubhouse, streaked and gray as the sky on so many Scottish mornings, testifies to that resolve.

"That building sits there so perfectly," says Sandy Tatum, "and expresses such authority and integrity, it borders on the metaphysical."

"On quiet days," British golf writer and R&A member Pat Ward-Thomas wrote, "when nothing of moment is afoot and a few members drowse in their deep chairs, one might look through the tall windows and dream awhile. So peaceful is the scene ... that it is hard to believe that almost every great golfer in the game's history has stood on the tee below and looked down the long fall of fairway to the hills beyond; and that on an upper floor the processes of guidance and government are constantly under way."

The portraits have not, in fact, fallen off the walls. The R&A endures.

IN THE ROUGH

◆ ◆ ◆

The Glory Game
At Goat Hills

BY   DAN   JENKINS

GROWING UP IN TEXAS, DAN JENKINS PLAYED A GAME WHICH
THE GENTEEL MEMBERS OF CLUBS LIKE WINGED FOOT OR MERI-
ON MIGHT NOT RECOGNIZE AS GOLF. IN THIS CLASSIC PIECE,
JENKINS FONDLY RECALLS THE DAYS HE SPENT IN THE COMPANY
OF CECIL THE PARACHUTE, MAGOO AND FOOT THE FREE.

*Goat Hills is gone now. It was swallowed up almost four years ago by
the bulldozers of progress, and in the end it was nice to learn that
something could take a divot out of those hard fairways. But all of the
regular players had left long before. We had grown up at last. Maybe
it will be all right to talk about the place now, and about the people
and the times we had. Maybe it will be therapeutic. At least it will
help explain why I do not play golf so much anymore. I mean, I keep
getting invited to Winged Head and Burning Foot and all those fancy
clubs we sophisticated New Yorkers are supposed to frequent, places
where, I hear, they have real flag sticks instead of broom handles. It
sounds fine, but I usually beg off. I am, frankly, still overgolfed from
all those years at Goat Hills in Texas. You would be, too, if....
Well, let me tell you some of it. Not all. I will try to be truthful and
not too sentimental. But where shall I begin? With Cecil? Yeah, I
think so. He was sort of a symbol in those days, and....*

We called him Cecil the Parachute, because he fell down a lot. He would attack the golf ball with a whining, leaping half-turn—more of a calisthenic than a swing, really—and occasionally, in his spectacular struggles for extra distance, he would soar right off the end of elevated tees.

He was a slim, bony, red-faced little man, who wore crepe-soled shoes and heavily starched shirts that crackled like crunched glass. When he was earthbound Cecil drove a delivery truck for a cooky factory, Grandma's Cookies, and he always parked it—hid it, rather—behind a tall hedge near the clubhouse. When the truck was there, out of sight of passing cars (or of cooky-company dispatchers snooping on cooky-truck drivers), you could be pretty sure that not only was Cecil out on the course but so were Tiny, Easy Reid, Magoo, Foot the Free, Grease Repellent, Ernie, Matty, Rush, Little Joe, Weldon the Oath, Jerry, John the Band-Aid and Moron Tom.

There was also the very good chance that all of us would be in one hollering, protesting, club-slinging fifteensome. Anyhow, when Cecil the Parachute had the truck hidden you knew for sure that the game was on.

The game was not the kind of golf that Gene Sarazen or any of his stodgy friends ever would have approved of. But it was, nevertheless, the kind we played for about 15 years, from the mid-'40s to the late '50s, at a windy, dusty, indifferently mowed, stone-hard, broomstick-flagged, practically treeless, residentially surrounded public course named Worth Hills in Fort Worth, Texas. Goat Hills, we called it, not too originally.

It was a gambling game that went on in some fashion or another, involving from two to 20 players, almost every day of every year. The game survived not just my own shaft-bending, divot-stomping presence, but heat, rain, snow, war, tornadoes, jobs, studies, illness, divorces, birth, death and considerations of infinity. If there were certain days when it seemed the game might help pay part of my tuition through Texas Christian University—a jumble of yellow brick buildings across the street from the course—there were others when it seemed certain to guarantee a lifetime of indebtedness. Either way you were trapped, incessantly drawn to the Hills, like Durrell to Alexandria.

Nearly all of the days at the Hills began the same way with

lazy conversations on the front porch of the small white club-house. We would be slouched in chairs, smoking, drinking coffee, complaining about worldly things, such as the Seventh Street Theater not changing its movie in weeks. Say it was August. We would be looking across the putting green at the heat. In Texas in August you can see the heat. It looks like germs under a microscope. In fact, say it was the day of the Great Scooter Wreck.

We were lounging. Matty, who had a crew cut and wore glasses and looked collegiate (and grew up to be a doctor), was resting against a rock pillar on the porch, playing tunes on his front teeth with his fingernails. He could do that. Learned it in study hall. For money he could even play *Sixty Minute Man* or *Rocket 88* or whatever happened to be No. 1 on the jukebox at Jack's Place on the Mansfield Highway, where most of us went at night to "hustle the pretties," as Moron Tom phrased it, and watch truck drivers fight to see who bought the beer. I was reading either *The Best of S.J. Pereman* or *The Brothers Karamazov*. Any kind of book would prompt needling whoops from Tiny, who was a railroad conductor, or Weldon the Oath, who was a postman, or Grease Repellent, who worked at the Texaco station three blocks away. ("Hey, Jenkins! What you gonna do with all them facts clangin' around in yer head?") Foot the Free, which was short for Big Foot the Free-loader, was there, practice-putting at a small, chipped-out crevice in the concrete of the porch, a spot that marked the finish of the finest one hole of golf I ever saw played—but more about that later. Magoo was around. And Little Joe. Presently John the Band-Aid showed up, striding grimly from the parking lot, clubs over his shoulder, ready to go. He had beaten a Turf King pinball machine somewhere on University Drive—had found the A, B and C lit, had lit the D, then hit the feature—and he had some money.

"You and you and you and you and you, too," said John. "All of you two, two, two automatic one-down presses, what-ever gets even on 9 and 18, and whipsaw ever'body 70 or bet-ter for five." John the Band-Aid had lost the day before.

We began tying our shoes.

Magoo said, "I don't guess anybody's gonna let me play, since I didn't drop but a young 50 yesterday."

"You're here, aren't you?" said John. "Joe and me got all teams for five match and five medal. Same game as yesterday. Come on, let's jack it up."

Little Joe, who played without a shirt and had a blond duck-tail haircut, said, "Sure wish I'd get to pick my own partner sometime." Then he said, "You gonna play good, John, or scrape it as usual?"

"There ain't no keep-off signs on me if you want some," John said, swinging his driver on the first tee.

"Five's enough," Little Joe said.

"You got it," said John.

Little Joe and I took a scooter, one of those two-seaters with three wheels, and John and Magoo took one. The rest walked. We were an eightsome. If others came later they would join up along the way, as always, and there would be some action for them, too. Plenty.

With only eight players it was a fairly simple game to book keep. You played each of the other seven individually on the front nine, on the back and on the 18—three bets each to start. Without any presses—new bets—that was a sizable investment right there. But new bets came quickly, because of an automatic one-down press rule and big, get-even bets on 9 and 18. It was certainly nice to birdie the 9th and 18th holes sometimes. Like maybe $100 nice.

Naturally, there was always a long pause at both the 9th and 18th tees to figure out how everybody stood. Like this particular day. John the Band-Aid, I recall, had shot even par but was down to everyone.

"I got to be the alltime world's champion unlucky," he said, beating his driver against the tee marker. "Magoo can't play and he's beatin' me, and Matty can't play and he's beatin' me, and my young partner's dead as an old woman and.... "

John the Band-Aid, who wore glasses and a straw hat and kept a handkerchief tied around his neck for protection against sunburn, rarely observed honors on the tee. In fact, the game sort of worked in reverse etiquette. The players who were losing teed off first.

"I'm gonna hit this one right into young Stadium Drive," said John, impatiently. The 9th at the Hills was a long par-4. The tee was on a bluff, above a desperate drop-off into a cluster of undernourished hackberry trees, a creek, rocks and weeds. Ideally, the drive had to carry over the trees and creek and into the uphill fairway, leaving about a seven-iron to the green. Stadium Drive was behind the green.

As John the Band-Aid went into his backswing, Little Joe said, "Hit it, Daddy."

John said, "Mother, I'm hittin' hard as I can." He curved a wondrous slice into the right rough, and coming off of his follow-through slung the club in the general direction of Eagle Mountain Lake, just missing Little Joe. The Band-Aid's shot irritated Little Joe, and so did the flying club. "Man, man," said Joe. "They ought to put me in a box and take me to the state fair for bein' in this game."

I was fairly mad, too. One under par and no money ahead. Maybe that's why I pointed the scooter straight down the hill and let it run. We were almost instantly out of control. "Son of a young ...," said Joe, holding on. The scooter zoomed, but the front wheel struck a boulder and, like a plane taking off, we were in the air. I sailed straight over the front, and Joe went out the right side. The scooter, flipping and spewing clubs, landed on both of us, mostly on my left leg.

I think I was out for about 10 seconds before I heard all of the laughter behind me and felt the clubs and rocks underneath. They pulled the scooter off, and off Joe's white canvas bag—or what was left of it. Battery acid had been jolted out of the scooter and was already beginning to eat away at the bag.

"I got two says Joe don't have a bag before we get to 18," said Magoo. Foot called it. Although my left ankle was so swollen I had to play the rest of the way with only one shoe, we continued. It was on the 14th green that we noticed Magoo was a winner. When Joe went to pick up his bag after putting out, the only things left were the top metal ring, the bottom, the wooden stick and the shoulder strap. Not only that, Joe's left pants leg was going fast.

In or out of a runaway scooter, our game frequently took odd directions. Bored, we often played Goat Hills backward, to every other hole, to every third hole, entirely out of bounds except for the greens (which meant you had to stay in the roads and lawns), with only one club or at night, which was stimulating because of all the occupied cars parked on the more remote fairways. One of the most interesting games we invented, however, was the Thousand-yard Dash. This was a one-hole marathon. It started at the farthest point on the course from the clubhouse—and ended at the chipped-out place in the concrete on the porch.

I have forgotten who invented it. Most likely it was either Foot the Free or myself or Matty, for we had once played from the Majestic Theater to the Tarrant County Courthouse in downtown Fort Worth—anything off Throckmorton Street was out of bounds—without getting arrested. At any rate, there were 12 of us who each put $5 in the pot and started flailing away, cutting across fairways, intruding on other games, cursing and carefully counting the strokes of those who had chosen the same route as ours. Some went to the left of the stone rest room, some went to the right. I followed Foot the Free because he could never afford to lose. He carried the same $5 bill, I think, for eight years. We hit a hooked driver, another hooked driver, a third hooked driver and then a hooked three-wood—you had to hook at the Hills to get the roll—and that got us both within pitching distance of the porch. The others were out of it by now, lost in the creek or in the flower beds of the apartment houses that bordered the No. 1 fairway.

My approach shot carried the concrete porch, hit hard against the clubhouse wall, chased Wells Howard, the pro, back inside the door, brought a screech from his wife, Lola, glanced off one of the rock pillars and finally came to rest—puttable if I moved a chair—about 20 feet from the hole.

Foot played a bounce shot, lofting a high wedge, letting it plop in front of the porch on some gravel, then hop up over the curb and skid against the wall. He was only 10 feet from the hole. Hell of a shot.

We quickly got a broom and began sweeping dirt particles off the porch and took off our cleats because they are very bad for a stance on concrete and put Wells and Lola at ease by convincing them that this would look good in our memoirs one day after we had all won the young National Open and got famous.

A couple of rent-club players strolled out of the golf shop, and Foot asked them not to walk in his line. My putt offered one distinct danger, tapping it too firmly and having it roll past the hole and into a row of golf carts lined up at the far end—which is precisely what happened. I tried to argue that the carts were an unnatural hazard and that I deserved a free lift; but Wells, the pro, no doubt believing the game was my idea, ruled I had to play it. On in five, I 18-putted for a 23. Against anyone else I might still have had a chance. But Foot was one of the great putters in history. He calmly tapped his putt and it dribbled slowly, slowly, over the concrete, wavering, wobbling—and *in*.

Foot's 6 was about the best hole I ever saw played, and I have seen several Odessa Pro-Ams. The only thing I ever heard of that came close to equaling it happened in Austin a year or so later. A friend of mine named Thor, a Hills man off and on, made a 517 from the Lake Austin Inn to a brown-leather loafer in the closet of an apartment near the University of Texas campus.

I am sure that the longest hole we ever played was from the first tee at Goat Hills to the third green at Colonial Country Club. It was about 10 blocks, regardless of whether you went down Stadium Drive, past the TCU football field, left on Park Hill and over the houses, or down Alton Road and Simondale.

The first time we played it, Tiny wore his bright-red elastic-waisted slacks—he was 6 feet 3 and weighed close to 300 pounds—and Rush's dad, a retired oilman, caddied for him, driving his big black Lincoln, and Cecil got bit by a cocker spaniel.

Playing through neighborhoods requires an unusual shot. The trick is to stay in the streets as much as possible to get the distance, so a good club to have is a blade putter. You can swat the ball low on the street and guide it pretty easily. We all kept one around. I happened to have sliced a putter shot into a bed of iris on Alton Road and was hunting for it when I saw Cecil the Parachute down the driveway considering an iron shot that would have to rise quickly to clear a towering oak. A dog in the backyard was barking at him.

Cecil leaped at the ball and drove it straight into a Cyclone fence—he seldom hit the ball higher than the tops of his rolled-down socks—and his follow-through sailed him forward onto his elbows, like a man who had been dragged behind a team of horses. It also brought him within range of the spaniel, which bit him on the leg.

Cecil scrambled up and came tiptoeing back toward me down the driveway, saying, "Hurried the shot. That sucker was agrowlin' at me, and just when I started to swing I seen a lady cussin' at me through the kitchen window."

We picked up—"I. P.'d," as one said at the time, meaning in-pocketed—and began searching for the others in backyards along the way to Colonial. Tiny had quit at a fishpond, and Easy Reid had met a friend and paused to sell him some insurance. The only two left in contention were Foot and Magoo, whom we found hitting seven-irons out of Bermuda-grass lawns over the fence and onto Colonial's first fairway. They had to hole out pretty fast because some Colonial members sent a caddie back to the clubhouse to get the manager, Vergal Bourland. Foot and Magoo each wound up with a 19 and hustled back over the fence before Vergal could get their names.

Quite an argument followed about the playoff. Magoo suggested playing back to the Hills. Foot wanted to play to Herb Massey's restaurant on Eighth Avenue because he thought he would win and be able to afford the specialty, a chicken-fried steak with cream gravy. I thought they should play to the Forest Park Zoo, which wasn't too far. They decided to split the money, so we all went back to the Hills and got in a putting game that lasted until midnight.

To at least partly understand why anyone would hang around a municipal golf course for one-third of his life playing games such as these you have to understand something about the town and the state and what golf means there.

First of all, Fort Worth is basically a quiet place with a river, the Trinity, a fragrant stockyard on the North Side (where no one who lives South, West or East ever goes except to eat Mexican food at Joe Garcia's), a Convair plant, a couple of newspapers, a lot of beer taverns, a few elegant neighborhoods, a downtown area sparkling with loan companies, and a university, TCU, which is primarily noted for producing Sammy Baugh and Davey O'Brien. It is a town where little has happened, outside of a few important football games, since Vernon Castle, the famous dancer, was killed when he crashed a plane into a field in Benbrook during World War I. Nor has anyone cared to make something happen except, occasionally, on the golf courses.

Fort Worth is where Ben Hogan and Byron Nelson came from, and this is one of the first facts I ever learned. It probably happened to other kids the same way. There you were one day, waving a yardstick like a sword, playing Errol Flynn in *The Sea Hawk*, when suddenly your parents decided you had a natural swing. They told you about Hogan and Nelson, and about Jimmy Demaret, who came from Houston, and about Ralph Guldahl, Lloyd Mangrum and Harry Cooper, who came from Dallas, and they shoved you onto the nearest course and said not to come home until you were ready for the Ethiopian Four Ball. So you stayed 20 years curing a shank and learning to love a duck hook.

Probably because of the climate—there are only two weeks out of the year when a man would not play golf, but even those February afternoons might be considered ideal in Pittsburgh—the sport has for 30 years been second in importance only to football. This is true throughout the state: in the north central area of Fort Worth and Dallas, through the thick pines of East Texas, in the hills and woods around Austin, along the palmed coasts of Houston and Corpus Christi and all across the peach-colored plains of West Texas and the Panhandle, where the fairways wind around mesquite and oil pumps and players are seen wearing silver tool-dresser's helmets and coveralls and carrying clubs in their hands instead of in bags.

Golf always received generous attention in the papers. As soon as you were old enough to read you saw headlines about people like Gus Moreland and Harry Todd playing in some weird thing called the Cisco Invitation. Almost every town with a hen house, some tin cans and broomsticks still has an annual invitational tournament. All kinds of places—Abilene, Lubbock, Tyler, Longview, Ranger, Eastland, Waxahachie, Midland. These invitationals begin in mid-March and last through mid-September. Each week there are from 10 to 20, and it is possible for an enterprising, neat-swinging high school or college golfer to play competitively for 22 weeks or more of the year, winning, if he is good enough, more sets of clubs, TV sets and silver trays than he can ever sell to get money to gamble with.

It was this vast amateur circuit that gave you Hogan and Nelson and Demaret, and later on Jackie Burke, Tommy Bolt,

Ernie Vossler, Earl Stewart, Shelley Mayfield, Don Cherry, Billy Maxwell, Don January, Joe Conrad and Wes Ellis, and now Bobby Nichols, Dave Marr, Miller Barber, Jacky Cupit, Rex Baxter, Billy Martindale, Homero Blancas, Terry Dill, Charley Coody, Don Massengale, Dudley Wysong and Jerry Edwards, to name a few.

Vossler and Edwards, I can relate with a certain amount of pride, came right out of our game at Goat Hills. Ernie was a relentless competitor who could not understand why anyone but him ever sank a putt. Sometimes, when someone like Weldon the Oath made one, Ernie would just walk straight to the clubhouse. He was never as proficient as myself at club-breaking. I often broke my eight-iron on the dinky 17th hole, a par-3 flip shot, because I was either long and in the creek or short and in the trap—but Ernie had his moments. He bladed a seven-iron one afternoon at the 6th hole, I remember, and almost killed us all. He hurled the club straight into the brick fairway, and the shaft snapped. Both parts of the club bounced into the air. One jagged end sprang back and hit Ernie in the palm of the hand, causing a five-stitch gash. The other glanced toward Weldon and myself. It looked like we had been attacked by flashes of lightning as the steel sparkled in the sun, and we dived for safety.

Later on that same day Weldon had one of his talking fits— talking to the ball. He took oaths. Wearing his postman's cap and without golf shoes because he had rushed to the game so quickly, he gave the ball a wonderful lecture on the 14th fee. "This is your last chance, you lousy little curd," he said. "If you slice on me just one more time I'm gonna bite you right in half and chew your rubber guts up. Now I'm gonna hit you straight, you hear me! There's no by God reason why you got to slice on me ever' time, damn it! You hear me? *You hear me tellin' you this?*"

Then Weldon hit a world-record slice. It crossed at least two fairways, but before it landed he turned around two, three times, slung the club and went sprinting after the ball. When he got there he jumped up and down on it.

"I'm dad-bam finished," he said, panting. "This is my last day on *any* golf course, ever. You picks have guyed me damn stick." He was so mad he couldn't talk straight. "Enough and

I'm done. Rotten, stinking, miserable game." He was, of course, back the next day.

After I holed out a 30-foot putt to halve a gimme birdie one afternoon, Vossler left for good. He moved on to bigger things, to the big-money games at Ridglea, to become city champion, state amateur champion, ultimately on to the PGA tour. I have always considered Ernie our honor graduate, although Edwards may outdo him.

Jerry could drive the ball four miles, or roughly the distance to old Paschal High School (now Tech), a Gibraltar of formative education that turned most of us out with degrees in Library Pass Forging, Double Lunch Period Registration, Boiler Room Smoking, Chug-a-Lug, Basketball and Marriage. Except for a recurring Goat Hills temper, Jerry has a sound game and has been in the money many times on the PGA tour. So far, however, his greatest publicity came when he was rumored to have gone AWOL from the Army in 1962 to play in the U.S. Open.

"A true Hills man," Magoo said.

Although Vossler and Edwards were the only two who succeeded, all of us at one time, I believe, envisioned a pro career. Easy Reid, for example, bought a huge black bag and an umbrella and some alligator shoes and turned pro, but the closest he came to the big time was missing the cut at the Odessa Pro-Am with me as a partner. Grease Repellent turned pro after he shot 62 at Goat Hills, eight under, breaking the course record that five of us held at 65. But he did not go on the tour, and I don't think he took a club job. He only refused to play in any more amateur tournaments, which he didn't play in anyhow.

Sadly, my own dreams were constantly interrupted by reality. The first time was early in the State Junior at San Antonio, when I was defeated 3 and 2 by a cross-handed Mexican wearing tennis shoes. Thirsting for some sort of revenge, I returned the following year and lost to a barefoot 14-year-old who had only five clubs.

But if those experiences were not enough to convince me, the Waxahachie Invitation should have. The Waxahachie Invitation was not exactly the Masters tournament of Texas, but it did draw a few celebrities: Cherry, Stewart, Maxwell, Conrad, for example. I know it was an unusually strong field one particular year because it took 70 to qualify for 30 of the 32 places in the championship flight. Unluckily, I shot 71 along with 11 others, so there had to be a playoff—swatfest, it was called—for the last two places. A playoff meant a gallery. Bad deal.

We began swinging, and nine players bogeyed the first sudden-death hole and were eliminated. (I envied them all.) One player got a birdie and was in. Two of us made pars and had to go another hole for the remaining berth or the privilege of being thrashed 6 and 5 the next day by a Cherry, a Stewart, a Maxwell or a Conrad.

My opponent was a tall fellow named Shelby, and I did not realize until a few years later that it was the same Carroll Shelby who raced sports cars. This might have been the thing that drove him to it. The crowd stayed—the ritualistic barbecue and dice game were still a good hour off—and it had no respect for either of us. As we stood on the tee, perspiring from fright, I heard someone say, "Who you want?" And the reply: "Aw, neither one. They both chili dippers."

Whatever Shelby did, I did better. He hooked, I hooked. He hit over the fence, I hit over the fence. The giggles trailed us endlessly. He got lost in the gully, I got lost in the gully. He landed in the bunker, I landed in the bunker. At one point I heard a man say, "Well, I been to the Dublin Rodeo, I've met the Light Crust Doughboys and I've stepped across the Mississippi where it ain't but a foot wide, but I never seen nothin' like this." Finally, perhaps through a bookkeeping error, I won the hole with a 10.

You did not have to venture out of town—out on the *tour*—to enrich the game that you always came back to at Goat Hills. You could go across town to one of the dozen other courses that Fort Worth had. You could certainly sneak into any of the country clubs and play from No. 2 through No. 17, placing all the flags in the bunkers for reasons that seemed hilarious then.

Our game, I think, was substantially influenced by those at other courses. At one time we thought the really good players were mostly at another public course, Meadowbrook. They did things like win the City Tournament, which is something neither Hogan, Nelson nor I could ever do. In our respective eras we each finished second. And then there was Ridglea, where Vossler went.

Ridglea had players who may not have been as skilled, but they could certainly outbet you. Occasionally one of us would be deluded by a 67 at wide-open Goat Hills and go to narrow Ridglea. You always came back busted, but at least you had been to the shrine where Titanic Thompson, the famed Evansville hustler, had once defeated Byron Nelson in a head-to-head match, taking $1,000 from Byron's backers. That was back in the early '30s, when Nelson was merely the best amateur in town.

At Ridglea you could hear all the good stories about Titanic Thompson, some of them maybe even true. They would tell how he would throw a ball down on the ground, waggle a driver and say he bet he could hit the green with his driver, although the green was 400 yards away. Somebody would call it. And Ti would calmly walk to the green and tap it with his driver and collect. And how he once bet he could throw a watermelon about as big as a baseball, went up on top of the building next door and threw it over. And how he would bet a man in Phoenix that he would have more mail waiting for him in Fort Worth than the other man, having mailed himself 50 postcards. And all those other stories. You would like to have known Ti more than any other celebrity.

Since that was impossible, the next best thing was just *being* at Ridglea, at the shrine, in the days before they turned it into a country club for Jaycees. There was one day when several of us were in the old golf shop and saw the pro, Raymond Gafford, on top of a wooden table with a four-iron, put a ball down on the table, address it and aim out the open door toward the first green, a par-5.

"Believe I can make five from here?" asked Raymond.

We all looked respectfully at Spec, who had a solemn face, and we saw him do what we figured he would do.

"Well, I ain't had nothin' this good lately," Spec said, taking out a roll of bills. Spec was an action man. Craved it. Once, even though he had a broken leg, he did not miss his game at Ridglea. He hired a caddie to pull him around the course in a red wagon.

"Can I get all that off you?" said Raymond. "I don't want to be greedy."

"I'll guarantee you, this man's got to make me rich some day," said Spec. "Yes, sir. Ever' meal's a banquet and ever' day's a holiday. We're gonna eat steak tonight and play golf tomorrow."

Raymond said, "All I know is I can make five."

"Well," Spec said, "I don't know a whole lot about it, but I know a man can't make five off a table."

"Just get it on," Raymond said.

"On?" said Spec. "On's here in my hand."

A few others got in, do or don't, and Raymond, who was a fine player, hit a crisp four-iron right off the tabletop, out the door and down the fairway. It was clear that he would have only a three-wood and a long iron to reach the green in three. Spec said, "Oops. Step on the fire and call in the dogs. The hunt's over, boys."

And it was. Raymond made an easy five.

After that, I remember, we hit a lot of shots off the shingle roof of the Goat Hills clubhouse and did a great deal of chipping off the hoods of our cars and, in fact, designed one hole that started on top of the gin-rummy table in the locker room, went through the restaurant, noted for its cheese crackers and R.C. Colas, out the golf shop, around the putting course and concluded on the first green.

It was in the last few years at Goat Hills, before the city sold those 106 acres to TCU so the school could build more yellow-brick buildings, that the games got too big, too outrageously expensive. One reason was that most of us were working by then, or were supposed to be. We somehow managed always to have the afternoons free. Anyhow, we virtually were wealthy. For instance, I had ingeniously slithered my way up to $87.50 per week at *The Fort Worth Press*. So I was a high player now. And then there was Moron Tom, who worked terribly hard at eight ball, poker, gin and pinball. He could high-play you.

Moron Tom was a likable, muscular West Texan who had gone to TCU to play football but had quit when he discovered you had to practice every day during the season. He was a brilliant hustler who talked in a fast code, often describing his long tee shots with such immodest expressions as "quadruple unreal." He almost never spoke English, only a weird gibberish that you had to learn or not know what bets you had with him.

There was one special day—the day of the last truly big game—that began with Moron Tom saying, "I'll take toops and threeps from Youngfut, Youngjun, Youngmut and Youngrus." Translated, that meant he wanted 2 up and 3 up from young Foot, young John, young Matty and young Rush. He wanted the same from Magoo, too, but Magoo said, "Kane go-fert," which was Moronese for "Can't go for it."

Somehow Magoo and I wound up as partners, and this was bad. Magoo was a good player, but he was unlucky. Once in the Glen Garden Invitation across town—that is the course where Hogan and Nelson caddied as kids—he hit a fine shot to a difficult green and found the ball in a man's mouth, being cleaned. Things like that happened to Magoo. Only this time, all the way around, it did not seem to matter. Frankly, we played superbly.

We birdied so many holes between us that Moron Tom, each time either of us swung, said, "Cod Ee-rack Fockle-dim!" That was his pronunciation of Doc Cary Middlecoff spelled backward, and a compliment. Sometimes Moron Tom said, "Wod Daw-ret-snif," which was Dow Finsterwald, and a cry of doom.

As we came off the 17th green, having birdied every hole since the 13th, Magoo and I calculated that if we could simply par the 18th we would not be able to get the money home in Cecil the Parachutes's cooky truck. With all of the double and triple presses, it was up to around $600, at least. And there was blood everywhere.

"Ain't this somethin'?" said Foot. "Man's gonna be took to Dump City by two clutch artists." Meaning us.

"Come off this, Magoo," said Rush. "Man, you're supposed to be standin' in line to give up."

Magoo said, "I don't guess anybody wants a young press to get even, do they?"

There were a few sarcastic snarls. The get-even press was automatic, of course.

Easy Reid said, "Oh, Lordy. I don't want the prize, I just want to get my hand out of the box."

The 18th was an easy par-4. You drove from a windy knoll, with the wind helping, to a wide, wide fairway across a creek and an embankment. There was always a tendency to come out of your shoes at the ball because there was so little danger, and a big drive would leave you with only a 50-yard wedge shot to the green. The only conceivable trouble was far to the right, beyond the bordering 10th fairway, where Stadium Drive was out of bounds. In all my years I never saw anyone slice that badly—only Magoo when Moron Tom spoke to him for all that money.

At the top of Magoo's backswing, Moron Tom quietly said, "Tissim, Oogam," which of course was "Miss it, Magoo" backwards, and my poor partner sliced out of bounds. Well, we had to laugh about the irony of it. Once again Magoo had blown the Open. And there could be no protest. Needles were common. Sneezing, coughing, dropping a full bag of clubs on a player's backswing were part of it. Normally, it was something you ignored.

Magoo simply looked at his club and then at me and said, "If you don't make four, I'm gonna stamp this Tommy Armour right on your young forehead."

Now, across the creek at the 18th, laid upright into the embankment, was a storm drain, roughly three feet around. We used to pitch at it with old balls from the ladies' tee, but it was a rare day when anyone ever actually hit it. From up on the men's tee 100 yards back, it was an awfully small target. In fact, it never even entered my mind. I was intending to drive the green, frankly, and get a birdie just to make up for Magoo's slice. That would have been quadruple unreal.

But at the height of my arc, Moron Tom whispered something again.

"Clutch, Mother Zilch," he said.

I did not fall completely down, but almost. The club head hit about two inches behind the ball. The shot snap-hooked into the ground just in front of the ladies' tee, took a giant hop to the right off some rocks and—I swear to you—went straight into the sewage drain.

It was the only hole in one I ever made, and the shot that semiretired me from golf. Forever.

Where A Golf
Nut Is King

BY DAN JENKINS

CONTRARY TO WHAT YOU MIGHT EXPECT, MOROCCO IS NOT
ONE HUGE SAND TRAP. WHEN DAN JENKINS VISITED THE LAND
OF *CASABLANCA*, HE DISCOVERED SOME FINE GOLF COURSES,
EVEN IF THERE ARE COBRAS IN THE ROUGHS. HE ALSO MET
KING HASSAN II, A MONARCH WITH A SERIOUS GOLF HABIT.

What could happen in the middle of this story is that the
writer might decide to hurl Morocco to the ground and rav-
age it. Nothing obscene, mind you. Just a gentle, loving tus-
sle in a platter of *couscous* while his heart thumps ecstatically
and the neckcloth on his Foreign Legion cap billows in the
soft Marrakesh breeze. The thing is, Morocco grabs you
here, right here, like a haunting song. But even before I
went there recently on a golf assignment—uh huh, golf among
the Arabs—I had been carrying on a rather violent affair with
the country. Casbahs and French Legionnaires had done it.
And harem girls. And Humphrey Bogart running a bar in
Casablanca. What chance did I have on a visit? None, of
course, which explains why I shall soon be rejoining a group
of contented Berbers in Tiznit, there to enjoy the quiet life
of carving silver gunpowder horns and perhaps helping tend

the greens of the Robert Trent Jones course that King Hassan II is certain to have constructed one day in the Anti-Atlas.

I thought I knew what to expect in the way of golf in Morocco. I knew the king was building courses as if he had heard that Charlie Farrell was opening a racket club in Agadir. I was aware he had also been flying in Claude Harmon between nines to put some altitude on his low darters. But a golf course there, I felt, would have to combine all that was beautiful and serene about the St. Louis zoo and the battle of the Kasserine Pass.

For example, it was easy for me to envision this wondrous Trent Jones par-4 where one drove from a nest of cobras, aimed for a meandering camel on the right, drew it back between a couple of Sahara dunes and hoped to avoid being stymied by the only living palm in the country. The second shot would require a full carry over an old Nazi ammunition bunker, would have to bounce safely over a herd of sheep, glance off a mosque and come to rest on a putting surface occupied by acrobats, storytellers and clusters of veiled women.

In all of my stupidity, in fact, I have to confess that I didn't really know where Morocco was. I knew it was over there somewhere in Africa or Arabia, somewhere in the land of Yvonne de Carlo and Peter Lorre, in the land of dark, narrow streets, magic rugs, tribesmen and a lot of guys wearing tarbooshes and trying to buy a visa.

I had inquired of Claude Harmon, "What do you do over there besides get your jewels stolen and watch Sydney Greenstreet auction off your wife?"

Like myself, Claude tends to exaggerate, but he has an excuse, having devoted his career to curing the slices of millionaires, presidents and kings. In any case, his reply was encouraging.

"It's the most beautiful country in the world," he said, "next to the good old U.S.A. And it's just as friendly as can be. You're gonna eat it up like a drive and a wedge. And, hey. The king is my man."

Claude Harmon was the king's man, actually. For a couple of years Claude had been going over to Morocco to bring Hassan II's game down from 110 to 85. Claude had been getting permission from his two clubs—Winged Foot in the summer and Thunderbird in the winter—to go over and watch the King take divots in Rabat, Marrakesh, Casablanca, Fez, Tangier, anywhere there happened to be nine holes hidden inside the palace walls or tucked away on a hillside or creeping through a palm grove or seared by the Atlantic or Mediterranean sun. This led some of Claude's friends to invent a slogan for him: have overlapping grip, will travel.

Originally, according to Claude, the king wanted Tommy Armour because he had come into possession of an instruction book by Armour and decided to invite him over. Tommy thought about it but eventually declined, his friends joked, because he discovered that Morocco wasn't in Westchester County.

Claude, the king was told, had a reputation as the most accomplished teaching pro in the U.S., a man who had once captured the Masters (1948) even though he hadn't played in a single tournament all that winter, who could go around Seminole in something like even 3s and in his later years had taught such power brokers, statusmakers, Bob Hopes and patriotic Americans as Dwight Eisenhower, John F. Kennedy and Richard Nixon.

Anyhow, that is the rough background on how this all got started. Claude and the king are mostly what this story is all about, but there will be something of Morocco in it too, I hope, and, of course, in the minor role of casual typist and thorough-going tourist there is, clearing the throat, me.

I find it fascinating that of the few monarchs left today—24 by my last count—one is not only captivated by golf but has sort of bent himself toward making his country one long par-5—to promote tourism—and has, at the same time, developed a very special relationship with an American pro. Claude Harmon had made four trips to Morocco before I joined him there last spring for his fifth. During this period of almost three years Claude and the king had exchanged more gifts than words. Claude had not known exactly what to expect in the way of reward until after his first visit. "I went out of goodwill," he said. Goodwill became a thousand a day plus expenses. Plus as many swords, daggers, plates, trays, leather goods and small jewelry as Claude could admire during his free-time shopping tours. Claude would pause to glance at something, a guide would notice it, he'd tell the king, and it would later arrive at Winged Foot.

A Mark III Continental arrived at Claude's home one day, and so did a cigar box full of cash—in case Claude wanted some undeclared income. "I declared it all," said Claude.

Things also turned up for Claude's wife, Alice, and for the country clubs he represented. For straightening out a duck hook, one might presume: some antique jewelry and a Moroccan belt for Alice. And then for ironing the curl out of a slice, one might also presume: a $25,000 silver tea service for Thunderbird and one on its way for Winged Foot.

But what could one give a generous monarch, Claude often wondered.

"I don't know," I told him once. "His very own junta?"

On each trip Claude would take along dozens of golf clubs and bags and shoes to pass around among the king's friends and aides. He would take the king a wedge or putter or odd club he might not have seen or heard about. He once had Ben Hogan make up a few dozen balls with "King Hassan II" engraved on them. He also had Hogan make an engraved set of clubs. Claude carried over balls, clubs, head covers, gloves, wedges, sand irons, weird putters, even a set of gold Winged Foot cuff links.

Morocco's oldest course is in Marrakesh and it consists of 18 holes woven through lovely woods, with occasional glimpses of the snow-peaked Atlas mountains. One doesn't find a swimming pool or tennis courts at Royal Golf de Marrakesh. In fact, one seldom finds any people there at all, much less caddies. You lug your own clubs and hope to find an Arab mowing greens along the way to tell you where the next tee is. He might say something in Arabic, like, "Car-rock, a-loc, a-loc," which I took to mean, "Tees are where you find them."

But it was handsome, quiet and pleasant, and always there were the mountains rising above the palms and poplars. The holes, as on all of the courses, aren't tremendously long, which does much for the golfer's ego. But I gather that no one spends much time looking for a stray shot in the uncultured rough, unless, of course, one has a fetish for disturbing cobras.

As one of the world's leading cobra haters, I had two experiences in Marrakesh that scarred the soul. First, entering the orange-walled city by car, having driven three hours from Casablanca through some amazing scenery changes—from dunes to brilliant green hills and over streams the color of café au lait—I came upon two grinning Arabs under a tree, waving at me. I stopped. They stood up. I smiled back. They pointed at two buckets they were holding. And smiled again. I smiled again. So they reached into the buckets and lifted out two wriggling, unhappy cobras.

"A-mock, car-rock, a-loc," one of them said, still smiling.

"Car-rock you," I said, and sped away.

Later on, in a square named the Djemaa-el-Fna, I found their mates.

Like 50,000 other people, I had been milling around the Djemaa-el-Fna, looking for the missing letters in the name and observing fortune-tellers, magicians, medicine men, gamblers, acrobats, Saharan dancers, donkeys, camels, children sitting and listening to story tellers and vendors cooking snails and sausages, when an Arab tapped me on the shoulder. He pointed to a carpet spread out on the dirt and to a basket turned upside down.

"Hmmm," I said. "Beeg black cobra? One dollar American?"

The Arab grinned delightedly, lifted up the basket and out he came, King S, to rear up, swell up and do his thing. And then out from under the carpet came another. Terrific.

"That's great," I said, putting a dollar in his hand. "Now do you happen to have a magic carpet to get me back to America?"

Like every other place on the globe, Marrakesh is finding itself being modernized. Only two blocks away from the Mamounia Hotel, a mammoth place of elegance and gardens said to have been Winston Churchill's favorite, is a Holiday Inn and a friendly neighborhood Avis office where a cute Arab attendant wore a miniskirt as short as any on a cocktail waitress along the Sunset Strip. Sadly, one thing is unavoidable in Marrakesh. You can't sit in a hotel lobby having your mint tea without overhearing an American in a summer sport shirt reaching to his navel, crepe-soled shoes and a Midwestern accent telling a Frenchman about his fun-filled days at the University of Ohio and what a damn hard time he was going to have trying to fit three sons-in-law into his roofing company back home.

The best golf course in Morocco for anyone, king or peasant—at least the best until Robert Trent Jones gets finished with all of the complexes he's designing in Marrakesh, Rabat and Agadir—lies about 40 minutes north of Casablanca, on the Atlantic. Royal Golf de Mohammedia, it is called. The resort town is Mohammedia, naturally. A couple of large luxury hotels sprawl on the beach, and there is a yacht basin, but the main attraction appears to be the golf club. The course is flat but heavily wooded and quite scenic along the bay, where the 9th and 18th fairways lie adjacent to the water. (In Casablanca proper there is another course to which the tourist has entree, but the serious golfer would be just as well off hitting a few chip shots in a public park. This is the Royal Golf d'Anfa, a nine-hole layout inside a small racetrack.)

But Casablanca had far more mystery when it was situated on Warner's back lot than it seems to have today. I couldn't find Rick's Café Américain or Ingrid Bergman or anybody.

There are only four other golf courses that any Moroccan knows about in his country. One is a nine-hole course in Tangier that is notable for only one thing. Playing it with Claude on an occasion a year ago, the king wmarmed up by hitting a few pitch shots onto a tennis court and then by driving a dozen or so balls off a cliff toward the Rock of Gibraltar. Another course is in the Tyrolean-type village of Ifrane, an hour or so by car from Fez. It isn't much—"A hotel par-3 that hasn't been mowed in a week" pretty well describes it—and the king plays it only rarely. Then there's Royal Guard in Rabat and Inezgane in Agadir, both nine-hole layouts.

So much for the courses that the public sees. There are others that only His Majesty and those who loiter with royalty can see and play. These are courses Hassan has had built inside the walls of his various palaces. There are nine holes, fully lighted, within the main palace in Rabat. There are 18 holes behind the walls of the summer palace on the Atlantic in Skhirat. There are nine holes inside the palace grounds in the ancient town of Meknès. And nine more inside the palace at Fez. All of which add up to 45 more than most of us have for working out our duck hooks in private.

But before anyone starts thinking that Hassan II is greedy with his golf, listen to all of the things Robert Trent Jones is doing for him—and Morocco.

Soon to be completed in Rabat, for instance, is the Royal Golf Club of Rabat, a 45-hole project complete with clubhouse and cottages. It should be ready next February. Not only has the king had Jones design a championship 18 holes—"Worthy of holding the World Cup," he ordered—but he also has had Jones build another 18 for package tours, and then finally a nine-hole course for beginners.

The complex is built on rolling terrain through cork and oak trees. One course has a multiplicity of bunkers, the other plateaued greens and an island hole. Dave Hill would love it.

As elaborate as the Rabat complex is, it only got Hassan warmed up. Rabat was for diplomats, and tourists jumping off toward other places. Places like Marrakesh. Yes, Marrakesh. That would be the city to do something really spectacular in. Jones was no more than half-finished with Rabat when His Majesty hired him again. Do me Marrakesh, he said.

So what's happening there these days is this: on 3,000 acres near the Marrakesh course I mentioned earlier, a modest little thing called the Club of the King's Friends is going out and up and around. Championship layout, of course. A bit of Dorado Beach. A bit of Sotogrande. A bit of Williamsburg. Trees. Sand. Water. And those Atlas mountains peering down on it all. Another 45 holes in all, like Rabat, but the Club of the King's Friends, the main course, is being confined within walls and encircled by a moat. A mall leads through the center to a cul-de-sac where condominiums will be built, overlooking the course. An apartment complex for members is also planned, and a polo field. Plus Alpine skiing in the Atlas most of the year, with helicopters available to take the golfer skiing in 15 minutes. (Jones was recently commissioned to start another project, this one farther south and on the coast, in Agadir. It, too, will contain 45 holes.)

For all of the work he has done, Jones has seen King Hassan only five or six times, and only then on a golf course,
walking along with him, chatting between shots. They have
never had a meal together, and the architect has never seen
him at night. This probably isn't unusual. I haven't dined that
often with kings, either.

As the guidebooks say, Fez is the "heart of Morocco," the
onetime capital, the spiritual and intellectual center of the
country. Thus, it was more than appropriate that in Fez,
which is about as ancient as a place can get and not be in
China, I finally caught up with Claude and his pupil.

One of the king's cars, bearing a driver who believed himself to be the Arab equivalent of Cale Yarborough, had trans-
ported me the 125 miles from Rabat to Fez in, like, zap.
There a two-engine plane was landing at a deserted airport.
Out of the plane stepped Claude and his personal guide-
friend-envoy for this particular trip, the Moroccan Consul
General in New York, Abdesslam Jaidi.

Jaidi spoke good English and good everything else, so the
heat was off. Jaidi's job was largely that of entertaining
Claude and seeing that he got where the king wanted him to
be each day. His job was also to bargain for Claude in the
Casbahs and try to prevent him from buying every brass tray
and Moroccan carpet in existence.

"Claude, you can't cure the economic ills of our country
singlehanded," Jaidi would say.

"Don't you understand?" Claude would reply. "I *love* your
country, Monsieur Jaidi."

Fez is cradled by hills, but it crawls up the sides of some of
them, its old fading cream structures and brown ruins ringed
by rich green beauty. For all of its age, you can do things in
Fez you wouldn't dare do or try to do in, let us say, Mexico
or Spain—like eat anything, drink the tap water and get one-
day dry cleaning. It is simply a remarkably pretty, enchanting
and friendly city with all different kinds of lofty balconies and
dark dungeons to dine and drink in and gardens to stroll in.

The Casbah or medina—or old city, as they call it—is twice
the size of any other in Morocco and twice blessed with
atmosphere. Deep in the Casbah of Fez one can wander into
a doorway, be led through damp corridors of carpet and

leather to antique jewelry room, there to be offered a chair, a glass of hot mint tea, a plate of cakes—and a pipe. Two puffs and you buy the whole store.

Frankly, despite all of Claude's stories I didn't really know what to expect from His Majesty. And when the day came that I would be invited to accompany Claude inside the palace walls at Fez and there to stroll nine holes with him—as Trent Jones had done six times—I was a little nervous.

"I hope there's some atmosphere around," I said to Claude. "I mean, it would be kind of nifty to see a king play golf around some ruins or something."

Claude said, "How does twelve hundred years old grab you?"

Inside the burnt-orange walls of the palace at Fez there was, sure enough, a nine-hole golf course. It had grass that was green. It had smooth putting surfaces with pins. Rough. Water hazards. A couple of par-5s. And all around it were these 20- to 50-foot walls, looking as though they had always been there, as if Idriss II, or somebody, had known a long time before the Scots about the rut iron.

On days when Hassan plays golf, a lot of people turn up. Mostly, they are aides and servants and simply close friends. Claude, Jaidi and I got there a few minutes ahead of His Majesty, and I got to notice a great deal of hustling about by everyone. A couple of Harley-Davidson carts were driven out, one carrying three sets of clubs, all belonging to King Hassan, the other carrying refreshments.

Several Arabs wearing fezes and djellabas neatly spread out a dozen pairs of golf shoes from which His Majesty would make a selection. They also spread out half a dozen sweaters in cellophane wrappers for the same purpose.

A number of men with briefcases stood by, obviously hoping to conduct some business between swings. Some diplomats, the Moroccan chief of world affairs and an official of the police were there, as were the head of the paratroopers and a very good Moroccan amateur. These last three would play with Hassan. Claude would walk around and give a tip now and then.

Suddenly something dawned on me.

"Listen, uh, Claude," I said. "How do we greet His

Majesty? I mean, I know I don't say, 'Hi, King! How's your mom and them?' Do I kneel or what?"

Claude said, "He's quite a fellow. A young man. Tough. Well educated. Speaks a lot of languages."

"So what do I do?"

Claude said, "He's a king, you know. No mistake about who the *king* is."

"Yeh, I know," I said. "So?"

"You're an American," Claude said.

"Yeah, right."

"Well, you just walk up to him and stick out your hand and say, 'How do you do,' and look him right in the eye."

"Oh, good," I said. "Then I don't have to bow and kiss his hand like I would Hogan."

I don't know whether I expected the palace gates to open so King Hassan could gallop in on an Arabian stallion with a hundred Bedouin warriors, or what. But I do know that I didn't expect him to arrive driving the lead car in a motor-cade himself, and for that car to be a Chevrolet station wagon.

"He loves cars," Claude whispered. "He'll turn up in a Maserati tomorrow and a Volkswagen the next day. He's probably trying this one out. Probably thinking about buying a fleet of them."

Everybody lined up to greet the king, including all of the people in all of the limousines behind him. The custom is that the king sticks out his right hand and a Moroccan gets to kiss the back of it. If the king holds him in favor, he also gets to kiss the palm. Very close friends and family get a back, a palm and a cheek. This went on for a while and then Claude shook hands and forthwith presented his writer pal.

Following Claude's advice, I self-assuredly stepped forward, took King Hassan's hand, looked him straight in the forehead and said, "Good Majes, your morningsty. Real pleasure. Fine. Sure is."

He was a bit tiny for a king, I thought. About five-six. He was swarthy and had black sideburns stealing down in mod fashion from thinning hair on top that he combed straight across. He was pretty mod, all around, in fact. He wore a pair of tight, pocketless flairs and buckled loafers, and he had gotten out of the car in dark granny glasses. I decided that he could pass easily in Beverly Hills for the script supervisor on a hit TV series.

He moved around briskly, choosing his shoes and sweater. But he didn't put them on. Somebody else did that for him. And the singular job of one valet was to hold an odd-looking instrument that resembled a large pair of tweezers. It was a cigarette holder. The king smoked a lot and rather than drop his cigarette on the ground between golf shots, he just held it out and the tweezers grabbed it.

Now he had a three-wood and went to the practice area to take several vigorous swings before the game. Claude trailed quietly after him with his hands folded behind his back. Two of Morocco's best pros, who have played in several World Cups, were present, and their jobs were equally divided. One selected each club for His Majesty, and the other saw that he never got a bad lie, even in the rough.

What most of this added up to, I realized, was that when kings play golf they never have to bend over.

The king's swing would not send Bert Yancey scurrying to the practice tee. He took a wide stance with both toes point-ed outward. Wearing gloves on both hands and with his shoulders hunched up he swung aggressively with a long, flap-ping backswing and a leaning-forward follow-through. Still, he hit some good ones, favoring a medium to low hook.

"Too fast," he cried of his swing a few times.

"Hmmm," Claude said, agreeing.

Turning to me, Claude said, "You can never let a pupil think you're disappointed in him. You can never let him think he isn't improving. The secret to teaching golf to someone is to show a deep interest in his game, no matter how bad it might be, and continually offer encouragement. If I just tell him one or two little things today, he'll be happy. I'll pick my spots."

The king, now ready, had a small surprise for us. He led us all, maybe 20 people, toward a corner of the palace wall, through an entranceway, up a long, high rock stairwell to the very top of the corner wall. Perched up there, overlooking all of Fez and all of the palace grounds, was a little grassy knoll—alas, the first tee.

"We tee off," said His Majesty, "from many centuries ago."
And he smiled.

The first hole was considered a par-4, a straightaway drive,
mindful of the wall running down the left side of the fairway
with a small pond in front of the green. Although the king
played it in four with a driver and a wedge, an American
touring pro would use about a three-iron. It would be a par-3.

As we walked along on the first few holes, Claude
explained that His Majesty likes a joke or two. Indeed, I
noticed in one of his golf bags there was a pop gun.

"He'll sometimes sneak up behind somebody who's getting
ready to tee off and shoot the gun between his legs, blowing
the ball off the tee just as the fellow swings," said Claude.

"Hey, that's really funny," I said.

There had also been a day when one of His Majesty's golfing companions from the court showed up in wild, multicol-
ored slacks. So the king ordered a pair of scissors, which
were promptly produced, and went about cutting off the
man's trousers above the knees.

Just before I got there, Hassan had played in Rabat with the
Apollo 12 crew—Conrad, Bean and Gordon—Claude told me.
"They didn't play too good. I told him, 'Your Majesty, they
can play the big ball in the sky but they can't play the little
ball on the ground.' He liked that."

Claude had said that although the king was never with you
in the evening, he arranged, personally, most of your entertainment. And he always knew where you had been and with
whom. Armed with this knowledge, I was not surprised
when he asked, "How was dinner last night?"

We had gone to the home of a wealthy businessman of Fez
named Mernissi. Whiskey and ice were displayed on a center
table in the living room, a help-yourself favor to the thirsty
Americans. Few Moroccans drink. Scads of servants moved
about, passing snacks and placing incense burners on the
floor. A Berber orchestra showed up and there was occasional dancing and singing. Scotch, incense and music do not
necessarily make an American hungry, but Claude had
warned the feast would be spectacular.

And here it came.

A tureen of soup first, with lamb and lentils and lemon.

Then shish kebab. Then a smoking platter of lamb knuckles with artichoke stalks and lemon. Then a huge bowl of meatballs with lightly fried eggs on top, floating on a mixture of paprika or chili pepper. Tex-Mex-Moroc, I thought. Next came an equally large serving of whole chickens highly seasoned and swimming in juices. This was followed by an entire barbecued lamb. Then came the *couscous*, served on this occasion as a dessert with powdered sugar. Finally, there was fruit and hot mint tea.

We dined Moroccan style, which means that one eats only with the thumb and first two fingers of the right hand. Just reach in and rip it out.

For a napkin there is only your very own huge loaf of crusty bread. You wipe your hand on it, or tear off chunks and dip it in the bowls and platters. Moroccans know where the best pieces of barbecued lamb and seasoned chicken are. My hand followed theirs, to the point, in fact, that one or two of them began to pull off delicate, lean slivers of meat and offer them to me. "Fine. Sure is," I said.

To say the least, it was the best meal I've ever had.

And so when Hassan asked how our dinner was last night, I couldn't resist preempting Claude.

"It was marvelous," I said. "And what I think I'll do is cut off my right hand and open a restaurant in New York."

His Majesty laughed and repeated the remark to some aides.

"He likes a joke," I told Claude.

Along about here, the king's golf suffered a bit. From the 5th or 6th tee he hooked a high one over the palace wall and onto the Boulevard des Saadiens.

"Golf go away, Monsieur Har-moan," he said to Claude.

"Golf will come back," Harmon smiled.

Whereupon the king hooked another high one over the wall.

"Very bad," he said.

"Golf comes and goes," said Claude.

Whereupon the king hooked still a third drive over the wall.

"Golf is gone," he said, shaking his head.

"Golf will come back," said Claude.

"When?" I said to Claude.

King Hassan finished out the nine holes in something like 43. He hit a few more bad shots, but he also hit some good ones, including a fine three-wood to the last green, where he picked up his fifth par of the round.

He went then to the practice tee, chatted with his friends for a moment, signed a few documents, read through some papers an aide handed him and then began soaring several practice shots off into the distance.

They were remarkably straight.

The king looked up and smiled.

"Golf come back," he said.

As we were driven back to our hotel in Fez, we passed along the Boulevard des Saadiens. Through the car window I saw an Arab in a djellaba sitting cross-legged on the grass looking at an object in his hand.

It was most likely a golf ball that had "King Hassan II" engraved on it. But the Arab would not know what it was, I figured. And he would never understand what it might mean to his country.

Love That Golf

B Y   R I C K   R E I L L Y

RICK REILLY SUFFERED A TOUCH OF *GOLF-KICHIGAI*—GOLF CRAZINESS—WHILE EXPLORING JAPAN'S NATIONAL OBSESSION WITH THE GAME. HE ALSO VISITED AN OXYGEN BAR, TRIED TO SALT HIS OMELET WITH A CIGARETTE LIGHTER AND ATE A BLOWFISH.

"No wonder we lost the war," the Japanese man said as I wore out the dimples on my ball with a 290-yard drive on the 18th hole....

Wait. Wait. Let's start at the beginning. What is this about you trying to salt your omelet with the cigarette lighter?

You don't want to hear about the drive?

The omelet.

Well, yes, that's true. I did try to salt my omelet with the cigarette lighter. But that was only because I had taken too much oxygen.

Hold on. Where was this?

This was at Koganei in Tokyo, the most expensive country club in the world. It takes about $2.5 million to join and even that might not do it; two years ago, a businessman reportedly made an offer of $3.57 million to join and was given the big raspberry. I mean, a divot at this place might go for $63. And not only do you have to cough up the 2.5 mil, but also there are the yearly dues. Of course, tees are free.

So you were having breakfast at Koganei....

Right. I'm having breakfast at Koganei, having talked my way into a big match on the Fourth of July in the most elite country club in the new money center of the universe, Tokyo. And I'm sort of on a mission. I mean, the Japanese are beating the microchip out of us these days, right? Did you know that nearly all the fax-machine makers in the world are Japanese? Did you know six of the 10 richest men in the world are Japanese and only one is American?

But I don't mind that so much, and I don't mind their buying so many great American golf courses, such as Riviera and La Costa. But when I heard a rumor that the Japanese had made an offer to buy Pebble Beach lock, stock and bunker, that really fried my sand wedge. I mean, can you imagine Pebble Beach for sale? That's like selling Mount Rushmore.

Or London Bridge.

Exactly. So I just wanted to go over there and see why the Japanese were so gaga over golf and also see if I couldn't win back just a little bit of face for America, you know? Just win back a small speck of dignity in my own little way.

So you set up this match.

Exactly. U.S. versus Japan. A 1,000-yen Nassau to the death. Loser eats flag and leaves town. I would play this six handicapper at Koganei, owner of a textile factory. As you know, I'm an 11, and....

Twelve.

O.K., a 12. He agreed to give me six strokes. So I had nine days in Japan to prepare for the match. I decided to learn all I could about Japanese golf—play like a Japanese golfer would play, eat what a Japanese golfer would eat, the whole ball of wax. I set out on a course of defeating my opponent by *becoming* him.

Very Oriental thinking.

Besides, I hit the ball the way they read.

How's that?

Right to left.

Yes. And you began this face-saving mission over an omelet?

No, at the oxygen bar.

Come again?

The oxygen bar. First, what you have to understand is that there is a word in Japan for "golf crazy": *golf-kichigai*. Golf has swallowed Japan whole. People will do almost anything, and pay almost anything, if it has anything to do with golf.

For instance, weekend greens fees at clubs near Tokyo are between $150 and $300. To play Koganei as a guest on a weekend will cost you $250, including lunch. Balls are sold one at a time, at about $8 each. Getting a tee time at even the ugliest course requires a telephone call one to three months ahead. Just to hit a bucket of balls at a driving range requires a reservation.

This is a country smaller than California, with a population half that of the United States, and Japan had only about 1,500 golf courses as of December '87. The U.S. had 12,500. Now the Japanese are building courses anyplace you can fit two phone booths. They think nothing of lopping off parts of mountains to build a course.

It's a mania, I tell you. Lawsuits have even been filed involving guys bonking people in the eye while practicing their golf swings on train platforms with their umbrellas.

One day, I played a public course called Akabane in northern Tokyo. The last guy to take a mower to this place must have been General MacArthur. It was as bad as any course in the U.S., yet it cost $100 to play on Saturdays. Doesn't matter. The golfers started lining up at two in the morning. The first foursome went off at 4:30 a.m., with 150 golfers waiting behind them. You don't know what it's like to have 150 Japanese watching you hit on the 1st tee.

What was it like?

I was shaking. But I managed to steer a two-iron into the fairway only after the caddie wrestled a seven-iron out of my hands.

Understandable.

In Tokyo there's even a brothel called Hole-In-One, with a putting green in the lobby. Can't you see some guy wandering in there? "Is there anybody here who can help me with my grip?"

So get to the oxygen bars already.

Right. I started at the oxygen bar because they're all the rage now in Tokyo. Some Japanese believe breathing pure oxygen improves your golf, though I never quite found out how. Apparently they think the rush of oxygen clears your head and lets you visualize the shot more clearly and hit it more smoothly, your muscles pulsing as they are with rich, right-off-the-shelf oxygen.

You walk in—most of the bars are in department stores and spas—pony up 100 yen (about 72 cents) and tell the bartender what your pleasure is: mint, coffee, orange or lemon. She flips a switch and turns over an egg timer, and you stick your face in an oxygen mask and suck for three minutes.

People sniff two or three rounds and then maybe buy a take-home can for later. The cans come in two sizes—5,000 and 10,000 milliliters—and run from $5 to $18. The girl at the oxygen bar in the Takashimaya department store says some customers come in once a week and take home a case.

I guess that's what's known as oxygen debt.

Right. So I ordered coffee, but the only thing I felt was woozy—and I had the overwhelming sense that I'd woken up in Juan Valdez's living room. Still, I bought a can to take with me for Koganei.

How in the world did this catch on?

There is a Japanese proverb: "The protruding nail gets hammered." Conform, or bring shame to yourself and your group. So if one person is sucking air, everybody wants to suck air. If your neighbor is bowling—as everybody in Japan was 10 years ago—then you bowl. And when they stop bowling, you stop. Which explains the giant bowling pins on roofs of warehouses all over Tokyo today.

So what makes you think golf will stick?

What could be better? You not only get out of standing-room-only Tokyo—where you now must be able to prove you have a place to park before you can buy a car—but also get to be in the group at the same time. To be alone and together.

And forget weekend golf. Golf is such a national jones in Japan now, that going to the driving range has become a hobby in itself. Of course, most of the ranges are on top of buildings, surrounded by nets. There's no land for golf. You can't buy three square meters in the Ginza for $1 million these days.

But the best and biggest range is freestanding—Shiba Golf, the world's largest practice range. When you first walk into Shiba Golf in downtown Tokyo, you notice that it's hailing. Or are those golf balls? One hundred and fifty-five golfers, stacked on three stories, turn the sky white. They hit their shots onto a 280-yard rubber-matted landing area, surrounded by nets 100 feet high.

This place is Japan at its finest. The balls roll downhill into a trough, which is banked so that the balls then roll outwardly to gutters on either side of the range. The gutters have conveyer belts that take the 500,000 Shiba balls to the basement to be cleaned and dried; then they are sent to two men who sit, day and night, pulling out the scuffed and damaged balls. Next the balls are whooshed up three floors by a pneumatic system and channeled into the reservoirs at each of the hitting stations, where the customer simply pushes a button and the clean, dried, cut-free balls come tumbling out.

Of course, unless you've arranged a tee time at the range in advance, you won't be pushing any buttons for an hour and a half or two hours. That's the usual wait, without a reservation, for a first-floor spot. No problem. Shiba Golf also has a swimming pool, bowling lanes, TV lounge, three restaurants, beer garden, massage, sauna, pro shop and golf-travel bureau with a giant board telling you where you might be able to get a weekend tee time within the next two months. Right now, that's nowhere.

So when do they play?

A lot of Japanese don't. There's a story about a PGA Tour player who, while visiting one of these driving ranges, comes upon a golfer with a beautiful, fluid swing.

"What do you shoot?" the pro asks the guy.

"I don't know," he says.

"Excuse me?" the pro says.

"I've never played on a golf course," the guy says.

Whether your wallet is full of dollars or yen, golf in Japan is expensive. Only 15% of the people who practice the game ever play on a real course, according to the *Sunday Times* of London.

♦ ♦ ♦

"We could have four floors and fill it up easily," says the Shiba manager, Atsushi Mitobe. Range practicing has become so popular in Japan that people carry "rangebags," minibags that hold only three clubs. You drape it over your shoulder on the way to work and then swing at Shiba by night.

The Seibu Big Box practice range—on the fifth floor of a sports and shopping complex—has an indoor sand trap, encased by glass and net on all sides. This is real sand and real golf balls. You have not lived until you've skulled a sand shot you were sure was heading for ladies' lingerie.

I'll risk it.

The Japanese are also perfecting simulated golf, in which you pick your course—they will allow you to play Pebble Beach, Augusta, St. Andrews—grab your clubs and crank it. You hit a regular golf ball into a huge canvas that has the picture of the hole you're playing projected on it.

Three cameras record how fast the ball comes off the club, with what spin, and at what trajectory. Then the canvas shows the view from what the computer says is your next shot. For instance, if you chunk one way to the right, the next thing you see on the screen might be a bunch of trees. When you hit the green, the computer tells you to putt from one of 26 different spots on the artificial putting green in front of you.

I understand you shot 133 on this course.

Yes, well, that was only because at the 14th, the computer was convinced I was hitting the ball out of bounds. I hit 17 shots of every direction and size, and it refused to call any of them in bounds. Finally, I picked up a ball and threw it into the canvas, and the computer let me play on. I made a 38 on that hole.

I see. Now, about those salted fish chips.

Yes, I was getting to them. As I've said, in my determination to defeat my Japanese opponent, I thought Japanese, practiced Japanese, and even ate the way Japanese golfers eat. At Fuji Lakes Country Club, surely one of the most beautiful places in the world, sitting as it does on the toenail of Mount Fuji, I came off the course and was served the standard post-golf snack: dried, salted fish and green beans. That and an ice-cold beer. You know, it just doesn't get any better than that.

At Kawana, Japan's gorgeous version of Pebble Beach, only without the seals, I had the traditional "golfer's breakfast" in my room: rice, raw egg, seaweed, soybean soup, dried fish, Japanese pickles and green tea.

Seize the day.

I even ate blowfish, a sushi delicacy that kills about 100 diners a year in Japan. I didn't eat at Steak of Steaks Holytan, however, where a steak costs $175.

You ate the blowfish but not the steak?

I figured the odds of the steak killing me were worse. I also learned how to drink beer at the 28th hole (the Japanese always try to play 27 holes): Your opponent pours your beer, and you pour his, even for fill-ups. To do otherwise would be like opening his shirt pocket and sneezing in it.

Please.

Another thing. The Japanese don't flip a tee before the round to see who hits first. Instead, they draw one of four metal sticks out of a metal canister. The man whose stick has one notch in it hits first. Two notches, second, and so on. Thus, the expression, "He swings a big stick."

You made that up.

I did. However, I am not making this up: Nobody in Japan wants to make a hole in one.

Come again?

It's true. The last thing you want to do is make a hole in one. I was curious why every time somebody would hit it close to the hole in Japan, but not *in* the hole, the players would holler, "Lucky!"

It turns out that in Japan the hole-in-one maker must pop for: 1) drinks for everybody in the club; 2) nice gifts for his best friends, usually silver pens with the feat engraved on them; 3) towels or the like, with the details of the feat embroidered on them for his B list of friends, about 100 of them; 4) a special tip for the caddie; 5) a tree to be donated to the course; and 6) a huge party within the month for all his friends, the witnesses and anybody else who knows about it. All of that can cost $5,000 and up.

Better luck next time.

Right. Also, for any bag that is overweight, the course charges extra. There's also an extra charge for playing on a

rainy day. Not that you have a choice. There are no rain
checks in Japan. We played at Kawana when it was raining
miserably, yet the course was packed. "Only two groups have
canceled today," the gleeful course manager told us.

In English?

Well, O.K., not in English. But what *is* weird is the English the Japanese use while playing golf. "Nishot!" they say a
lot. They give it a contortionist's twist of the body and
scream out, "Bunkahh!' They seem to love saying that.
There's also "nisapproach" and "nistouch" and "bardie!" It's
like somebody sent them the back of a cereal box with those
golf expressions on it and everybody in Japan knows them.

I asked nearly every person I met on courses in Japan to
tell me his favorite golf joke and nobody could tell me
one. I guess they are so fascinated with the game that they
have not yet gotten around to making fun of their fascina-
tion, as we do. Finally, one man said, "What do you mean,
'jokes'?"

"You know, jokes," I said. "Jokes about golf. Like the one
about the guy who comes home and says to his wife, 'Boy,
what a tough day on the course today.' And his wife says,
'Really? What happened?' And the guy says, 'Well, Charlie
dropped dead of a heart attack on the 3rd hole.' And his wife
says, 'Oh, no, that's terrible!' And the guy says, 'You're
telling me. All day long it was hit the ball, drag Charlie, hit
the ball, drag Charlie.'"

The Japanese man did not laugh.

"Do you get it?" I said.

"I do not think that you showed much respect for this
Charlie," said the man. "Nor for his wife."

*This is what you are adding to the Japanese golf culture? Sick
jokes?*

Darn right! These guys need a laugh or two. Do you know
how long it takes to play golf in Japan? All day and half the
night is how long it takes.

The typical Sunday golf game for the average Japanese
golfer goes like this: The night before, you ship your clubs
off to the course, via a courier that specializes in transporting
clubs, saving you the trouble of carrying them the next
morning when you catch the six o'clock train, which will

take you to your 9 a.m. tee time at a course far from Tokyo.
Courses anywhere near Tokyo are much too costly.

You get to the course and tee off. But since the courses are
so crowded, the wait is often 10 minutes between shots. You
play nine holes in about three hours. Now you have lunch,
drink beer and sake, soak in a Japanese bath and generally
just waste time until your back-nine tee time.

Back-nine tee time?

Because so many people want to play golf in Japan, clubs
send foursomes off both the front and the back nines all day.
After you play one nine, you have to be squeezed into the
other nine. O.K., so you play the other three-hour nine, get
back in the bath, have a few beers and catch the train home.

One reason golf is so slow in Japan is that most of the
players practice on the rooftop driving ranges. The most
their shots travel is 20 yards before they hit the net. That's
why the Japanese lose so many balls when they play on a
course.

It's also slow because many Japanese are just plain rotten at
it. "We don't play enough," is how Japanese course designer
Takeaki Kaneda explains it. "The Japanese have no time. They
work so hard. Most people's club is an hour to two hours
from work. Jack Nicklaus grew up five minutes from Scioto."

Another thing is that a lot of Japanese golfers don't want to
be golfers in the first place. It is only *otsukiai*—"socializing for
business"—that has them out there. For a Japanese businessman, the golf course has become more workplace than playing field, and his handicap more a résumé line than a hobby.

A decade ago, a businessman might have taken his client to
a fine dinner in the Ginza and a few hours in Shinjuku titter-
ing at a hostess bar; now he might take a client to a round of
golf. Even if you hate golf, it would be committing career
hara-kiri not to play if asked.

"If you're a businessman and you don't play golf, you're
out of the promotion scene," says Toshio Aritake, an editor
for McGraw-Hill in Tokyo.

The protruding nail gets hammered. So you play, but if you
play lousy, you shame your group and business. "The stress is
terrible," says Aritake.

Yes, I have heard about a Japanese malady—karoshi, "death from overwork." It sounds as if golf may be adding to the problem rather than solving it.

It's true. Luckily, the clubs try to make golf as relaxing as possible. At one course, Murasakizuka, north of Tokyo, a boy comes out during your bath and scrubs your back for you.

Very civilized.

Better yet, Japanese courses come equipped with the best caddies in the world, almost all of whom are women. Even on the hottest days, their uniforms never change: heavy walking shoes, long pants, matching long-sleeved smock, white gloves, hard hat with an eight-inch bill, and a tablecloth draped over the hard hat and tied loosely under the chin. The full effect is like Sister Bertrille of *The Flying Nun* pulling a double loop.

Our Holy Order of Bogey.

Right. The caddie's entire face is usually in shadow, and the only thing you hear is a voice way inside there saying, "Iz O.B."

With only one caddie per foursome, it is a mystery how she gets it all done. She marks and cleans the balls—not done in the U.S.—hands out everybody's putters, takes whatever clubs they're holding, advises everybody on the putting line, handles the pin, excuses three-putts, smooths egos and traps, takes the putters back, hands out drivers for the next hole, and makes it halfway down the fairway, ordering your clubs numerically as she goes, before you're ready to hit.

For this, she makes about $19,000 a year—plus a tip from the entire foursome: a pair of socks or a box of chocolates from one of the on-course teahouses. At some clubs she gets free lodging in a caddie dormitory. For most golfers, though, the thought of a caddie dormitory is chilling.

Why?

Because you can imagine the conversations that go on in a place like that: "So the guy says to me, '235 yards, what do you think it will take?' I wanted to say, 'With your swing? Two three-woods and a seven-iron.'"

Have we exhausted your store of information about caddies?

Well, there is one more thing. The caddies are seriously high-tech. At a lot of courses, when it's foggy or you can't see the hole, a caddie will whip out her walkie-talkie and check with the caddie ahead to see if it's clear to hit.

At the GMG course, west of Tokyo, the bags travel by an elaborate monorail system operated by the caddies by remote control. The four bags are loaded on a little tram—sort of a par-72 Futureland—and the caddie "walks" it along with the foursome up the side of the fairway, stopping it when she needs clubs and sending it whirring off when she doesn't. It's sort of like playing C-3PO's home course.

Japan may also be the only place on earth with escalators on the golf courses. Instead of making the players actually *walk* up hills, on many courses there are "skylators," rubberized moving sidewalks that whisk the player up the hill to the next tee.

So the players won't have to wait in order to begin waiting for their next shots.

And when you're done playing, you don't just scrape your shoes on the mat a couple of times and walk inside. You blow your shoes spotless with a high-pressure air hose.

Pardon me. This is all fine and good, but how does cleaning your shoes with a high-pressure air hose relate to your Nassau-to-the-death match on the Fourth of July at Koganei?

It's just in that I wanted to familiarize myself with the way of the Japanese golfer before I played my match on the Fourth of July, for undying respect and home-country glory.

Is that when you tried to ignite your omelet?

Yes, more or less. See, before the round I inhaled the whole can of oxygen. Then we went to have breakfast before the round. So we were having breakfast, and you must understand that things are not always as they seem at Koganei. For instance, Koganei, the most expensive course in the world, looks like a really nice muni. What makes the price so high is the prospect of the club's selling out to real estate developers. Each member would stand to make $4.4 million.

So...

So ... the same goes for the table condiments. They are not all what they seem. I was looking for the salt and at first tried the little silver dish, but that was red pepper. Then I tried the gold thimble with the holes in the top, but that held toothpicks. I'm a little lightheaded from the oxygen, remember.

Certainly.

I thought I had solved it with the burnished-silver object. I held it over my omelet and tried to turn what I thought was a crank, as in, "Fresh ground pepper, sir?"

And when did you realize no salt was forthcoming?

When I saw the horror on my host's face, matched only by the ashen face of my interpreter. "No, this is not America," said my interpreter, snatching it from my hands and lighting it.

Thus you were set at a decided disadvantage to your opponent.

I was. Even though he pretended to stare out the window, he knew the humiliation I felt. So he goes out and beats me on the front side 2 up.

Of course. And did the nine-hole lunch and bath affect your timing on the back nine?

Horribly. For one thing, it is a bit disconcerting at a Japanese bath to have a *woman* handing you a towel as you get out. So, naturally, I hit my first shot out of bounds on the 10th tee. By the 13th tee, I was three holes down on the back-nine bet alone.

Deep shame was yours.

Yes, but then I thought of the adage: "Even a thousand-mile journey begins with a single step."

In that you took strength?

I did. I won the next three holes by parring two of them while he made three straight 6s.

Even monkeys fall from trees.

True. But we split the next two holes, and so it was that we came to the par-5 18th hole all tied. And, as I said, I stepped up and absolutely hit a two-cheeker of a drive that went 290 yards and caused one man in our group to say, "No wonder they won the war."

We heard that.

Meanwhile, my Japanese opponent had hit his ball out of bounds. He was lying three, 50 yards behind where I was lying *one*. A win on the back nine was most certainly mine. I could gain a split on the man's home course, which, naturally, I would take back to America as a glorious victory.

You were gladdened.

Yes. Unfortunately, I had forgotten the Japanese proverb: "Darkness lies one inch ahead." In my excitement to save

American face, I tried to reach the green in two and make an eagle.

Very symbolic.

Instead, I topped my three-wood sideways into a trap, hit a tree coming out, bombed my approach 30 yards over the green, hit a bad chip and two-putted for a 7. During all this, he had recovered nicely and made a 15-foot putt for a 6 and a one-hole victory.

You choked worse than Heimlich.

This is true. But afterward, I got to thinking about the world as a global village. I remembered how George Bush wants to share our defense secrets with Japan. And I recalled seeing news of a joint microchip venture between Hitachi and Texas Instruments. And I thought about what a good time I'd had among the friendly and generous people of Japan. Suddenly, I felt proud just to have participated.

In other words, he bought the beers.

Exactly.

THEY ALSO SERVE

❖❖❖

'Man, I'm Dropping Your Bag Right Here.'

BY GEORGE PLIMPTON

PROFESSIONAL CADDIES ARE AN INTRIGUING BUNCH. THEY POSSESS THEIR OWN LANGUAGE, CODE OF HONOR AND FAVORITES AMONG THE PLAYERS THEY WORK FOR. WHAT'S MORE, AS GEORGE PLIMPTON DISCOVERED, THEY PROBABLY KNOW MORE THAN ANYONE ABOUT THE GAME'S EXCRUCIATING PSYCHOLOGY.

Just about the liveliest place to listen to golf conversation, though of a slightly different nature from what you hear in the clubhouse, is along the rail fence or out back by the shed where the touring caddies perch between the big golf bags they tend. Their rialto is here, and they rock back and forth and compare notes and swap yarns and gossip and talk of their rounds, and particularly about money and how their pros let them down: "Oh my, we're doin' jes' fine and then my man he goes an' *dies* on me," etc., etc.

There are about 40 professional caddies—touring caddies, they are called—some of whom, the fortunate ones, stay with one golfer throughout the winter tour (the PGA does not allow the touring caddie system during the summer months when the high schools are out; at that time a caddie must stick to a home course), while the others, less fortunate, travel uncommitted and hope to pick up a bag, or "pack a bag," as the phrase goes, when they turn up on the eve of a tournament.

The touring caddies are a wildly individual clan, not at all to be confused with the local caddies. They are a nomadic group—some of the more disapproving professionals refer to them as "the traveling brewery"—that moves from tournament to tournament, usually four or five to a car, and suddenly appears around the caddie shacks with the abruptness and aplomb of extremely competent men sent to do an expert job. The local caddies stare at them with as much awe as they work up for the professional golfers. Johnny Pott once told me: "I can't imagine what it's like to travel with the touring caddies. I remember once a car with six of them in it, going cross-country, came through my home town, and they stopped by to pick up a club I had promised one of them. Well, I opened up the trunk of their car to put in the driver and there wasn't anything in there at all—no suitcases, kits, anything. Real gypsies. They travel in just their shoes."

I got to know some of these caddies by wandering down from time to time and asking questions. It was very lively listening. Most of them are Negroes, though there are exceptions, notably Arnold Palmer's caddie, Bob Blair, a loner I never saw with the others, and a caddie Jack Nicklaus often uses, Angelo Argea.

The caddies had a splendid variety of nicknames: Cut Shot, Violence, Texas Sam, the Wolfman, the Rabbit, the Baron, Cricket, the Rock, Big Ted, the Golfball ... their names peppering their conversation, as in, "Hey, Cricket, you seen the Golfball?" "No, ask Wolfman." Ted Randolph was the one called Wolfman. He was given that nickname in the Boy Scouts where, he told me, he had once done a very impressive imitation of a werewolf. I could not imagine such an imitation.

Walter Montgomery was the one they called Violence. He had had his hair straightened. He kept it flattened slick against his skull, so that the sheen of black seemed newly painted on. He was named after his short temper—a characteristic he had worked in recent years at curbing.

"What did you use to do, Violence?" I asked, relishing the odd nickname and the strangeness of it on the tongue.

"I've cooled it, baby. It don't make no sense. It don't do no help to the guys I was packing for."

"You mean you took it out on the golfers?" I asked.

"A cat'd make some crazy play like miss a putt of two foot. Now a cat like that, why he's cuttin' my money, making a bad shot, dig? So I go up and kick his bag. I really bang it."

"Well, how did they take that?"

"Like I say, it don't make no sense, 'cause it don't do no good. They start keepin' a side eye on me, like maybe I'm fixin' to lift a shoe into *them* the next time."

"What else did you do?"

Violence frowned slightly. "Oh," he said, "I slam the pin back in the cup real hard, jes' to show the guy, y'know, what I think of his messin' up the shot. Threw my cap quite a lot. Once I sailed it across the green and it hit Doug Sanders in the back of the head. But then, like I say, I cool it. I pack for Julius Boros and he like me and he say, 'Man, act like me, very calm, all the time, and you do O.K.' "

Alfred Dyer, out of New Orleans, was called the Rabbit. He was very self-assured. "You talk to the Rabbit," he said, "an' you're getting the stuff straight from No. 1. If it's caddyin' you're talking 'bout, the Rabbit's your man. Why, at those big Jewish country clubs in the East it's the Rabbit they's always calling for—'Where's the Rabbit? Where's the Rabbit?' They say, 'You think I'm takin' one step on this course less'n the Rabbit's packing my bag, you is loco in the *head*.' Why, I make $40 a day in the East jes' on my name alone. Autographs? Man, the Rabbit's always signing autographs...."

At this, there was a bit of good-natured hooting from the others down the fence. Someone shouted: "Rabbit, you can't write, man, an X, much less'n your name."

I asked: "Rabbit, what do you think you do best as a caddie?"

The Rabbit thought, and he said: "Well, calm my man down, I think that's what I do very good. Pull him off to the side when he's got a lot of pressure on him, and I tell him, let the Rabbit share it with you. Maybe I get him telling what he done the night before—jes' to get his mind off the pressure and make him relax. 'Course sometimes you got to do jes' the opposite—fire yo' man up. Now take Tom Weiskopf in the Colonial one year. We're comin' down the stretch with a jes' fine lead, but then Tom bogeys three holes in a row and he comes up on the 13th about ready to fall to pieces. He's chokin'. He's got this big ball in his throat. He says, 'Rabbit, we're going to have to play for second place. I'm playing it safe.' So the Rabbit says, 'Man, I'm dropping yo' bag right here if you don't go for the flag. You take a two-iron and put the ball up there nice an' easy. Smooth.' I can say 'smooth' like you never heard nobody say that word, like silk. Well, he done it. It wasn't my fault he got in trouble afterward and shot 80 or something" (actually 81).

Quite another sort was Dale Taylor, Billy Casper's caddie, a soft-spoken polite man in his 40s, I would guess, and with very much of a no-nonsense attitude about his profession. I had heard that he was an excellent golfer. He told me that he caddied for his man with pleasure because Casper always tended to the business at hand—their rounds together on a golf course had no other purpose.

"But don't all golfers go out on the course with that same attitude?" I asked.

"They should," Dale said. "But then you get a golfer like Ken Still who has this really great talent, this fantastic potential...." He looked around at the other caddies. "That's right, isn't it?" They all nodded. "And yet when he goes out on a golf course his mind just isn't on what's what. He's interested in sports, Ken Still is, and if there's a ball game going on somewhere, he's thinking about it. He's likely to have a transistor plugged in his ear, and sometimes he yells things like, 'Come on, belt one for ol' Ken.' "

"It don't take much to make 'em a duck," someone said.

"A what?" I asked.

"A duck."

A duck turned out to be a word they used a lot for the young professionals rather than the word "rabbit," which the golfers used. A caddie would say: "I got me a duck who *faints* on me at Napa—lies down on the course and goes to sleep with two holes to go and we got the cut made cold."

Some of the terms they used were rather arcane. One caddie referred to a golfer as a "Union Oil."

"What's that?" I asked. "A Union Oil?"

"He's like those fancy oil stocks," I was told. "He goes up and down jes' like they do—man, he's got a 69 one day, and the next he shoot up to 89. So we call him a Union Oil."

From the earliest days of golf, caddies have been the originators of golfing terms and also masters of the quip, the laconic remark that seems so often the legacy of menial jobs. I particularly like the caddie's retort to the novice golfer who slices an enormous divot out of the ground and asks, "What do I do with this?"

"Take it home," the caddie says, "an' practice on it."

Or:

Beginner, after repeated failures: "Funny game, golf."

Caddie: " 'Taint meant to be."

Traditionally, caddies have been showboat characters. For example, when Johnny Pott sank a chip shot to win the Crosby in 1968, his caddie, Raydel Scott, flung his arms up and fell down in a heap. The television cameras caught him in his prostration of pleasure, and he told me that his mother had seen him on national television, and most of the neighborhood, and he had become a celebrity.

When I spoke to him, he got to reminiscing, and he said that he thought he might *patent* his collapse and do it every time he came on the 18th with a tournament winner, or even with someone back in the pack if that golfer recorded a good shot on national television. "Just throw up my arms," Scott said, "and fall in a heap on the green."

"Scott, do you ever throw up your arms and fall in a heap on an *early* hole—if your man makes a great shot on the 3rd hole, say?"

I sensed his answer and was right: "Oh, I give a good yell," he said. "But for falling down, I save that for the finishing holes and the television. I mean it takes something out of you to fall down like that. It's a question of timing. Of course, the trouble is you got to find someone to pack a bag for who's going to do *his* side of the falling-down act. I mean, make that shot, baby. I been all set to fall down for some months now, but I ain't had no *kind* of cat to give me the opportunity. It seem like I'm fighting to make the cut every time.

"I dunno," he added mournfully. "Maybe the next time we make the cut I'm goin' to fall down in a heap jes' to keep my hand in...."

I asked them about perhaps the most famous contemporary caddie—the one the golfing public would know about from

watching TV—Arnold Palmer's Iron man, the tall, gaunt dean of
the caddies at the Masters in Augusta, the caddie everyone
remembered for his long, slow, loping walk up the last fairways
in the white coveralls, the old, thin face under the cap, and
how he sat on the bag at the edge of the green with his knees
drawn up under his chin, or stood out behind Palmer and
leaned over and spoke his notions into Palmer's ear as the two
of them inspected the lie of a putt on those huge last greens.

A chorus of disapprobation rose, particularly from Scott.

"Iron Man? What he know 'bout packing a bag? He know
know nothin', man."

"That's right. You get the Iron Man offen the Masters
course, an' he *lost*—why he stumble 'round like he gonna be *bit*
by something."

Another caddie chimed in: "He been confused since he was
2 years old—man, how you talk about Iron Man?"

"Well," I said, "what about all that advice he gives Palmer.
On the green. You see him there, leaning over, advising ... at
least he's whispering things for Palmer to hear."

"He's jes' movin' his lips. He don' know what he's sayin'."

"Why, he ain't *got* nothin' to say. He don' know golf enough
to say beans."

One of them leaned forward. "I'll tell you what he's sayin',
man. He's leanin' into Palmer's ear and he's saying, 'Jes in case
you wanna know, Mis' Palmer, it's gettin' on to 'bout four fif-
teen in the afternoon.' "

The caddies all grinned and hee-hawed.

The one caddie all of them spoke favorably of—a hero among
them, apparently—was Wayne Hagan, semiretired now, they said,
who worked out of the Riviera Country Club in Pacific Pal-
isades, Calif. They spoke of him as being the first caddie who
made a scientific art of the craft—checking the course early in
the morning for pin positions and pacing off the holes and noting landmarks on a card so that if a golfer asked what the distance was, Hagan would say, looking at his card, "Well, from
that tree it's exactly 135 yards to the center of the green." All of
this, when Hagan began, was unknown, but it is now widely
practiced, not only by the caddies, but by the golfers themselves.

"Tell me more about Hagan," I said.

"He really knew what he was doing," one of the caddies

said. The others nodded. "Big pride in his work. There was this time he was carrying for Tommy Bolt. So Bolt says, 'What do you think?' and Hagan says, 'It's a six-iron.' Bolt says, 'No, it's a five.' Hagan says, 'No, it's a six and when you hit it, just hit it firm and don't press.' Bolt says, 'You're crazy, Hagan,' and he takes a five-iron and hits it 20 yards over the green. So Bolt takes the five-iron and he breaks it over his knee. Well, Hagan, who's been holding the six-iron, *he* breaks *it* over *his* knee, and he drops Bolt's bag right there and begins striding off down the fairway. He's done with him. But Bolt comes hurrying on down after him and he's all full of apologies. He says, 'Wait for me, Hagan, ol' Tom's right sorry. You was right. Listen, I'm on the tournament committee and I'm fining myself $150 for what I done.' "

"Do caddies ever get fired?" I asked.

The caddie called the Baron spoke up and said that Bob Goalby had fired him three times on one hole.

"He says to me, 'How far is the flag?' I tell him, and he says, 'You're fired.' Well, I stand around and he comes up with a bad shot and he sees I was right and he looks around and he hires me again. But he's all riled up inside, and when he misses his next shot he bangs his club around and his eye lights on me and he fires me again. So I drop his bag. I stand around. I don't know who else he can hang the bag on. A couple of grandmothers. He don't have any big gallery. His wife maybe. She was there. Or maybe he'll pack the bag himself. He must be thinking the same thing, 'cause after a while he says, 'Hey, Baron, pick it up,' which means he's hired me again. We get up to the green and we confer on a putt and he misses it real bad—he don't *begin* to do what I tell him. So he wheels around and he fires me again in this big loud voice. That's enough for me. I drop the bag and I head for the caddie shop. His wife comes running after me. She don't want to pack the bag. She says, 'Come back, Baron, please, Bob don't mean none of that, he *needs* you.' She's a great girl. I know he don't mean no harm. Golf does things to people. So I tell her that and I go back and I pick up his bag."

"Does a caddie ever really drop a bag on a pro?" I asked.

"Who was it—Tony?—who dropped Finsterwald's bag on the 15th at Denver in the Open in '60."

They nodded.

"Yah, Arnold Palmer won that one with a little short white caddie, didn't he. You recall?"

Palmer had had some strange caddies, I was told. For a while, one caddie said, Palmer had a fellow who was a Marine Corps colonel on the lam—his wife was trying to sue him. The colonel thought he could lose himself in the traveling life of the caddies—which he imagined, I suppose, as the American equivalent of the French Foreign Legion. It worked for a while, until suddenly he was Palmer's caddie, appearing on television, and it rather went to his head. "He tried to pass himself off as a big shot," the caddie said. "Man, he had a terrific wardrobe. He was a good-looking guy. He turned up at the country-club dances in a tuxedo—man, he was more at home in a tuxedo than Palmer. I don't know what ever happened to him."

"Maybe his wife caught up with him," I said.

"Well, it was sure a funny place to hide," the caddie said. "I mean, every Sunday, if his wife got a look at her TV set, there her husband would be—standing behind Arnie."

When I asked the caddies along the fence if there were any players they were not wildly anxious to work for, there was a quick reaction.

"Oh my!"

A chorus of dismay went up.

"Frank Beard!"

"Man, Bert Yancey's got to head that list."

"Baby, I'll tell you, Bobby Nichols is sure on the list, and there don't have to be no squeezing to get him on!"

"Cupit!"

"Tommy Aaron!"

"Shut yo' mouth. Richard Crawford, he's the cake."

"I'm telling you Frank Beard! Nobody's alive like him. I mean, I don't expect a man to be careless with money, you know, but...."

It seemed most of their assessment was on a financial basis.

"You know Deane Beman?" somebody said. "When he han' the money ovah, he look at you like you done stab him in the knee!"

"How about the caddie's friends?" I asked hastily.

The mood grew respectful.

"Dan Sikes, he's sure one, I'll tell you."

"Nicklaus. You know what he did for this caddie, this guy called Pappy?"

"What was that?" I asked.

"Pappy took his earnings at this Las Vegas tournament and he got hot on the crap tables and he had a pile—$22,000—sitting in front of him. He thought his luck was never going to stop. He was going to take that entire town and stuff it in his back pocket. Well, someone run and got Nicklaus and he come on the double and there's Pappy, the big crowd around him, with this wild gleam in his eye and rolling the dice like crazy. Nicklaus says, 'O.K., hand it over, Pappy, 'fore it's gone.' He leaves Pappy $2,000 and he takes that 20 grand and invests it for him in Arnold Palmer's equipment company. I tell you that fellow Pappy's sitting pretty these days."

"My man Doug Sanders is a caddie's friend," Cricket said. There was general agreement.

"I tell you," someone said. "the caddies' best friends are the golfers who finish in the top 15. You don't pack a bag for one of those cats and you like to have troubles."

"You're talking," said Cricket. He reported he had made $2,700 in a month of Florida tournaments carrying Sanders' bag. Normally, if their golfer finishes out of the money, the caddie gets paid $100 to $150. Usually he can rely on 10% of his professional's winnings.

The caddie called Doc stirred and said that when it came to money they were all spoiled. He had been on the tour for 22 years. When he started to caddie he was lucky to get $2 for packing a professional's bag for 18 holes. Out of the first prize for tournaments in those days—maybe $3,000—why, a caddie'd be pretty lucky to clear $150. Doc's real name was Foster Eubanks. He was called Doc because he carried all his gear—his rain hat and so forth—in a doctor's satchel. He was one of the caddies with a car. Five other caddies drove with him—spelling each other at the wheel. He shook his head thinking of their conduct. "They don't know what a dollar is. The gambling! Those boys from Dallas, I tell you, they'll bet you a hoss fell out of a tree."

The caddies themselves kept track of each other's fortunes. "You can tell if a caddie's doing O.K. on the tour by his shoes," one of them told me. "If he ain't wearing rubber-sole

shoes to get a grip on the hills, and he's got on his regular
shoes with wax paper in them to keep the wet out of his
socks and slidin' under those bags—those big Haigs, they'll
weigh over 100 pounds—and he's wearing a quarter in each ear
to keep out the cold on the dew patrol, well, you got a caddie
who hasn't got a deal, an' he'll be thinking real low."

One of the main topics that the traveling caddies talk about
is the "Rule." They inveigh against it at any opportunity, and
one can hear such odd legal phrases along caddies' row as,
"I'm telling you, baby, it's restraint of trade ... and besides it
ain't fair practices."

The Rule is the condition enforced by the PGA that touring
caddies cannot work the tour from June 1 to September 1
when school is out and the caddie forces are largely made up
of kids caddying for their summer jobs.

"Those kids snap up our bread," the Rabbit said. "Why in
San Francisco this one time when they play the Open there in
June, this boy from the University of Stanford packs for Bill
Casper who makes the playoff and wins it. Kid's name was Jim
Stark. Casper says, 'Stark, what's your fee for packing?' And he
says, 'Seven dollars a day. Five dollars for the playoff 'cause
that's extra.' Billy gives him $2,000."

A moan went up along the fence.

"We're treated like dogs," one of the caddies said. "We got
to park 50 miles over in the woods. The public don't understand this. We got a lot of trouble. We should have credentials
just like the touring pros. We're worth it to them. In the
seven years I been a touring caddie I can't think of a touring
pro who's lost a penalty shot 'cause of some mistake."

It was true that many of the golfers were sympathetic to the
caddies' woes. When I asked Doug Sanders about the Rule, he
was very insistent. "I wish they'd waive it," he said. "You have
to be lucky to get a good caddie in the summer. You don't
want an intern operating on you; you want a doctor. A good
caddie can help you maybe only one shot a week—but that adds
up. Try that on the money list. It makes a big difference, particularly if you're anywhere near winning a tournament. It's like
combat. You want someone you can really depend on."

But some of the golfers disapprove of the touring caddie
arrangement. Tom Nieporte, for example, told me that he

thought a team of a professional and his caddie, if they had been together for a long time, might be tempted, well, to try something. To give an extreme example, a caddie, with or without the knowledge of his pro, might edge a ball into a slightly better lie. Nieporte had never heard of this happening on the tour, but his point was that an arrangement should not be condoned that could so easily lead to such a temptation.

I asked the caddies about this, and they were scornful. "It never happen," one said. "Man'd be crazy to take a chance like that. You get caught, that's the end, baby. You ain't goin' to find any long-toed boys on the tour." When I asked, he said what he meant by "long-toed boys" was in reference to the old-time barefoot caddie who could envelop a ball with his toes and move it to a better lie.

The main attribute of the caddie, some professionals seem to feel, is to reinforce their pro's decisions, or even to dispute them, and make the golfer think hard before hitting his shot. But other golfers believe that the caddie's importance is overrated.

Claude Harmon was scornful of a caddie's advice. He said his instruction to them was always very simple: clean the clubs and the balls and show up on time and be in the right place and always be quiet. "My idea of a caddie is the one I won the Masters with. Never said one word. He won two other Masters that I know of—with Ben Hogan and Jackie Burke—and I think he won a fourth one. We compared notes and only Burke could remember him saying anything. That was on the 72nd hole, and Burke, who was looking over his putt, heard this calm voice just behind him say: 'Cruise it right in there, Mister Burke. Cruise it in.' And he did, too."

Harmon said he never could remember asking a caddie's advice. He said: "How can a boy know what you spend your life learning? For instance, how's a caddie going to judge your adrenaline supply? Think of Trevino in the '68 Open. He comes down the stretch just about ready to take the whole thing and he asks his caddie to club him and the guy suggests a five-iron. Trevino's all hopped up, crazy strong, and he knows it, so he grabs himself an eight-iron and hits the flag with it. Well, imagine where a five-iron would have taken him. Right out of the whole caboodle, that's where."

Players sometimes have doubts about caddies, but caddies

rarely have doubts about themselves. This is especially true in England, where the caddie ranks with the cook and butler as a personage not to offend. Bobby Cruickshank told me that on his first practice round at Muirfield in 1929 he had a 75-year-old caddie, Willie Black. Cruickshank hit a good drive on the 1st hole. "Willie," he said, "give me the two-iron." "Look here, sir," Willie said, "*I'll* give you the club, *you* play the bloody shot." And I've always liked the story about the caddie at St. Andrews who interrupted his "boss" (which was the current term) at the top of his backswing and shouted, "Stop! We've changed our mind. We'll play the shot with an iron!"

What a tradition caddies come from. They don't know it, sitting down there on the fence wondering what they'll get at the next tournament, probably a duck for sure, but their heritage goes way back to the game's beginnings. I suppose the first of their number who achieved prominence was Scotland's William Gunn of the early 19th century. Caddie Willie, he was called—an odd and famous character referred to in the chronicles of the time as "peculiar but harmless." His habit was never to refer to those he caddied for by name, but rather by profession. Mr. Brand, for example, his landlord and an amateur gardener, he called "the man of the cabbage," as in "You'll be needin' a cleek, sure as not, man of the cabbage, to reach the green."

He wore his entire wardrobe on his back, one suit above the other—four or five of them at a time, including their vests. An old worn fur coat was outermost. He wore three bonnetlike hats, each sewed within the other. Had he been driving from one tournament to another, Johnny Pott would have found nothing in the trunk of his car, that's for sure.

And there isn't a caddie down there by the rail, not one, who doesn't agree with my favorite caddie of all. He was a Frenchman—Vardon has told the story about him—who packed the golf bag of an Englishman playing the course at Pau, just north of the Basque country. The Englishman made a particularly fine approach shot, and he turned to his caddie with a wide smile for some indication of approval. "Well, good heavens! What? What?"

The caddie's English was very limited. He struggled and offered what he had often heard uttered but did not fully understand. He said, nodding happily in reply: "Beastly fluke!"

A Town's View
Of the Affair

B Y   R O Y   B L O U N T   J R .

EACH APRIL THE WORLD COMES TO AUGUSTA FOR THE MASTERS
TOURNAMENT. ROY BLOUNT JR. TOOK A PEAK BEHIND THE AZA-
LEAS AND DISCOVERED A WORLD OF TATTOOS AND HAM HOCKS,
BAPTISTS AND POOL HALLS, IN SHORT A TOWN WHOSE CITIZENS
CONSIDER THE FABLED TOURNAMENT A MIXED BLESSING.

They are well-connected, or they wouldn't have tickets. They
are easy on the eye, in crisp spring outfits of predominantly
red, white and blue. They are unresentful about being pro-
hibited from running and they are duly responsive to green
litter bags marked PLEASE PLEASE PLEASE. They constitute
what is often referred to as "one of the most orderly crowds
in the world."

They are just about nice enough, then, for the grounds: a
landscape impeccable as to greens, lush and rolling as to fairways, white as to bunkers, blue as to ponds and resplendent
as to red dogwood, white dogwood, azalea, juniper, redbud,
Nandina and holly.

The crowd sips cool drinks on the clubhouse veranda or
flows around the sward. Seeing, being seen. Emitting rich,
mellow "Ahs" for good shots and lower, softer

"Awwwwwws" for missed putts. Clapping some, too. And pulling for, say, Oosterhuis to birdie Flowering Crabapple, which is the official name of the 4th hole.

That is the general atmosphere of Augusta National Golf Club during Masters Week. Lovely. But where are hijinks? Where is mystery? Where is funk? Who picks up the cigarette butts? Where can a person go to get tattooed?

The answers to these questions lie—in some cases—beyond the soft-focus scene at the course. But not beyond Augusta, an east Georgia town of 60,000 whose main-street monument to the Confederacy says, NO NATION ROSE SO WHITE AND FAIR, NONE FELL SO PURE OF GRIME, and one of whose smaller newspapers, *The Mirror*, in a front-page headline during Masters Week last year proclaimed:

WOMAN CUTS 3, TRIES TO CUT 2 OTHERS, ATTEMPTS TO CUT NITE CLUB MANAGER, IS SHOT.

No doubt the Masters is Augusta's most illustrious feature, and it affects the lives of a great many people in town. But as one resident declares, "Somebody tried to tell me that nobody would live here if it weren't for the Masters. That's not true. There's the nitrogen plant, Fort Gordon and the Medical College of Georgia, with all those doctors and things." Furthermore, there are country music shows, live wrestling, Elizabeth Taylor's gynecologist, the John U. Strother Old Folks Home, a barbershop advertising STYLISH HAIRCUTS/FLAT TOPS, and the Woodlawn Baptist Church, whose marquee last April read on one side, TODAY LET THE MASTER MASTER YOU and on the other side, IF YOU'RE TEED OFF, PUTT IN HERE. In 1972 it read, WHEN CHRIST AROSE GOD PLACED THE MASTERS JACKET ON HIM.

Another local religious operation with a tie-in to the Masters is a one-man effort run by W.A. Ethridge. He is a short, elderly, serene-seeming man who lives in and evangelizes out of a red panel truck that has PREPARE TO MEET THY GOD, JOHN 3:16, REV. 20:15 and JESUS SAVES THE LOST written on it. Augusta is Ethridge's home base, but he gets around.

"I've been in 48 state capitals and handed out six million Gospel tracts since 1960," he said one afternoon last Masters Week after driving back and forth outside Augusta National for a while, playing Gospel music loudly on his tape deck. "I never picked up a ball. I never hit one. But you look at all this money that's put back of golf. And that's for flesh entertainment. Now, how much more for spiritual entertainment?"

Around Ethridge's neck is a small medallion that says MISSIONARY. "But still and all," he says, "any kind of clean entertainment is spiritual. Anything that precious souls get joy out of. It all fits in a pattern—long as it's clean. Precious souls see that other things need comforting as well as the deep spiritual. Everybody knows we're living in peerless times, but thanks for golf to comfort the precious souls. There's precious souls that follow golf all over the world—your mind opens when you travel."

The souls from out of town are more precious financially to some Augustans than others. The hotels and motels are booked months in advance at jacked-up prices. Many visitors rent houses, at up to $1,500 for the week, from local people who go away on vacation. Masters veterans avoid the few good restaurants in town because they know people will be lined up to get in. A flush week is had by the niteries.

It remains uncertain what will be the most popular spot for television and press people this year. For the past two or three it was a place called The Cadaver, over by the medical college (the waitresses were dressed like nurses). But since last April The Cadaver has gone out of business and become a Lum's hot-dog palace, so it doubtless has settled down considerably.

Other enterprises take a more oblique advantage of the Masters. "Southern Roofing Co., Home of Christian Metal Screens and Awnings, Welcome to Augusta Our Masters Guests," said a sign on the way into town from Bush Field (which has a sign on one pyracanthus-covered wall identifying it as THE COUNTRY CLUB AIR TERMINAL). "Welcome Masters. Ballard Flour 5 lb. 49¢," said a grocer's sign, and "Beautiful Hanging Baskets for Masters," said a florist's. The Augusta bookstores report that the Masters brings them little extra custom, but last year they prominently displayed several golf books, and also—perhaps coincidentally—*A Nobody Gives Hell to Everybody*, by Augustan Robert L. Balfour, with whom Chi Chi Rodriguez has stayed on Masters visits. In

his lively book Balfour decries a number of modern trends
and reports that in college he had a friend with an artificial
leg who would go into a restaurant and order a toasted lim-
burger sandwich. When the waitress would demur, the
friend would "throw a perfect fit and gain the attention of
everyone present. He would then reach into his inside pocket, pull out an ice pick and jam it through some old trousers
into his artificial leg. While it stuck there he would snap it,
and as it vibrated back and forth the waitress would practically pass out."

Balfour also notes, as an example to the young, that "five
years ago I knew nothing about golf cars or batteries....
Through study and research I've had 19 different articles on
golf cars or batteries published in 14 national magazines and
the editorial comment at the end of one ... reads: "The article by Robert L. Balfour has been cited by battery industry
experts as one of the finest reports on battery maintenance
ever made available to the golf car industry.'"

The Masters no doubt has a beneficial impact, direct or
indirect, on Balfour's company, which makes golf carts, but it
does not do the Star Cafe on Eighth Street, in the downtown
commercial area, any good. In the Star, "Next to Home the
Best Place to Eat," last year you could get ham hocks and
three vegetables for $1.24 or a plate of fried chicken gizzards
for 99¢ and hear some diverting conversation. But you do
not catch the Masters crowd eating at the Star.

There are some grand old gabled homes near the Star, with
elderly people rocking on their porches, but this end of
town has always been set apart from the western, uphill area,
where the golf club and a number of fine residential streets
are located. Originally this area was not even part of the
city. Known as Summerville, it was established as a rich
man's high-ground refuge from yellow fever, which prevailed
in 19th century Augusta from June to October. The fever
period was also the social season—gentry came into Summerville from as far away as Charleston to escape the vapors
given off by rotting cottonseeds, which were believed to
carry the disease.

Down on Broad Street close to the Savannah River, where
the bales of cotton were piled, is Ted's Tattoos, which has a

sign in the window that states, "Speak up for the ART OF TATTOOING, for ART it is, and can be if properly handled. TATTOOING, in its proper clean and more beautiful form is far superior to costly jewelry."

However, it appears that no one has ever thought enough of tattooing in this town during Masters Week to have one of those Masters emblems—a United States map with a little golf flagstick stuck in the approximate area of Augusta—tattooed on his chest. Eddie Peace, whose studio is near Ted's, says, "We do have people down here for the Masters come in, but they get the usual tattoos like other people would. Right now it's a peace emblem that's popular. And girls get the butterflies. In sports they get motorsickles—aw, I don't know what all. But not directly golf, no."

The tournament is no boon to the taxi business, according to a driver. The first week of every month, Masters month or not, is the peak taxi-taking period, what with the old people, their welfare checks just in, calling cabs to take them shopping, and the just-paid Fort Gordon troops being lured into town by such enticements as the "almost topless girls," which were advertised at the Motel Warrick.

For black Augusta in general—which is to say 50.3% of the population, mostly clustered around the downtown area— Masters Week is not exactly a festival. The *Night Beat* column in *The Mirror* during last year's tournament did not mention the Masters, though it was pleased to note that Archie Dell and the Dwelles, at an unspecified nightspot, "did a wonderful job.... They are always popular and always put forth their best feet—and partner, their best foot is something else."

The *Augusta News-Review*, a more sedate black paper, carried a front-page editorial last year that said in part, "Augusta wouldn't think of having all Black policemen, all Black firemen, all Black teachers, or all Black appointees to positions of responsibility. Then why all Black caddies...?

"In movies, we are used to watching the African safari where the natives carry the gun and the MASTER shoots it. In Augusta the 'native' picks up the ball and the MASTER hits it...."

Mrs. Carrie J. Mays is one of three black members of the

city council. "I wouldn't know a bad golfer from a good one," she says, but "purely because of politics" she has an option on four tickets, "which I'm real proud of. A lot of white folks would give anything for them."

One such white person is David Peet, a past vice-president of the Augusta Jaycees and head of the civic project that transformed a formerly impassable, water-moccasin-laced area down by the river into perhaps the nicest spot in Augusta—an excellent park for riverside strolling, a small, public Summerville-on-the-bottoms. Peet has been in town for just three years and therefore, he says with some impatience, is merely "on the list to get on the list" to get tickets to the tournament.

Mrs. Mays claimed only two of her tickets last year and gave those to friends, who would account for a good 20% of the nonworking black spectators observed on the course daily during the week. But she says that if Jim Dent, a black Augustan who started as an Augusta National caddie and has gone on to win some recognition and money on the tour, were ever invited to participate in the Masters, "I might drag out there to see him play."

However, Mrs. Mays doesn't want to see any special exceptions made for Dent. If that were done, she says, Tournament Director Clifford Roberts "could apologize to his friends—who would certainly be white—and say, 'Well, we allowed Jim to play because he's a local boy, we felt like we wanted to do that much for him.' That would be a dressed-up bunch of hogwash." She wants (as does Roberts, according to his public statements in recent years) a black player to be invited under the rules like everybody else.

The Masters does do something for various blacks economically. Mrs. Mays' son Willie, who works with her in the family funeral parlor, usually chauffeurs distinguished visitors around town during the week in the parlor's limousine, and a good many other blacks pick up extra money in service capacities. For instance, James Dunn, now acting principal at Tubman Junior High School, for several years worked as a waiter in the clubhouse during the tournament week. After the schools with which he had been associated were integrated he occasionally found himself serving one of his students. He says it did not get him down.

Another Masters job performed by blacks is going around puncturing trash with a 12-pronged, spring-release stick and placing it in a big green bag. Representatives of these litter pickers, boys of high school age, were interviewed glancingly, since they felt a certain pressure not to goof off, but the following exchanges did take place one afternoon last year as, in the distance, J.C. Snead was bogeying Golden Bell, which is the 12 hole:

"All the kids in town get out of school all week so they can work here, huh?"

"That's so."

"But what are you going to do now that the tournament is extended over into Monday?"

"Not going to school Monday, either. I got good grades. No point in going to school and maybe doing something to mess 'em up."

"Have you found any interesting things, picking up trash?"

"Have I found a *lot* of interesting things? Have I found a *whole lot* of 'em? I found a hundred dollars."

"Don't believe him," says a friend. "He lie more than the average liar."

"I found a pint liquor bottle," says the first.

"How does Masters Week affect you?"

"A *lot*. Whoo."

"You tired?"

"Yes, goodness. And I don't get to see my woman."

"When you do see her, though, next week, you'll have plenty of money."

"That's exactly the week I *don't* want to see her."

"How much do you make?"

"$1.70 an hour; $150 a week."

"That's pretty good."

"For working 12 hours with one 15-minute break?"

"Aren't there any white kids picking up paper?"

"Naw. They holding ropes."

"Black kids pick up paper and white kids hold ropes?"

"Naw. Some black kids hold ropes. And they would take whites to pick up paper. But I don't know how long they would hold up under the work."

Two white kids who were game to try were ROTC stu-

dents ("they picked kids with short hair to represent the
school") from Butler High. They were employed posting
scores on the board near the 8th hole, or Yellow Jasmine.
Sloping up from the tee is a hill, one of the places where the
nonworking young traditionally sun themselves under the
scrutiny of security men. The score posters were using binoc-
ulars to get a load of strange girls going by in halters. ("A lot
of girls from Ohio are here every year," a local high-schooler
observed. "Those Ohio girls are funny. They just want to listen to the way we talk.")

One of the score posters took a break to change Tommy
Aaron's number from three under to four. A cheer went up.
The poster took a bow. "Thank you, thank you. I put up
that score," he said.

"Scoreboard guys get $5 a day meal money," his friend said,
"and $10 on Monday, when we should be in school. We're
going to break the color line next year. We're going to pick
up paper."

"Why?"

"Those cats told us they were getting $2.10 an hour."

One major problem during the Masters is the influx of
automobiles. "We've got 1930 streets, and here it is 1973,"
pointed out a city policeman. The department works overtime, some men 16 hours a day for seven days, to handle the
extra traffic. Last year an officer on crutches had to be
pressed into duty for office work.

The traffic can be turned to the advantage of some, of
course. Last year there was a man selling trampolines outside
the main gate to the club. He said he had taken orders for
five in six days. He had a sign up reading TRAMP-O-LINES.
TRY IT, YOU'LL LIKE IT. But he did not have an actual trampoline assembled on the scene.

"Oughta put one up and have a broad in a bikini bouncing
on it," a man told him.

"Kids would get on it," he said.

"Kids wouldn't be all," the man said with a leer.

Next to the trampoline man's lot, right across from Gate 3,
Mrs. Dorothy Bryant was running a $400-a-week business in
her front yard. Ordinarily her home doubles as the Washington Road Beauty Salon, which is why she has a beauty-parlor

chair and a hat tree covered with wigs ("ones people've left") in her living room, and hair-style photographs tacked up on her walls. She makes only about $100 a week from beauty. During Masters Week she and her kids and her friends park cars and sell refreshments on the lawn.

"In a couple of months the grass comes back up," she says. "I'm not even interested in golf, but this year we're getting $3 a car."

A great number of people in Augusta enjoy the Masters, but it can hardly be said that any one emotion pervades the town during the tournament. On Saturday night at the height of the week last year there was a party at the Sans Souci apartment complex, which offers its singles and young marrieds a seven-hole putting green and other comforts. Outside the party, in a Volkswagen, there was a pretty blonde young woman crying.

Her husband wouldn't let her go out by herself, she said, and he worked at night and she worked during the day, and she wasn't happy being married, and she'd been drinking, and her husband had a gun, and she liked to dance, and she had to go home.

"What," she was asked as gently as possible, "does the Masters mean to you?"

She spoke in terms of traffic. "The Masters," she pondered before starting up her car to go home. She was still crying. "The Masters means 45 minutes to make an eight-minute drive."

But few local reactions are as world-weary as that. One of the white-coveralled trusties cutting weeds with a sling down by the river last year under minimal supervision—Augusta has a model work-release program—said that there was considerable interest in the tournament at the jail. "I'm looking to January," he said.

"You get out then?"

"No. *Don* January. I got him in the pool."

Down on Broad Street a thin old man was riding a big bicycle. PRAYER was written on the mudflap, there were Palm Sunday fronds on the back and the big basket contained a radio and a number of less identifiable items. HOKE was written on the side of the bike.

Hoke stopped to talk to another, somewhat less vigorous, old man standing on the sidewalk.

"I've known you a long time," Hoke said. "I've known you since you were on the police force."

The man lifted a tube to a hole in his throat and said through it, in a distant voice, "That's right."

"Keep on," Hoke said to the man. "Don't stop.

"That's right," the man said.

"That's why I come out here every day," said Hoke. "Don't stop." And he pedaled on.

A little farther down the way Hoke was asked, "Do people in town get excited about the Masters?"

"Some do," he said. "Some don't."

"Do you?"

"Oh, yes. I listen to it on the radio here," Hoke said. He nodded his head firmly. "You got to have some recreation," he went on, "or your mind'll just go ... plunk."

Care to Join Our Little Old Game?

BY EDWIN SHRAKE

"IT'S MUSIC TO A GAMBLER'S EARS, THE SOUND OF SUCKERS CRYING." SO SAYS SAM SIMMS, ONE OF 58 COLORFUL GOLF HUSTLERS EDWIN SHRAKE ENCOUNTERED WHEN HE COVERED THE PROFESSIONAL GAMBLERS INVITATIONAL IN LAS VEGAS.

Using money as the measure of size, they played the biggest golf tournament in the world in Las Vegas last week. You could take the purses from a dozen Greater Open Classics and still be barely within range of the amount of cash that 58 guys teed up for in the third Professional Gamblers Invitational at the Sahara Nevada Country Club.

The players bet each other more than $2 million during the three-day tournament. Nobody is quite sure who the winner was. A bookmaker from St. Louis came out well over $100,000 ahead, but he didn't win all his matches. The only one who did was Don Keller, who owns some drive-in cafés around Dallas. Keller is built like a monster squash and carries in his mouth a cigar that looks like an exhaust pipe. He couldn't break 90 if he had the only pencil on the course. But the way the PGI is handicapped, it is heart and luck that count, and Keller bounced his grounders onto enough greens to win the trophy—if there was one. "I think we ought to give Keller a pistol and a ski mask so he doesn't have to come all the way out here to rob people," said Jack Binion, who organized the tournament, made the matches and in his own wagers got "drown-ded," as the gamblers say.

Several of the country's king poker players were in the tournament. In fact Doyle Brunson, who won the World Series of Poker the last two years at Binion's Horseshoe Casino in downtown Las Vegas, not only inspired Jack Binion to start the PGI, but he also was one of its attractions to the other players.

Since early May, when he picked up $340,000 at the poker tournament, Brunson has lost enough money playing golf to pay the electric bill for a medium-sized nation. Nobody is supposed to have as much cash money as Doyle is said to have lost on the golf course in the last 2½ months. Brunson is a very high player who has the reputation of never flinching from a bet on the golf course or at the poker table. He has won millions at poker in games with the other king players and all challengers in Las Vegas, which is where you have to win at poker to be a king player.

But Brunson is what he calls "a bona fide golf 'dengerarate.'" He is preparing a book, which he will publish himself, with the title *How to Win $1,000,000 Playing Poker*. "I may do a sequel called *How to Lose $1,000,000 Playing Golf*," Doyle said the night before the PGI began. He was eating watermelon in the Sombrero Room at Binion's Horseshoe. The next morning he was to play Butch Holmes, a commodities broker from Houston. The match had been rated even by Jack Binion, whose decision in such matters for the PGI is supreme. Doyle thought he ought to get a stroke.

The entry fee to play in the PGI was $1,900. That was broken into three $600 Nassaus on the three days of the tournament, plus $100 for carts and greens fees. Binion thinks of the $600 Nassaus as just a way to say hello to the person you are matched with. If you're not willing to go for a lot more action than that, you will not be invited to return.

"Action don't mean the same to Doyle as it does to most people," says Pug Pearson, himself a former winner of the

261

poker world series. "I asked Doyle one day if he was going out to sweat some players, and he said, 'Naw, there wasn't enough action.' Doyle had $70,000 bet on the deal."

So when Brunson is losing at golf, there is blood in the water. Some of the sharks who came to Las Vegas for the PGI will stay and play golf with Doyle the rest of the summer. The only reason the gamblers quit playing golf in the fall in Las Vegas is that betting on football requires much time for study.

"My goodness, they go crazy over football," says Louise Brunson, Doyle's wife. Louise is a pretty woman with a quick smile. Like the wives of several other king poker players, Louise is very active in Christian work. She sends Bibles to Taiwan and cassettes of Christian testimony to folks in prison. Before they got married, Doyle promised Louise he would give up gambling. Then Doyle was operated on for a melanoma and given four months to live, at the outside. Louise was working as a pharmacist. She was five months pregnant and prayed Doyle would live long enough to see the baby. Doyle got up and started raising every bet, and the cancer went away.

"The doctors at M.D. Anderson Institute said it was a miracle," Louise says. "Everybody thought Doyle was as good as dead. One day when he came home between hospitals to make out his will, more than 200 people showed up at the house to tell Doyle goodby. But the Lord lifted Doyle out of that bed. I know the Lord has got some kind of a plan for Doyle.

"On holidays like Thanksgiving or Christmas I always cook a big, huge meal because I know Doyle will bring home a bunch of his friends who have no place to go. Last year I was in the kitchen fixing a turkey and country ham with redeye gravy, and Doyle and his friends were in the den watching the football game on TV. I heard Doyle say he had $60,000 bet on the game. Can you imagine that? All I could think of was how many hours I would have had to work in that drugstore to clear $60,000. Doyle lost the bet. His friends lost, too. They were kind of sullen at dinner. That's about the only way I can ever tell if Doyle is winning or losing."

There is no such thing as an obscure golf pro coloring his hair and changing his name and arriving in Las Vegas—or in Fort Worth, or Mobile, or other towns where the king gamblers play golf—to lift Doyle Brunson's bankroll. You check them out. Too much is at stake to let a thief in the game. A couple of weeks ago, Doyle was driving his golf cart down a fairway and reading the bets he had written on a paper place mat from a coffee shop. Doyle added up the numbers and felt an ice machine go off in his chest. It turned out he had bet $276,000 on that particular round of golf. "That is enough money to make you think about what you are doing," Doyle says. "You're not just playing for numbers on a big scoreboard. This is real money out of your pocket if you lose. I'd like to see Jack Nicklaus, sometime, with a six-foot putt that if he misses he's got to go in the clubhouse and peel off $50,000."

"We don't bar golf hustlers from our PGI tournament," Jack Binion says. "Most of the guys in our tournament *are* golf hustlers, on some scale. But I try to handicap them so if they play their regular game, they've got an even match. Guys I don't know so well, I make some phone calls. Golf handicaps have always been a swindle. Suppose you play to an eight at Olympic in Seattle. That might be a three here. Who knows? But if you know the guys, you'll know Doyle Brunson and Butch Holmes will both shoot 78 to 81 on this course, day in and day out, and they ought to be an even match."

Binion got the idea for the PGI while playing golf in Fort Worth with Doyle, Pug Pearson, Sailor Roberts and other friends who have since persuaded Jack to retire from the game for a while. Binion's last game of golf cost him $11,000. But he thought high-playing golfers around the country should learn about each other. There are guys who shoot 105 but are willing to bet $6,000 per hole if the match is fair. The rules of the PGI allow players who shoot 100 or so to tee up the ball anywhere they please, including sand traps. The 90-shooters can roll the ball around to improve a lie. The 80-shooters are supposed to play it as it is. Stamping down the line of a putt is permitted. You can tote as many clubs as you wish. Doyle Brunson carries four putters. Also, you can use grease.

Johnny Moss, the famous poker player and golf gambler who is now in his early 70s and runs the poker room at the Dunes, recalls using grease from time to time in big games with Titanic Thompson. Brunson says he first learned about grease 12 years ago from a jeweler in Arlington, Texas. Pearson says he learned about it from Doyle. Mostly they use grease in Texas and in Las Vegas. Many a sucker has seen grease used in Florida or California or New York without realizing it.

Any sort of grease will do, although Vaseline is the most popular. What you do is smear grease on the club face before a shot. The grease cuts the spin off the ball. The ball is thus inclined neither to hook nor to slice, and it flies farther. At the PGI you might hear a player wondering whether to hit a dry three-iron or a wet five-iron. Of course the use of grease is against USGA rules. "But you've got to use grease if the other guys are using it," says Dolph Arnold, who is Butch Holmes' partner in the commodities business and something of a king poker player in Houston, which is close to big league.

"Some people say the grease is psychological," says Jack Strauss, a gambler of note. "Well, the people who say that must not have tried it. Grease puts 10 to 20 extra yards on a shot. If you happen to be playing somewhere grease is not familiar, they'll look at you funny if they catch you doing it. I told some people one time I was putting on the grease to keep my clubs from rusting. It hadn't rained there in two years."

The players at the PGI were king gamblers, bookmakers, ranchers, pizza-chain owners, restaurateurs, car dealers, accountants, brokers and whatnot. They shared the love of gambling. Some were better at it than others. They all knew where their choking price was. If prodded, most of them would admit to a suspicion of superiority over the ordinary golf pro. The feeling is that the pros don't play for enough real money to be able to tell how much heart they've got.

One day last week Jack Strauss made a side bet of $600 to $100 that he would beat Red Whitehead of Dallas on at least one hole. Red can play about twice as good as Jack. "I've never paid off on that bet in my life and I've given it to better players than Red," Jack said. He then birdied the first hole, where he'd made a nine the day before, and beat Red's par.

On the opening afternoon of the PGI, Bobby Baldwin from Tulsa hit his drive at the 18th in high grass behind a tree near a fence. Whatever other bets he may have had, Baldwin was losing $9,000 to Brunson and he had pressed. In the opinion of Jack Binion, Baldwin is already a king poker player and is on his way to becoming the premier poker player. Brunson is the premier poker player right now in no-limit games. Baldwin is thin, has curly hair and wears glasses. Brunson calls him Owl.

"How come you call him Owl?" asked Amarillo Slim Preston on the 18th tee. Slim was riding around the course in a cart checking his bets. On one match Slim said he was betting a Cadillac a hole. A $9,500 Cadillac, he said. "Don't he look like an owl to you?" Brunson said. "Naw, an owl is a wise old bird," said Slim.

"I thought I was wise until I got into this can," Baldwin said.

The 18th is a par 5. Doyle was at the front edge of the green in two. Baldwin threshed his ball out from under the tree. He was now in the fairway 190 yards from the green in two. If he lost the hole, he would be out $18,000 to Brunson. The day was lemon-colored. It was 117°, a record for the date in Las Vegas. The carts of the bet sweaters were drawn up around the green, which is guarded by sand traps and water. Baldwin does not have the training to deal with that situation in golf. He pulled out a four-iron and hit the ball five feet from the pin and saved his money with a birdie putt.

"Some guys can roar like a forest fire back in their hometown," Amarillo Slim said, "but out here with real big money up, so much dog comes out in 'em that they could catch every possum in Louisiana. Those would be the guys that grew up scraping and hustling and playing for every cent they had every day."

Slim doesn't play golf. But last year at the PGI he won $5,000 in a footrace with a football player. They raced from Jack Binion's tee shot to the green. Slim also won a bet from

Leon Crump, who, Slim says, is the best good golfer in the world for money. Crump bet he could drive a golf ball over the top of the Hilton Hotel. He hit the eighth floor.

Brunson had some bad news in his match on the second day of last week's PGI that made Baldwin's birdie disappear from mind. Sam Simms from Nashville was five under par on the back nine. Simms was matched against Brunson, and the betting had been heavy.

"You might as well go back to Nashville, because that five under par of yours ain't getting you no more action here," Doyle said.

"The only time I'm out of action is when I'm out of money," Simms said. "It's music to a gambler's ears, the sound of suckers crying. Good thing this ain't 50 years ago. I know what you'd have done to me then."

"Damn right," Brunson said.

THE GAME

◆ ◆ ◆

That Old Sinking Feeling

BY DAN JENKINS

PUTTING, LIKE WAR, IS HELL. IN THE COURSE OF HIS LONG CAREER AS BOTH GOLFER AND GOLF WRITER, DAN JENKINS HAD THE CHANCE TO STUDY PUTTERS OF EVERY STYLE. IN THIS AMUSING PIECE HE REVEALS AT LAST THE 10 BASIC RULES FOR HAPPY PUTTING.

There is no question that golf would be a more fascinating and altogether more bearable game if it were stated in the rules that once the golfer reached the green he could call upon a Rumanian soccer-style placekicker to handle the rest.

The problem with putting is that it has absolutely nothing whatsoever to do with golf and hasn't for decades. Putting only came about with the invention of the smooth, cultured green, which must have been in the pre-cursing era of the game. Good greens have done nothing but give the golfer a split personality.

First, he is the violent, physical athlete who tries to slash enormous divots out of the fairways, as if he is hoping to bring in another East Texas oil field, or as Dave Marr once said, as if he's preparing Ewell Gibbons' lunch. But when on the green, the golfer becomes something else. He is a solemn,

timid, prayerful soul who wants only to peck tenderly at the
ball, to dance quaintly behind it or perhaps trot along beside it
reading a few pages of Keats, fearing that if he doesn't do any
of this, the ball will glide up, over, down, around and so far
away from the cup he will have to place an order with room
service to get it back.

For almost as many years as golfers have been trying to putt,
there have been professional golfers trying to tell golfers how
to putt. In their wisdom, they have told everybody to be
bold—"Never up, never in," some Scot once said, smoldering
in his tweeds—and they have told everybody to let the putt
"die at the hole," pointing out that a ball that rolls *past* the cup
is more than likely *not* going in, and they have told everybody
to do something in between, such as "lag." Old Laurie McLag
said that one day at Leith.

Further, the professionals have told us to use rear-shafted
putters, center-shafted putters, mallet-head putters, blade putters and putters that plink a tune at the strike of the ball—*We'll
Meet Again.* They have told us to stand with our feet close
together, with our feet spread apart, with our weight on the
left foot, with the weight balanced and sometimes to just "get
comfortable" and putt. They have told us to putt like a pendu-
lum, to putt as if a door is closing, as if a nail is being driven,
as if we see an "imaginary line," as if we have "feel." They
have told us just about everything except that you can't putt in
a coffin unless you sit up straight.

For all of this, it has been proved by the simple playing of
the game that no one—pro or sausage hitter—can putt well consistently. Jack Nicklaus will stare at a short one that missed and
claim it hit "nothing but air." Arnold Palmer will be unable to
get his knees unlocked in time for dinner. Gary Player will bar
God from South Africa for a week. Lee Trevino will say, "I
putt so bad I'm gonna eat a can of Alpo." And Jimmy Demaret
will remember that "Tommy Bolt's putter has spent more time
in the air than Lindbergh."

Fortunately, there is now hope for everyone. A spiral notebook recently was found in the hollowed-out portion of an old
sycamore tree that borders a par-5 hole on a municipal course
in Fort Worth, Texas. Also in the tree were the rusted head of
a cashed-in putter and a suicide note from the putter itself,

saying it was sorry for all of the grief it had caused the owner. The notebook has been sent to this office by the man who found it. He has asked that his name be withheld in the fear that someone will think he still plays golf.

In any case, the notebook contains 10 Basic Rules for Happy Putting, and they are now to be shared.

1. Don't attach any cork or foam rubber to the shaft of your putter unless you want it to float.

2. Always drag your cleats when walking on bent grass greens.

3. Any sidehill putt over 25 feet in length requires either whistling or humming.

4. Backhand anything four feet long or under and pretend you heard somebody say, "It's good."

5. Never squat down in tight pants.

6. Before tapping in a gimme birdie, light a cigarette, comb your hair and twirl the putter like a baton.

7. Never waste time squinting at a 3-footer that breaks to the right. Nothing will help.

8. If somebody says a putt breaks toward a mountain or an ocean, find out why you aren't there instead of on the golf course.

9. At least twice a round while marking the ball, try stumbling and falling forward.

10. There are many ways to punish a putter, such as burning, rusting and drowning, but the most torturous is to drag it along on pavement out of the door of a fast-moving vehicle.

There will be those golfers whom none of the above will help. In that event, they will be left with the time-preserved words of Ben Hogan. Hogan once was asked by a long-suffering player what he should do about his wretched putting. He had tried every stance, grip, club and attitude. But nothing was dropping. Said Hogan, "Have you considered hitting it closer to the hole?"

Choose Your Weapon

BY E . M . S W I F T

GOLF TECHNOLOGY HAS BECOME THE PROVINCE OF ROCKET SCIENCE. WITH CLUB SHAFTS GETTING LONGER AND CLUB HEADS LIGHTER, SOME WORRY THAT THE GAME WILL BECOME TOO EASY. E.M. SWIFT TAKES A LOOK AT HOW SPACE AGE EQUIPMENT IS THREATENING AN ANCIENT GAME.

You begin to get the idea that maybe golf manufacturers are out of control when you find out that they are making clubs and balls out of components used in nuclear weapons and bulletproof vests. I mean, progress is great and all, but when a sleeve of golf balls sets off the alarm at airport security, and when alloys once used in the struts of a Gemini space capsule show up in your irons, you wonder whether we're on the right track. What we are talking about here is a game.

A game whose increasingly sophisticated tools are compromising, in the opinion of many, the time-honored elements of skill, practice and judgment. Want to hit the ball far? May we suggest an aerodynamically designed graphite-headed driver from Yonex, the A.D.X. 200. The half-grapefruit-sized club head, with a sweet spot 20% larger than normal, is oversized but lightweight, and it is attached to a 45-inch graphite/boron shaft that is two inches longer than standard. Increased club length translates, by the oxymoron of simple physics, into increased club head speed; ergo, greater distance. You'll drive the ball, the company estimates, an average of 11.7% farther than usual.

Or perhaps you would prefer something in cobalt chromium, a metal so hard it is used to make artificial hips. Combined with a graphite shaft, a cobalt chromium club head will add 10 yards to your drives or your money back. The Lynx company guarantees it.

Are synthetic polymers more your style? Cobra recently came out with the Ultramid, a driver made of a high-tech thermoplastic originally developed by scientists for use in bulletproof vests.

Whichever set of clubs you prefer, you will want a golf ball that explodes off the club face. Something in lithium, perhaps, the metal of choice of nine out of 10 nuclear physicists who have designed a hydrogen bomb. Talk about getting more bang for your buck. Just don't let the Iraqis get their hands on the Ram Tour Lithium Plus.

Windy day? Want to hit it low? Forget choking down and pretending you're Lee Trevino. It's simpler to run out and buy a three-pack of Titleist's 384 Low Trajectory balatas, whose icosahedron-patterned dimples have been designed to cheat the wind, not to mention the club pro who teaches good shot making.

The fact is, for almost any difficulty in golf, there is a high-tech remedy for sale that was not on the market 10 years ago. Got the yips? Buy a long putter, the pendulumlike contraption that uses the player's sternum to anchor the top hand. This is a golf swing?

Got a slice? Perennial banana-bonkers can now whale away with abandon, knowing that metal woods used in conjunction with two-piece, Surlyn-covered balls will absolutely, positively impart less spin on impact than their old persimmons did.

The sweet spot of a golf club, once the size of a dime—the exact location of which, worn smooth, can be found on Ben Hogan's one-iron, on display in Golf House, the United States Golf Association museum in Far Hills, N.J.—is now the size of an Oreo cookie. Shots that once squirted off the toe of a six-iron now fly straight and true toward the green, thanks to the miracle of perimeter weighting. And who knows what lies ahead as golf manufacturers race to harness the powers of Kevlar and ceramics and compounds unknown?

Where will it all end? And who, pray tell, has been minding the store while the club and ball manufacturers have busied themselves with all manner of schemes—some bogus, some legitimate—to diminish the skill factors in golf, making it increasingly difficult to distinguish the great golfers from the nearly great, and the good golfers from the pretty good? Is the game becoming too easy?

"Easier, yes. Too easy? No," says Don Callahan, head pro at The Country Club, in Brookline, Mass., which was host to the 1988 U.S. Open. "The ball is livelier and the club heads more forgiving, which is making the game more fun for the average golfer. But instead of hitting a dozen good shots a round, he's probably hitting 18."

Wally Uihlein, President and CEO of Titleist, echoes those sentiments: "I talk to very few amateurs who say, 'Wally, I'm playing too good. Let's make the game harder.' I know that my handicap isn't the lowest it's ever been. Is yours?"

As a matter of fact, no. And according to the USGA, which historically has safeguarded the best interests of the game, neither is the average golfer's. The median handicap for men today is 17, the same as it was 25 years ago. So why all this fuss about equipment?

Because, at the professional level, scores are dropping every year as the game's best players take advantage of superior equipment in ways that amateurs can only fantasize about. "The better the player, the more the equipment becomes an advantage," says teaching pro Jim Flick. "It's like you and I trying to drive a race car at Indianapolis. We wouldn't know what to do with it. For the real expert, technology has made a measurable difference, particularly in the so-called scoring clubs, the driver and the wedges."

Statistically, the changes have been subtle, but the trends are uniformly in the same direction: longer shots, straighter shots, and lower scores. Between 1981 and 1989, the average score on the PGA Tour dropped almost a full stroke, from 72.06 to 71.09. The average drive crept up nearly two yards, from 259.9 to 261.8. Fairways hit off the tee—a factor attributable, most believe, to the sudden preponderance of metal drivers—have increased from 61.8% to 65.1%.

None of those numbers, individually, is especially alarming. Athletes in all other sports are improving measurably—why not in golf? And traditionalists can take comfort in the facts that the record 59 that Al Geiberger shot in 1977 has never been duplicated on the PGA Tour and that the lowest seasonal stroke average remains Sam Snead's bench mark of 69.23, set in 1950.

There are other factors besides equipment to consider when analyzing the trend toward lower scoring. Greens are more consistent, and courses are generally better conditioned than ever before. The days of Tommy Bolt marching off a golf course and saying "How do you read mud?" are pretty much a thing of the past. Yardage measurements are more precise than they were 20 years ago, and rough is not as penal.

With more money at stake, the best golfers are working harder. Swing doctors—the pros who teach the pros—are on hand at every tournament, ready to fine-tune Jack's or Payne's swing. "It looks like the Mayo Clinic on the practice tee on Wednesday afternoons," says Uihlein. "You never used to see that. The facilities have improved, equipment has improved, and individuals have improved. It's the one-plus-one-plus-one-equals-five phenomenon."

But not everyone is happy with that equation. How long will it be before some new distance-enhancing shaft or spin-inducing club head enables one-plus-one-plus-one to suddenly equal six? Golf architects are already building 600-plus-yard par 5s in an effort to keep the game's longest hitters from getting home in two. Can an 8,000-yard course be far behind? And what about the older, classic 6,500- to 6,600-yard courses, like Merion and Cypress Point, that were designed in the era of the hickory shaft?

"I think it's important to preserve the shot values of those old courses," says Deane Beman, commissioner of the PGA Tour. "There's not room at most of them to add back tees. The game should not be controlled by the manufacturers.

There are problems already out there that are threatening the integrity of the game."

The square-groove issue is one that certainly qualifies. Let us synopsize that ongoing controversy, by flatly stating that square grooves add spin to a golf ball. Spin, to a player, means control. The USGA, after testing the square versus the triangulated groove, decided that it could live with the square groove's conformation but that the most popular square-grooved club on the market, the Ping Eye2 iron, had its grooves too close together to conform to USGA standards. Thus, it declared the club illegal. The PGA Tour went the USGA one better, declaring all square-grooved clubs illegal, beginning in 1990.

Karsten Manufacturing Corporation, makers of the Ping Eye2, sued. The USGA revealed itself to be a paper tiger by settling with Karsten out of court for an undisclosed amount of money. The two sides also agreed that the Ping Eye2's would remain legal and fully sanctioned by the USGA if Karsten would make the clubs' grooves farther apart in the future.

Karsten's case against the PGA Tour is still pending, and Beman considers it a landmark piece of litigation. An out-of-court settlement is unlikely, because at issue, he feels, is whether the PGA Tour has the power to put a leash not just on square grooves but also on all developments in equipment that are at odds with the best interests of the game.

"The historical role of ruling on equipment is not ours," says Beman. "But the technology and sophistication of the manufacturers has outstripped the ability of the USGA and the R&A [the Royal and Ancient Golf Club of St. Andrews, which is golf's ruling body everywhere except in the U.S. and Mexico] to oversee the game. Litigation will continue to play a role in that."

Beman's right. "The USGA has never been staffed to keep pace with the manufacturers, and I don't see how they ever will be," says Uihlein, whose futuristic vision of golf has Blade McPhyviron walking into his local pro shop, taking a few swings in front of a high-speed camera, which then feeds that information back to Titleist's central computer in New Bedford, Mass., which immediately analyzes the data and spits back information on the ideal swing weight, shaft type, flex proportions and ball design for that golfer's individual game. The USGA, meanwhile, will in all probability still be teeing up Iron Byron, their ball-testing robot.

The USGA, essentially, governs American golf only with the consent of the governed, since it lacks the clout to dictate what club and ball manufacturers can and cannot offer on the open market. When the USGA ruled that Polara's self-correcting golf ball was illegal in 1978, Polara sued and the USGA ended up paying them nearly $1.5 million. More recently, Weight-Rite, a company that manufactures golf shoes, brought suit against the USGA for ruling that the wedge sole in Weight-Rite shoes ran afoul of USGA rules. That trial is still pending. And, of course, there was the fiasco with Ping.

What do you think would happen if the USGA suddenly reversed itself in the matter of the long putter? Or if it decided to set limits on how long a manufacturer can make the shaft of a golf club? (As it is now, the shaft must be at least 18 inches long but can be any length greater than that.) What if the USGA ruled on which materials can or cannot be used in a club's construction? Don't blow a fuse trying to figure it out. The USGA would be sued.

Why? Because the USGA does not anticipate difficulties before they arise. It only reacts after new products are on the market. The USGA's guidelines on equipment are so vague and outdated that any attempt it makes to draw the line on technological development can be interpreted as capricious. Nowhere in the Rules of Golf is there mention of approved or disapproved materials. And while golf balls must be submitted to the USGA annually for official certification (meeting, among other things, an overall maximum distance standard of 296.8 yards when struck by the USGA's Iron Byron machine), golf clubs are innocent until proved guilty. So while ol' Iron Byron, with a standard-length, steel-shafted driver and a swing speed of 109 mph, might still be smacking balls 295 yards in the year 2050, Huey Longknocker, driving leader on the PGA Tour, will be averaging 360 by using a club head made of moon rock at the end of a 55-inch plutonium shaft forged in Mizuno's space laboratory.

"Right now, we only test golf balls," says USGA's director of operations, John Matheny. "What we need—and this is coming—is another Iron Byron machine so we can get more involved in the testing of clubs."

Don't hold your breath, golf fans. USGA executive director Dave Fay admits that even with another machine, it will take a lot of time and effort to come up with a series of tests that can meaningfully compare the various materials that are being used today to manufacture golf clubs. At which point, even if it were determined that, say, a graphite head on a 45-inch titanium shaft gave a golfer an unfair competitive advantage by violating the USGA's Overall Distance Standard ... well, bring on the lawyers. Says Fay, "Sure we're concerned about litigation. But we still believe we're the people in the best position to oversee the game."

Not unless the manufacturers call off the legal eagles—an improbability, given the cutthroat competition created by a fraternity that has grown to more than 60 members, with more companies leaping into the golf market every year. "We're in America, aren't we?" says Karsten Solheim, founder and CEO of Karsten Manufacturing. "If people want to buy a Chevy or a Cadillac, they should be able to buy one. If you can build a better golf club, you should build it. When a lot of us have trouble hitting the ball 220, or even 120 yards, why should we be punished because Greg Norman can hit it 320 yards?"

That's a point well taken. Which is why it is becoming increasingly apparent that golf must begin to follow two separate paths: one professional, one amateur. "We need to have two sets of rules," says The Country Club's Callahan. "I understand that it would be pure and nice to have one set of rules for all golfers, but that's not realistic anymore. It's the same thing as major league baseball sticking with wooden bats when at almost every other level players are using aluminum. The game is played at two levels: one for fun, and one for entertainment and profit."

Most members of the golfing establishment cringe at that suggestion. "One of the game's charms is that we're playing with the same equipment on the same courses with the pros," says Solheim. "You don't want to lose that."

"If one group breaks away and forms its own set of rules, it won't stop there," cautions Pat Rielly, one of the directors of the PGA. "The PGA Tour will be playing by one set of rules, the European tour by another, the USGA by another. Pretty soon local clubs will start making up their own sets of rules. Let's all keep playing the same game."

But as things stand, golfers aren't all playing the same game today. Jim's steel club head and graphite shaft give him measurable advantages over John's persimmon club head and steel shaft. And as anyone who has watched a golf tournament firsthand can tell you, the idea that amateurs are playing the same game as the pros is as fanciful as suggesting that your local slo-pitch softball home run champ is playing the same game Jose Canseco is. The club professional isn't even playing the same game as these touring pros, a fact that is painfully apparent every year at the PGA Championship, in which club pros make up 26.6% of the field.

As for the argument that golf's popularity is based, in part, on the amateur using the same equipment as Arnie or Jack, Beman dismisses it as poppycock. "Amateurs and pros are already playing with different equipment," Beman says. "Ninety-five percent of amateurs don't use the wound balata ball, and almost all our players on the Tour do. I don't think that by placing restrictions on certain pieces of equipment we'd be hurting the popularity of the game at all."

Indeed, it is just as logical to assume that equipment restrictions would enhance the popularity of pro golf. Not only would it keep some popular old courses from becoming obsolete, it would establish a foundation for comparing the best golfers of one era with the best golfers of another. When someone breaks Jack Nicklaus's and Ray Floyd's record 271 total at the Masters, it would be nice to think he broke it because he was a better golfer over four days, not because he was playing with better equipment.

Here are four areas that Beman should look at:

• Golf clubs should have a maximum length. How long will it be before a touring pro who can control a 48- to 50-inch shaft and has a short game to match arrives on the scene, reducing 500-yard par 5s to a drive and a wedge?

• Golf balls used on the PGA Tour should be standardized in

regard to dimple depth, dimple patterns, cover material, core construction and flight characteristics. Can you imagine Andre Agassi being permitted to serve with one brand of balls and Ivan Lendl with another? Absurd.

• The long putter should be banned. Never mind that the shaft is 52 inches long—nine inches longer than the standard driver—and that it can therefore be of use away from the green, on those occasions when a golfer is allowed two club lengths of relief. The long putter is not swung with a golf stroke. The way the top hand is anchored against the sternum violates the spirit of Rule 14-3 in the Rules of Golf, which states: "... the player shall not use any artificial device or unusual equipment ... which might assist him in gripping the club [or] in making a stroke...." The sole purpose of the long putter is to help the golfer make a stroke by allowing him to "grip" the shaft against his chest, stabilizing his swing path.

• Clubs should be sanctioned on a case-by-case basis before they are permitted in PGA tournaments. They should be tested by whatever criteria can be established to insure that golf, as it is played today, will be the same in 20, 50 or 100 years. No one is suggesting that golf return to the days of the hickory shaft. But today's graphite will soon be yesterday's persimmon.

As for the amateurs, we need all the help we can get. If NASA's technology can somehow help me reach a 425-yard par-4 in two when I'm 64, then bring on the future. Just as long as golf manufacturers are careful what they put in the core of those new low-flying, distance-enhancing, sunlight-seeking, self-propelling balls with auto-reverse. It would be a shame to accidentally start a war.

S.O.S. From
The AT&T

BY   RICK   REILLY

RICK REILLY USED TO SIT IN THE PRESS TENT AT PGA TOURNA-
MENTS CHUCKLING AT THE INEPTITUDE OF SOME OF THE PEO-
PLE WHO DARED TO CALL THEMSELVES PROS. BUT AS REILLY
DISCOVERED WHEN HE TOOK HIS 15-HANDICAP GAME TO THE
1993 AT&T AT PEBBLE BEACH, IT'S NOT AS EASY AS IT LOOKS.

YOU MAKE ME SICK.

You have no idea what it's like, do you? You sportswriters
are all alike. You sit in your press tent and eat your catered
lobster bisque and look up at the scoreboard and cackle. *He's
bogeyed three holes in a row! What's he playing with, gardening
implements?* If Greg Norman isn't leading the tournament, you
file an official grievance. *Who cares? This guy will be running the
Topeka Putt-Putt inside of six months.* You howl about how any
pro could make a 7. *For chrissakes, I could do better than that!*

No. You *couldn't* do better than that. I know. I know
because that's exactly what I used to howl in the press tent
over my catered lobster bisque. But now that I'm out of the
press tent and actually *playing* on the PGA Tour regularly ...
well, now that I've played in one Tour event, last week's
AT&T Pebble Beach National Pro-Am ... I have only one

thing to say to the whole lot of you do-nothing, late-sleeping, easy-living media swine:

Can I come back now?

It is difficult to tell exactly *when* I realized that playing in the AT&T was a mistake on the order of, say, New Coke, but it was probably at some point between the sight of 1) my first shot of the tournament still rising as it sailed over the first crested waves of Carmel Bay on its way into the vast Pacific and 2) Charles Schulz, the harmless 70-year-old creator of "Peanuts," beating my butt by seven shots—gross—last Thursday.

No. I take that back. I probably knew it the day before, during a rainstorm at the putting green at Spyglass Hill, when I noticed all the other caddies holding umbrellas over their players. I hollered over to my friend and caddie, "Two-Down" O'Connor, the world's most avid golf gambler, that maybe now was a good time to start thinking about getting out the umbrella. "Good idea," yelled Two-Down, who pulled out the umbrella and held it over his head. "Gettin' kinda wet there for a while."

Like the 1970s, this all seemed like a good idea at the time. This is how it happened: Boss throws out his back. Boss already shelled out $3,500 to play in the AT&T Pro-Am. Boss has no choice but to send freeloading 15-handicap writer in his place. Writer nearly pulls groin yanking invitation from mailbox. Writer immediately regrips ball retriever, buys 11 new sweaters and steam-cleans head covers. Tournament still three months away.

If you didn't have a bad back before coming to this tournament, you might get one from hauling home the loot. For the $3,500, an amateur player gets an AT&T answering machine-phone, a Waterford crystal clock, an ugly decanter with golf tees in it, invitations to three celebrity-stuffed parties and a framed picture of his foursome, which in my case included my pro, Dennis Trixler, and Schulz and his pro, Jeff McMillen. Of course, since I paid exactly nothing for this tournament—and since it wasn't really me who was invited in the first place—I realized it wasn't fair that I get to keep all these expensive gifts. I am sending my boss the ugly decanter.

The phone was nice. It made me think it would be a smart

thing to go up to Robert Allen, the chairman of AT&T, one of the most powerful and busiest businessmen in the world, and say, "Hey, thanks for the phone." As though he'd actually packed it himself. As though he might say, *Did you like it? I wasn't sure if brown was O.K. or what. I've got the receipt if it doesn't work out.*

What I really wanted, of course, was what every Pebble Beach amateur wants: to play on Sunday. At every party and lunch and practice putting green you hear it:

"You gonna play Sunday?"

"Let's get serious and play on Sunday for once, huh?"

If you play on Sunday, it means that of the 180 teams entered, yours is one of the 25 to make the Saturday-night cut. Jack Lemmon has not made it to a Sunday for 20 straight years. At one tournament party Bill Murray, Clint Eastwood, Dan Quayle and Donald Trump went unnoticed by the poor saps who were trying to figure out the key to making Sunday. "It took me five years to learn this," one man told me. "Forget your total score. Just make 10 pars." I asked him how many Sundays he had ever played. "None."

Trixler, 35, my partner for the week, was a touring pro from San Mateo, Calif. Oh, I know, some people might want Curtis or Payne or Fred, but there are a lot of us out on the Tour like Trixler, guys who have to arm-wrestle the marshals for every birdie they get, guys who have lost their cards more often than their keys. Guys who know what a rigged game golf is. Ask yourself this: Does Michael Jordan get to shoot his free throws from eight feet? Does Kirby Puckett take his pitches from second base? Why then do golf stars get the best tee times and the "c" category players, like Trixler, get the worst? Why should a Trixler have to putt greens that look like they just hosted an Arthur Murray class?

It is such a disadvantage to be a "c" category player that this year one of the penalties the Tour will hand out for slow play is a "c" category tee time. What did guys like Trixler do to get penalized?

"Do you know how many times I've had some guy on a Toro lawnmower on my butt as the sun is going down and I'm trying to make a six-footer to make the cut?" says Trixler.

"The marshals? When Greg Norman comes through, they're wide-eyed and alert, all ready to watch *exactly* where his ball goes. But by the time I come through at six o'clock, they're snoozing, sunburned, tired. They've had nothing to eat or drink. And you say, 'You didn't happen to see where my ball went, did you?' And they say, 'Get bent.' "

Trixler is also the funniest thing in pants. When he is playing horribly, he will say, "God, I'm playing well. I'm hitting it sooooo good. I've got tickets for the doubleheader Saturday." Once he hit a perfect shot that flew the green. Later he described it to a friend this way: "I'm pumped. I flag a four-iron. I'm posing. Every shutter in the place is releasing on me. The world at my feet. Then, goodbye, gone, see ya. Does the word *alcoholism* mean anything to you?"

Great guy, Trix. Besides, I *tried* to get Fred, Curtis or Payne. They were taken.

As tough as it is for us out here on the Tour, I have to say we are treated with a modicum of human decency. Most players get courtesy cars, usually brand-new Buicks. There is a nutritious breakfast waiting for us at the driving range. And, best of all, there are hordes of fully grown men waiting to give us free things when we come out to play. The balls, clothes and clubs are free. A man from Titleist gave me two dozen balls free, someone from U.S.T. shafts offered to reshaft me, and some guy from Founders metal woods gave me a very fresh three-wood—all at absolutely no cost. I really considered pitching a tent on the range and leaving it at that. Two-Down was agog at all this.

It quickly became apparent that choosing an old pal as my caddie was perhaps not a wise move. Two-Down does not do bibs well. He had never caddied before in his life. The gambling jones is incurable in him. For instance, here's what he carried in his so-called rain-delay kit: five sets of dice, three minibottles of Scotch, a juggling book, moonwalking instructions, Sam Snead's guide to golf hustling, a bottle of Brain Pep and a miniroulette wheel. The man is a walking pigeon trap.

Before he even arrived in Monterey, he was talking about "subletting" the job, which would keep him fresh for the evening card games.

"Why not?" he said. "I'll just walk along with you, and

when you say, 'Five-iron,' I'll turn to the kid holding the bag and say, 'Five-iron.' " In our first practice round, on Tuesday, I hit a ball out-of-bounds, then hit one down the middle. Two-Down walked with me to the fairway ball. "Aren't you going to look for the first one?" I asked.

"What for?" he said, incredulously. "The guy just gave you two dozen free ones!"

Trix gave me some pointers about 1st-tee jitters before our opening round at the Pebble Beach Golf Links on Thursday. "Just think about this," he said. "In 15 minutes not one person standing here will remember how your shot went. Actually, even right now they don't really give a rat's ass. So screw 'em and have fun."

I also thought of James Garner's secret to playing televised golf tournaments. "Set up to the ball," he advises. "Squint into the sun. Take your swing. And no matter what happens, no matter how bad you've hit it, start walking right down the middle of the fairway." Unfortunately, Garner admits, there was one time when it didn't work: "The time my ball hit the camera lens."

With all this in mind, I went out Thursday and hit two over the cliff at 10. Trixler hit one over the cliff there himself. Then I hit another one over the famous cliff at 18, and Trixler hit one off the majestic cliff at 8. By the end of the day we had searched more cliffs than the heroine in *Wuthering Heights*. After one hole we were two over par as a team, which meant that we were only 44 shots behind last year's pro-am team winner.

When we finally putted out on that first hole, Schulz, the creator of Charlie Brown, actually said, "Good grief."

Still, the day was not a total loss. At one point Trixler advised Two-Down and me that we could take a ball out of play as long as it was "out of round." We both found it a fascinating phrase and decided it would be quite useful in other situations in life.

Hey, Fred, I heard you're getting a divorce.

Yeah, Bob, I am. Gladys got a little out of round.

By the end of the first day, Trixler had shot a four-over 76. Our team shot 68, six behind the leaders. I say this with all honesty and candor: Linus and Lucy could've beaten us.

We Tour players sleep fitfully if we end the day on a bogey or, in my case, six bogeys in eight holes. That is why Tour players practice after their round, often until dusk. In fact, Tour players feel the need to practice after their round even if they've shot 66. I asked Trixler why. "Mostly guilt," he said. "Most of the time it doesn't help anyway. You're just out there doing penance. You see another guy out there putting, and you don't want to get passed, so you do it yourself. If Catholicism had an official sport, it would be golf."

The truly devoted keep practicing long after the sun punches out. They say Billy Casper putted so much at home that he had to change the carpet in his house every few years. Nowadays Andrew Magee may be the Tour's best hotel/motel practicer. I asked for a few tips.

"First thing you have to do is get a room with blackout curtains," Magee said. Apparently you shut those big, thick drapes and, voila, instant golf range. "Start with full wedge shots," he said. "The window won't break. You can pretty much go through all your short irons and not break the window." I had only one question: Wouldn't you break a lot of windows until you found just the right thickness of curtain? "Well," he said, "one night I'd had a few beers, and I was ticked off because I missed the cut, and I went back and started hitting full wedge shots into the curtain. I guess I didn't care if the window broke or not, but it didn't."

Magee also recommended getting a cheap hotel room whenever possible. The cheaper the hotel, the thinner the carpet pad, which means the faster and truer the putts roll. Anything over $69 a night isn't going to help your putting a damn.

On Friday, Trix and I went out to Poppy Hills and didn't knock it into the Pacific Ocean once. Instead we hit it into and off of every tree in the Del Monte Forest. I had to chip out of the trees on holes 4, 5, 9, 10, 12, 14, 15, 16 and 17. It was my personal Arbor Day.

O.K., so Trix was not at his best this week, either. He threw a little six-over 78 at the field on Friday, which left him only 15 shots behind the leader. He was really playing great. Hitting it long. Putting well. He has brunch reservations Sunday.

And yet, somehow, we shot a team score of 65 on Friday. The AT&T Pro-Am is a best-ball tournament. Since my handicap is 15, I got a free shot on each round's 15 hardest holes. Pros, of course, get no free shots. So if Trix made a 4 and I made a 4 on one of my free-shot holes, then our team score for that hole was 3. Things just seemed to work out on Friday. Every time I was stuck chipping out from behind a Georgia-Pacific crew, Trix was making par. And every time Trix was finding new and inventive ways to make a 6, I was banking one off two blue spruces, a pine tree and Bambi for par. After two days we were only two shots off the cut. I could just *feel* Sunday morning coming down.

Schulz and his pro were still three shots ahead of us, though. Schulz not only has a great sense of humor and more money than Saudi Arabia, he also has a helluva golf game. On Friday he knocked the ball four feet from the hole on a par-5—*in two.* I loathe that man.

During a wait I asked Trix what he would do if he won a tournament. He talked as if he'd had his answer ready for years. "First of all, I'd cry," he said. "Then I'd hug my wife. Then I'd rent the Golden Gate Bridge and throw the largest party in the history of San Francisco. The best wines and abalone for everybody. Spend $50,000 on it. Limos. The works. And everybody would go home knowing the greatest feeling in the history of life."

There was a long pause.

"Orrrr . . . I'll just continue to miss cuts by 28 shots, play myself off the Tour and become the prep cook at the Des Moines Denny's."

I asked Charles Schulz if, in 42 years, Charlie Brown has ever worn anything but that yellow sweater with the red zigzag stripe. "Yes," he said. "For the first two weeks of the strip, he wore a plain white T-shirt. But then I realized the strip needed more color, so I drew the sweater." Great trivia question.

I decided on Saturday that if Two-Down got any more out of round, I was going to have to put him to sleep. First, he started hinting that if we won, he was going to be "very upset" if there was no caddie crystal. Then he began complaining about the weight of the bag. I think he purposely tried to leave my two- and three-irons behind on the range, but Andy

Bean yelled, "You forgot something." I gave Two-Down a
dirty look.

"Wouldn't have mattered," Two-Down said with a shrug.
"You haven't used them all week."

Did I mention that the driving range for the AT&T is quite
possibly the coolest place on earth? There is only one for all
three courses, and so all the stars and players meet there before
and after their rounds. It's like when you were kids and met at
the tree house before school. It's maybe the only place in the
world where, in 100 yards, you can see Joe Pesci hitting next
to Davis Love hitting next to Dan Quayle hitting next to John
Daly hitting next to a 15-handicap schlump like me. This can
only happen in golf. I have yet to see Pesci down punting
with the Raiders before one of *their* games.

The problem is, as you stand there on the sixth day, having
already played five rounds and scaled five-story hills, you realize that if you set up over one more five-iron, your aching legs
and back might decide to spasm you to death.

"The average amateur," says pro Roger Maltbie, "gets a look
at these beautiful free Titleists on the range and hits 5,000 balls
the first day and then walks 18. Then, the second day, he
overhears some pro talking about a swing change, and he picks
that up and tries it and hits 5,000 more balls and walks 18
more. Then, the third day, some Tour rep handing out drivers
gives him one, and he decides he's going to use that. So by
the time the tournament starts, he has hit 15,000 balls, walked
54 holes, got a new grip, a new swing and new equipment,
and he's exhausted. And he wonders why he can shoot 85 at
home with the boys and never break 100 here."

Sounds exactly like me.

Our final day, Saturday, was at the toughest of the three
courses, Spyglass. But Team Trix felt Sunday in its blood-
stream. Why not? We had it right in front of us. We were at 11
under. Most people figured 18 under would make the cut, so
all we needed was seven net birdies. We had averaged that the
two previous days. Besides, Trix hadn't made a birdie since
Thursday. "I got seven in me today," he said. He looked like
he meant it, too.

But Trix got his glove on correctly, and that was about it.
He crossed up the field and threw a little 82 at them. For the

week, that was 76-78-82—236, just 31 shots off the pro pace. He couldn't get a break. At the 8th hole he hit a shot just off the green, on a little hill. No problem. But as we were walking to the green, the ball suddenly decided to roll back down the hill into an impossible bunker lie. His face got all purple, and I thought he might just bite the rake in half. At one point, as he was crouched behind me reading my putt, I said, "What do you think?"

"I am quitting the game," he said with teeth clenched. "Put that in your [expletive] article." I really felt miserable for him. He was trying so hard. The thing was, we still had a chance. I came within one foot of a hole in one on the 12th hole, and we were 14 under at the turn. We had guessed that if we could make five net birdies on the back nine, we would be at Pebble on Sunday. Posing. Shutters releasing. Autograph sessions.

Instead we played like diseased yaks. We not only failed to make four more net birdies, we hardly made any more net pars. Our tournament ended on the 14th hole at Spyglass, an easy par-5. We both had 100-yard wedges over a pond to an uphill green. Trix went first and spun it back into the pond. So, naturally, I skulled mine down a 40-foot ravine to the right. We both made seven. Two-Down pulled something out of the bag and showed it to me. The bottle of Brain Pep. Trix never did make another birdie. However, on our 16th hole of the day, he missed a five-footer for birdie, walked over to a nearby pond and very calmly deposited his putter within. Good move. His putting improved. He made a nice four-footer with his driver on the last hole for par. We finished at 12 under, seven shots from making the cut, 15 shots behind Magee's team, the pro-am leaders.

I never did make 10 pars in one day for my pro. I'm not sure my pro made 10 pars for my pro. We were so bad, we tied with Jack Lemmon. Make it 21 *years* in a row. More bad news: Schulz missed the cut by one lousy little shot. Good grief.

There would be no Sunday services at St. Pebble for Team Trix. Still, I want to mention that we defeated Joe Montana, Orel Hershiser, Johnny Bench and Bobby Rahal, every one of 'em a Hall of Famer. Why don't you media types write that?

Next time, I've got to have 18 shots.

And Trix needs at least six.